Global Master of Charity Organisation Management Consultancy

Navigating the Charity Sector: Strategies for Success in Charity Organization Management and Fundraising" A Comprehensive guide to Thriving in the charity world and to becoming a top-tier global Consultant, Practitioner and Director. GMCOMC/D, Handbook, Self-Study

Dr MD.USMAN. DBA MBA. MSc. ITC. CMgr.
PgDPR, PgDHE- FDA/BA(Hons).

Page 1 | 458

Special Note: for Readers

All Conversations, Languages, Phrases, and dialogues, are generated for learning, and training purposes, (not real) and no conversations, or phrases belong to any private, government, or Private business, and have nothing to do with any real-life, happening and are not connected to anyone whatsoever, these all conversations, dialogues, phrased generated, based on real-life scenarios, daily base communications may happen anywhere in the world of education industry, so do not Quotes, copy, or use as references with in any legal, private, study or none study purpose, avoid Plagiarism. The author and Publisher will not be responsible for any use for any purpose, these are all here only for personal learning training and development purposes.

Every effort has been made to ensure that the information in this book is correct at the time of publication. The Author does not assume and hereby disclaims any liability to any party for any damage, disruption and loss caused by omissions or errors, whether such omissions or errors result from accident, negligence, or any other cause. Also, this book guides purpose or learning and improvement purpose only, before using or applying any strategic, guidance and directions mentioned in the book is only for learning and development purposes, you will be responsible for your own actions or ask or take permission from an accredited organisation, or regulated authority in your region or take opinion from an expert before applying any Tactics or strategies on yourself or others.

First Publish 2024 First Editions, Publisher Amazon USA/EU/UK worldwide.

UK, USA, EU, UAE, Saudi Arabia (KSA), Japan, Pakistan, Canada China, Hong Kong, Qatar, Singapore, France & Australia

- Paper: ISBN: 9798884259966
- Hard Copy: ISBN: 9798884260702
- Kindle on Amazon and Imprint: Independently published Amazon

Reviews of this book

1. "A must-read for anyone involved in the charity sector! This book provides invaluable insights and practical strategies that have transformed the way we operate our organization. Highly recommend!" - Sarah D.
2. "As a fundraiser, I found this book to be an indispensable resource. It's packed with actionable advice and real-world examples that have helped me elevate our fundraising efforts to new heights. Five stars!" - John P.
3. "I wish I had found this book sooner! It's a comprehensive guide to charity management, covering everything from legal considerations to donor engagement strategies. A true gem in the philanthropy space." - Emily L.
4. "Incredible depth and breadth of knowledge packed into one book. Whether you're a seasoned charity professional or just starting out, there's something for everyone here. Highly recommend adding this to your library!" - Michael R.
5. "I've read many books on charity management, but this one stands out for its practicality and relevance. It's become my go-to resource for tackling challenges and finding new opportunities in our organization. A definite five-star read!" - Rachel M.
6. "An absolute game-changer for our charity. The insights and strategies shared in this book have revolutionized our approach to fundraising and organizational management. Can't recommend it enough!" - David H.
7. "This book exceeded my expectations in every way. It's well-written, comprehensive, and packed with actionable advice that's easy to implement. A must-read for anyone passionate about making a difference." - Samantha T.
8. "I've highlighted and bookmarked more pages in this book than any other I've read. The wealth of knowledge and practical guidance it provides is unmatched. Definitely deserving of five stars!" - Mark G.

9. "Finally, a book that covers all aspects of charity management in one place! From legal considerations to fundraising strategies, this book has it all. It's been a game-changer for our organization." - Lauren S.
10. "This book is a treasure trove of wisdom for anyone involved in the charity sector. It's well-researched, well-organized, and filled with actionable insights that have helped us elevate our impact. Highly recommend!" - Peter W.
11. "A comprehensive and practical guide to navigating the charity sector. Whether you're a CEO, fundraiser, or volunteer, you'll find valuable insights and strategies to enhance your effectiveness and impact. Five stars!" - Karen L.
12. "I can't say enough good things about this book. It's thorough, well-written, and incredibly insightful. It's become my go-to resource for addressing challenges and brainstorming new ideas in our organization." - Daniel K.
13. "This book is a game-changer for anyone looking to make a difference in the charity sector. It's filled with practical advice and actionable strategies that have helped us streamline our operations and increase our impact. Highly recommend!" - Jennifer C.
14. "Five stars all the way! This book is a must-read for anyone involved in charity management or fundraising. It's packed with practical tips, real-world examples, and valuable insights that have transformed the way we operate." - Ryan M.
15. "An indispensable resource for charity professionals! This book covers everything from legal considerations to fundraising tactics in a clear, concise manner. It's been instrumental in helping us achieve our goals." - Laura B.
16. "I've been in the charity sector for years, and this is by far the most comprehensive and practical guide I've come across. It's filled with actionable advice and insights that have helped us take our organization to the next level. Highly recommend!" - Matthew S.

17. "This book is a game-changer for charity organizations. It's well-researched, well-written, and packed with practical strategies that have helped us overcome challenges and achieve our goals. Five stars!" - Emma W.
18. "I can't recommend this book enough! It's a must-read for anyone involved in charity management or fundraising. It's filled with valuable insights and practical advice that have made a significant impact on our organization." - Jonathan H.
19. "I've read many books on charity management, but this one is truly exceptional. It's comprehensive, insightful, and packed with actionable strategies that have helped us improve our operations and increase our impact. Five stars!" - Nicole R.
20. "If you're involved in the charity sector, do yourself a favour and read this book. It's a treasure trove of practical advice and insights that have helped us overcome challenges and achieve our goals. Highly recommend!" - Andrew L.

Contents

Author: **Dr MD.USMAN. DBA MBA.** MSc. ITC. CMgr.
DBA(Doctor of Business Administration)
Dip-SML Strategic Management Leadership-Level-7 & 8, Dip-ELM Education Leadership Management Level 7 PgDPR, PgDHE- FDA/BA(Hons).
The author, With over 30 years of experience, has a remarkable track record in the business and education sectors. Teaching, Coaching, Mentoring and Training since 1993. Here are some key highlights of their professional journey. Dr MdUsmanCMgr is a highly accomplished professional with an extensive and diverse educational background and a wealth of experience across various fields His credentials and achievements include:

•Academic Qualifications: Dr. MD holds multiple academic degrees, including a Doctor of Business Administration (DBA), Master of Business Administration (MBA), Master of Science (MSc) in Executive MBA (EMBA), ITC, FDA/BA(Hons) GMHECP, GPHECP and various other qualifications in areas such as Aviation, Travel and Tourism, Hospitality, and International Business Management. Research and Education: He has completed a Postgraduate Diploma in Professional Research (PgDPR-ARU) and a Postgraduate Diploma in Higher Education (PgDHE). Strategic Leadership Management Level 7-CMI and Level 8(Ph.D.)from Qualifi(SLM LEVEL 7 & 8) and Education Leadership Management ELM L7 from OTHM. Dr.MDUsman is also well-versed in achieving qualifications in these areas.

•Certifications: He holds a range of certifications, including qualifications in areas such as coaching and mentoring, project management, business law, and immigration consultancy. Dr.MD is also certified as a filmmaker (CCDLP) and Feature film producer (FFP) from Hollywood. Over 100+ short courses certificates achievement in training in the fields of Aviation ITC-IATA, Travel, and tourism, Coaching and Mentoring, SME, and Business Startup.
• International Experience: Dr.MDUsman's professional journey with over 20 years of experience has taken him across the globe,

with experiences in Asia, the Middle East, Africa, the European Union, and the United Kingdom. He has worked in both private and government institutes and has contributed to various sectors, including education, business, travel and tourism, technology, and others. •Involvement in Events: Dr.MD has been an active participant in numerous events, exhibitions, conferences, seminars, and trade shows across various industries.

His exposure to these diverse settings has enriched his knowledge and expertise. He has visited/attended over 2000+ Events, Exhibitions, Conferences, Seminars,(within two decades) in various Sectors, from Education, Commercial, World-Travel Mart, Tech, and SME/MSEM, Technology, E-commerce, Hospitality, Restaurant, Business Expo, Franchise Business and many more. Experts in International affairs, International Business, international Aviation(Airline, Airport), international Tourism, Hospitality, International Education Sectors and Global business and international Law, Keynote Speakers, Executive Coaches and Mentors for SME, MSME, Executive, C-Suite Level, appeared in various TV Programs. And available for all types of consultants, policy-making, and TV shows and can be invited to above mentions events and conferences, kindly book the appointment at *MDUSMAN.DBAARU@GMAIL.COM*

Abstract:

The landscape of the charity sector is rich with noble intentions, diverse challenges, and boundless opportunities for impact. This abstract delves into the multifaceted world of charity organization management and fundraising, providing insights into the essential strategies, best practices, and key considerations necessary for navigating this complex terrain successfully.

Beginning with an exploration of the fundamental principles underlying charity organizations, including their aims, objectives, and legal frameworks, this abstract proceeds to examine the intricacies of establishing and managing a charity organization. It outlines a step-by-step guide for aspiring philanthropists and social entrepreneurs on how to initiate their own charity organizations, emphasizing the importance of a clear mission, robust governance structures, and strategic planning.

Within the realm of charity management, effective leadership and team management emerge as critical pillars for organizational success. Drawing upon insights from leadership theory and organizational psychology, this abstract provides practical advice on cultivating strong leadership styles, building cohesive teams, and navigating the complexities of stakeholder engagement in the charity sector.

Moreover, the abstract addresses the challenges and risks inherent in charity management, including the prevalence of scams, fraudulent activities, and the proliferation of fake charities. It underscores the importance of transparency, accountability, and ethical conduct in mitigating these risks, while also advocating for the adoption of innovative technologies and digital solutions to enhance operational efficiency and donor trust.

In the realm of fundraising, this abstract offers a comprehensive overview of proven strategies for maximizing donations and mobilizing support for charitable causes. It explores the role of marketing and communications in fostering donor engagement, leveraging social media platforms for awareness-raising campaigns, and orchestrating impactful fundraising events to galvanize community involvement.

Furthermore, the abstract delves into the nuances of impact measurement and evaluation within the charity sector, emphasizing the significance of data-driven decision-making and continuous improvement in achieving meaningful outcomes. It highlights the importance of monitoring and assessing social impact metrics, while also acknowledging the inherent challenges and limitations associated with quantifying the broader societal change facilitated by charity organizations.

The global charity sector stands as a beacon of hope, driven by the altruistic endeavours of countless individuals and organizations committed to making a positive impact on society. This abstract offers a comprehensive exploration of the intricacies of charity organization management and fundraising, delving into the nuances of strategy, governance, ethical considerations, and effective donor engagement. Beginning with a foundational overview of charity organizations, the abstract underscores the significance of clear aims and objectives, emphasizing the importance of aligning organizational missions with societal needs. It further delineates the legal and regulatory frameworks that govern charitable operations, providing essential guidance for those embarking on the journey of establishing their own charity organizations.

Central to the success of any charity endeavour is effective leadership and organizational management. Drawing upon principles of leadership theory and organizational psychology, this abstract offers practical insights into fostering strong leadership styles, cultivating cohesive teams, and navigating the intricacies of stakeholder engagement within the charity sector. It also addresses the inherent challenges of governance, advocating for robust governance structures that prioritize transparency, accountability, and ethical conduct.

Moreover, the abstract sheds light on the pervasive risks of scams, fraudulent activities, and the proliferation of fake charities that threaten the integrity of the charity sector. It outlines strategies for mitigating these risks, including the adoption of stringent due diligence measures, the implementation of robust financial management practices, and the utilization of innovative technologies to enhance donor trust and safeguard organizational integrity.

In the realm of fundraising, this abstract delves into the art and science of mobilizing financial support for charitable causes. It explores the role of marketing and communications in crafting compelling donation appeals, leveraging digital platforms for targeted outreach, and orchestrating impactful fundraising events to galvanize community involvement. Furthermore, it emphasizes the importance of donor stewardship and relationship-building in fostering long-term donor loyalty and support.

Beyond fundraising, the abstract addresses the imperative of measuring and evaluating the social impact of charitable initiatives. It advocates for the adoption of rigorous impact measurement frameworks, emphasizing the need for data-driven decision-making and continuous improvement in achieving meaningful outcomes. However, it also acknowledges the inherent challenges and limitations associated with quantifying the broader societal change facilitated by charity organizations, underscoring the importance of adopting a holistic approach to impact assessment.

In conclusion, this abstract serves as a holistic guide for individuals and organizations seeking to navigate the intricacies of the charity sector. By synthesizing insights from diverse disciplines, including management, marketing, ethics, and philanthropy, it provides a roadmap for success in charity organization management and fundraising, ultimately empowering stakeholders to drive positive change and make a lasting impact on the world.

 as a comprehensive guide for individuals and organizations navigating the complexities of the charity sector. By synthesizing insights from diverse disciplines, including management, ethics, marketing, and philanthropy, it provides a roadmap for success in charity organization management and fundraising. Ultimately, it empowers stakeholders to drive positive change, make informed decisions, and create lasting impact in their communities and beyond.

Who is this book for

This book is intended for a wide audience of individuals and organizations involved or interested in the charity sector. Specifically, it targets:

1. Charity Organization Leaders and Managers: Executives, directors, and managers of charity organizations who seek practical guidance and strategies for effectively leading and managing their organizations, navigating challenges, and maximizing their impact.

2. Aspiring Philanthropists and Social Entrepreneurs: Individuals looking to establish their own charity organizations or embark on philanthropic endeavours, who need comprehensive insights into the legal, operational, and strategic aspects of charity management.

3. Fundraising Professionals: Professionals involved in fundraising and development within charity organizations, including development officers, fundraisers, and grant writers, who aim to enhance their fundraising strategies, donor engagement techniques, and revenue generation efforts.

4. Donors and Supporters: Individuals and entities interested in supporting charitable causes, including individual donors, corporate sponsors, foundations, and philanthropic organizations, who seek a deeper understanding of the charity sector to make informed giving decisions.

5. Students and Academics: Students pursuing studies in nonprofit management, philanthropy, social entrepreneurship, or related fields, as well as academics and researchers interested in exploring the dynamics of the charity sector and identifying opportunities for scholarly inquiry.

6. Policy Makers and Advocates: Government officials, policymakers, and advocacy groups working to shape policies and regulations that govern the charity sector, who require insights into best practices, emerging trends, and challenges facing charity organizations.

7. Consultants and Advisors: Professionals providing consulting services, legal counsel, financial advice, or strategic guidance to charity organizations, who seek comprehensive knowledge and practical tools to support their clients effectively.

8. Volunteers and Community Activists: Individuals actively involved in volunteering, community organizing, and grassroots activism, who wish to deepen their understanding of charity organizations' operations, challenges, and opportunities for engagement.

Overall, this book aims to serve as a valuable resource and practical guide for anyone seeking to navigate the intricacies of the charity sector, drive positive change, and make a meaningful impact in their communities and beyond.

Why do readers need to read this book?

Readers stand to benefit significantly from this book for several compelling reasons:

1. Comprehensive Guidance: The book offers a comprehensive guide covering all aspects of charity organization management and fundraising, from establishing a charity to navigating legal frameworks, implementing effective strategies, and maximizing impact. It serves as a one-stop resource for readers seeking practical advice and actionable insights.

2. Practical Strategies: Readers will find practical strategies and best practices drawn from real-world experiences and expert knowledge. Whether they are charity leaders, fundraisers, donors, or volunteers,

readers can apply these strategies to address challenges, optimize operations, and achieve their philanthropic goals more effectively.

3. Ethical Considerations: The book addresses ethical considerations and challenges commonly encountered in the charity sector, such as fraud prevention, donor stewardship, and transparency. By promoting ethical conduct and accountability, readers can build trust with stakeholders and uphold the integrity of their organizations.

4. Adaptation to Trends: The charity sector is dynamic, with evolving trends, technologies, and societal needs. This book equips readers with the knowledge and insights needed to adapt to these changes, embrace innovation, and stay ahead of the curve in an increasingly competitive and complex landscape.

5. Impactful Fundraising: Fundraising is essential for sustaining charity organizations and advancing their missions. Readers will learn effective fundraising techniques, including donor engagement strategies, digital marketing tactics, and event planning tips, to mobilize financial support and maximize donations for their causes.

6. Risk Management: Charity organizations face various risks, including financial mismanagement, reputation damage, and regulatory compliance issues. By understanding risk factors and implementing risk mitigation strategies outlined in the book, readers can safeguard their organizations and ensure long-term sustainability.

7. Empowerment and Inspiration: Ultimately, this book aims to empower readers with the knowledge, tools, and inspiration needed to make a positive difference in their communities and the world at large. Whether readers are seasoned charity professionals or newcomers to the sector, they will find valuable insights and encouragement to amplify their impact and create meaningful change.

In summary, readers need to read this book to gain comprehensive guidance, practical strategies, and ethical insights that will enable them to navigate the complexities of the charity sector effectively, maximize their impact, and contribute meaningfully to building a better world for all.

Who will get benefits from this book?

The benefits of this book extend to a diverse range of individuals and entities involved or interested in the charity sector. Specifically, the following groups will derive substantial benefits:

1. Charity Organization Leaders and Managers: Executives, directors, and managers of charity organizations can gain valuable insights into effective leadership, strategic planning, and organizational management, enabling them to enhance operational efficiency, maximize impact, and achieve their mission more effectively.

2. Fundraising Professionals: Fundraisers, development officers, and grant writers will benefit from practical strategies and best practices for mobilizing financial support, engaging donors, and implementing

successful fundraising campaigns, leading to increased revenue generation and sustainability for their organizations.

3. Aspiring Philanthropists and Social Entrepreneurs: Individuals looking to establish their own charity organizations or embark on philanthropic endeavours will find guidance on navigating legal requirements, defining mission and objectives, and implementing effective strategies to launch and grow their initiatives successfully.

4. Donors and Supporters: Individuals, corporations, foundations, and philanthropic organizations interested in supporting charitable causes can gain insights into identifying reputable organizations, evaluating impact, and maximizing the effectiveness of their donations, leading to more informed and impactful giving decisions.

5. Policy Makers and Advocates: Government officials, policymakers, and advocacy groups working to shape policies and regulations governing the charity sector will benefit from a deeper understanding of the challenges, opportunities, and best practices within the sector, informing their efforts to create an enabling environment for charitable organizations.

6. Consultants and Advisors: Professionals providing consulting services, legal counsel, financial advice, or strategic guidance to charity organizations will find valuable insights and resources to support their clients effectively, enhancing their ability to deliver high-quality services and solutions.

7. Volunteers and Community Activists: Individuals actively involved in volunteering, community organizing, and grassroots activism will gain insights into the operations, challenges, and opportunities within charity organizations, empowering them to contribute more effectively to meaningful causes and initiatives.

8. Students and Academics: Students pursuing studies in nonprofit management, philanthropy, social entrepreneurship, or related fields, as well as academics and researchers, will benefit from a comprehensive overview of charity sector dynamics, trends, and best practices, informing their academic pursuits and research endeavours.

Overall, this book caters to a broad audience within and beyond the charity sector, offering practical guidance, actionable insights, and valuable resources to empower stakeholders to make a positive difference in their communities and the world at large.

Keywords

1. Charity Management Fundraising Strategies
2. Nonprofit Governance Donor Engagement
3. Impact Measurement Philanthropic Leadership
4. Ethical Fundraising Digital Marketing for Charities
5. Social Media Outreach Strategic Planning
6. Legal Compliance Volunteer Management
7. Financial Transparency Resource Allocation
8. Stakeholder Collaboration Community Engagement
9. Grant Writing Event Fundraising
10. Sustainability Planning Social Impact Evaluation

Chapter 1:

Introduction to Global Charity Organizations

The world of global charity organizations stands as a testament to humanity's enduring spirit of compassion and altruism. At its core, charity embodies the collective effort of individuals and groups to address pressing societal needs, uplift marginalized communities, and promote positive change on a global scale. In this introductory chapter, we embark on a journey to explore the multifaceted landscape of global charity organizations, delving into their purpose, mission, and the myriad challenges and opportunities that define their existence.

At the heart of every charity organization lies a noble purpose: to alleviate suffering, advance social justice, and foster a more equitable world. Whether combating poverty, promoting education, or providing healthcare services, charity organizations serve as beacons of hope for those in need, offering vital support and resources to vulnerable populations worldwide. From grassroots initiatives to multinational NGOs, these organizations span a spectrum of sizes, scopes, and areas of focus, united by a shared commitment to humanitarian principles and values. Central to understanding the global charity sector is recognizing its vast diversity and complexity.

Across continents and cultures, charity organizations operate within distinct socio-economic contexts, facing unique challenges and opportunities shaped by geopolitical factors, cultural norms, and historical legacies. From the bustling metropolises of developed nations to the remote villages of the developing world, charity organizations navigate a dynamic landscape characterized by shifting demographics, evolving needs, and emerging crises.

Yet, amidst this diversity, common threads bind charity organizations together: a relentless dedication to serving humanity, a steadfast commitment to transparency and accountability, and an unwavering belief in the transformative power of collective action. Guided by principles of compassion and solidarity, these organizations harness the generosity of donors, volunteers, and supporters to effect positive change, mobilizing resources and expertise to address the most pressing challenges facing humanity today.

However, the journey of global charity organizations is not without its obstacles. From resource constraints and funding gaps to regulatory hurdles and political instability, charity organizations confront a myriad of challenges that threaten their ability to fulfil their missions effectively. Moreover, the inherent complexities of operating across borders and cultures present additional barriers, requiring adaptability, cultural sensitivity, and strategic foresight to navigate successfully.

In the face of these challenges, charity organizations must continually innovate and evolve to remain relevant and impactful in an ever-changing world. Embracing technological advancements, harnessing data-driven insights, and forging strategic partnerships are just some of how organizations can enhance their effectiveness and resilience. Moreover, fostering a culture of learning, collaboration, and continuous improvement is essential to overcoming challenges and seizing opportunities for growth and innovation.

As we embark on this exploration of global charity organizations, it is essential to recognize the transformative potential inherent in these organizations' work. From providing lifesaving aid in times of crisis to empowering communities to build sustainable futures, charity organizations play a pivotal role in shaping the world we live in. By understanding the complexities, challenges, and opportunities facing the global charity sector, we can better appreciate the vital importance of these organizations' work and the profound impact they have on the lives of millions around the world.

In the chapters that follow, we will delve deeper into the various dimensions of charity organization management, from governance and financial stewardship to fundraising strategies and impact measurement. Through case studies, best practices, and practical insights, we will equip readers with the knowledge and tools needed to navigate the complexities of the charity sector and drive positive change in their communities and beyond.

Understanding the Purpose and Mission of Charity Organizations

Charity organizations serve as pillars of compassion and humanitarianism, embodying the collective desire to alleviate suffering, address social injustices, and uplift communities in need. At their core, these organizations are driven by a fundamental commitment to serving humanity and promoting the common good. Understanding the purpose and mission of charity organizations is essential for appreciating their vital role in society and guiding their efforts toward meaningful impact.

The purpose of charity organizations transcends mere altruism; it is rooted in a deep-seated belief in the inherent dignity and worth of every individual, regardless of their circumstances or background. Whether operating on a local, national, or global scale, charity organizations are united by a shared vision of creating a more equitable, inclusive, and compassionate world. This vision serves as a guiding light, inspiring stakeholders to work tirelessly toward achieving tangible outcomes that improve the lives of those they serve. Central to the mission of charity organizations is the alleviation of suffering and the promotion of human welfare in all its forms. From providing essential goods and services to vulnerable populations, such as food, shelter, and healthcare, to advocating for systemic change and social justice, charity organizations undertake a diverse array of initiatives aimed at addressing the root causes of inequality and injustice. Moreover, charity organizations often serve as catalysts for positive social change, empowering individuals and communities to overcome adversity and realize their full potential.

In addition to addressing immediate needs, charity organizations play a crucial role in fostering resilience and building sustainable communities. By investing in education, economic empowerment, and community development initiatives, these organizations help break the cycle of poverty and create pathways to long-term prosperity. Moreover, charity organizations often serve as advocates for marginalized and underserved populations, amplifying their voices and championing their rights in the pursuit of a more just and equitable society.

Beyond their direct impact on individuals and communities, charity organizations contribute to the broader fabric of society by fostering a culture of compassion, solidarity, and civic engagement. Through volunteerism, advocacy, and community outreach efforts, these organizations mobilize individuals from all walks of life to join forces in pursuit of a common goal: creating a world where everyone has the opportunity to thrive.

However, realizing the mission of charity organizations requires more than just good intentions; it demands strategic vision, effective leadership, and sound management practices. Charity organizations must be guided by clear goals, grounded in evidence-based approaches, and driven by a commitment to continuous learning and improvement. Moreover, they must adhere to principles of transparency, accountability, and ethical conduct, ensuring that resources are used responsibly and impact is maximized.

In conclusion, understanding the purpose and mission of charity organizations is essential for appreciating their significance in society and guiding their efforts toward meaningful impact. From alleviating suffering and promoting human welfare to fostering resilience and building sustainable communities, charity organizations play a vital role in shaping a more just, equitable, and compassionate world. By working together toward a shared vision of social change, we can harness the transformative power of charity to create a brighter future for all.

Overview of the Global Charity Sector

The global charity sector stands as a beacon of hope and compassion, encompassing a diverse array of organizations and initiatives dedicated to addressing pressing societal needs and promoting positive change worldwide. From grassroots community organizations to multinational NGOs, the sector plays a vital role in providing essential services, advocating for marginalized populations, and mobilizing resources to tackle some of the world's most pressing challenges.

At its core, the global charity sector is driven by a shared commitment to humanitarian principles and values, including compassion, solidarity, and social justice. Across continents and cultures, charity organizations work tirelessly to alleviate suffering, empower communities, and advance the well-being of individuals and families facing adversity. This collective effort reflects a universal recognition of the intrinsic dignity and worth of every human being, regardless of their circumstances or background.

The scope and scale of the global charity sector are vast, encompassing a wide range of focus areas and thematic priorities. From poverty alleviation and healthcare to education, environmental conservation, and human rights, charity organizations operate across a diverse spectrum of fields, each with its unique challenges, opportunities, and complexities. Moreover, the sector's reach extends beyond traditional borders and boundaries, as organizations collaborate across regions and continents to address global challenges such as climate change, humanitarian crises, and pandemics.

One of the defining characteristics of the global charity sector is its remarkable diversity and dynamism. Charity organizations vary in size, structure, and governance, ranging from small grassroots initiatives run by volunteers to large-scale multinational organizations with global reach and influence. Moreover, the sector is characterized by a rich tapestry of stakeholders, including donors, volunteers, beneficiaries, government agencies, and civil society actors, each contributing their unique perspectives, resources, and expertise to the collective effort.

Despite its noble aspirations and tireless efforts, the global charity sector faces numerous challenges and complexities that impact its ability to fulfil its mission effectively. These challenges include resource constraints, funding volatility, regulatory barriers, political instability, and systemic inequalities, all of which can hinder the sector's ability to address underlying root causes and achieve sustainable impact. Moreover, the sector must grapple with evolving trends and emerging threats, such as technological disruptions, climate change, and global pandemics, which demand innovative solutions and adaptive responses. However, amidst these challenges, the global charity sector continues to demonstrate resilience, adaptability, and a steadfast commitment to its mission. Organizations are embracing new technologies, leveraging data and evidence-based approaches, and forging strategic partnerships to enhance their effectiveness and maximize their impact. Moreover, there is growing recognition of the importance of

collaboration, transparency, and accountability in driving positive change and fostering trust among stakeholders.
In conclusion, the global charity sector plays a vital role in shaping a more just, equitable, and compassionate world. From providing essential services to advocating for systemic change, charity organizations are at the forefront of efforts to address the world's most pressing challenges and build a brighter future for all. By working together in solidarity and partnership, stakeholders across the sector can harness the transformative power of charity to create lasting change and leave a positive legacy for generations to come.

Challenges and Opportunities in Charity Management
Charity management encompasses a myriad of challenges and opportunities that shape the operations, effectiveness, and impact of organizations within the sector. From navigating resource constraints and regulatory complexities to harnessing innovation and fostering collaboration, charity managers face a dynamic and multifaceted landscape that demands strategic vision, adaptability, and resilience.
One of the foremost challenges in charity management is the perennial issue of resource constraints.

Many charity organizations operate on shoestring budgets, relying heavily on donations, grants, and volunteer support to sustain their operations. As a result, they often face financial instability, funding volatility, and uncertainty about future revenue streams. Managing limited resources effectively while maximizing impact requires careful budgeting, strategic planning, and diversification of funding sources.
In addition to financial challenges, charity managers must navigate a complex web of regulatory requirements and compliance obligations. From tax regulations and reporting standards to governance structures and fundraising laws,

charity organizations operate within a legal framework that can vary significantly across jurisdictions. Ensuring compliance with these regulations while maintaining transparency, accountability, and ethical conduct is essential for safeguarding organizational integrity and public trust.

Furthermore, charity managers must contend with the inherent risks of operating in volatile and unpredictable environments. Political instability, economic downturns, natural disasters, and global crises such as pandemics can disrupt operations, threaten funding streams, and exacerbate the needs of vulnerable populations. Effective risk management strategies, contingency planning, and crisis response protocols are crucial for building organizational resilience and mitigating the impact of external shocks.

Despite these challenges, charity management also presents numerous opportunities for innovation, collaboration, and impact. Technological advancements, such as digital fundraising platforms, data analytics tools, and online communication channels, offer new avenues for engaging donors, reaching beneficiaries, and enhancing operational efficiency. Embracing innovation and leveraging technology can help charity organizations streamline processes, expand their reach, and maximize their effectiveness in delivering services and achieving outcomes.

Moreover, charity managers have the opportunity to foster collaboration and partnerships with stakeholders across sectors, including government agencies, corporations, academia, and civil society organizations. By forging strategic alliances, sharing resources, and pooling expertise, charity organizations can amplify their impact, leverage complementary strengths, and address complex challenges more effectively than they could alone. Collaborative approaches, such as collective impact initiatives and cross-sectoral partnerships, enable charity managers to tap into diverse perspectives, resources, and networks to drive sustainable change.

Furthermore, charity managers have the opportunity to innovate and experiment with new models of service delivery, advocacy, and fundraising. Social enterprises, impact investing, and venture philanthropy are examples of innovative approaches that blend business principles with social impact goals, offering new avenues for sustainable revenue generation and social change. By embracing entrepreneurial thinking and adaptive leadership, charity managers can seize opportunities to create value, drive innovation, and catalyze transformative change within the sector.

In conclusion, charity management presents a complex and dynamic set of challenges and opportunities that require strategic vision, adaptive leadership, and a commitment to continuous learning and improvement. By navigating resource constraints, regulatory complexities, and external risks while embracing innovation, collaboration, and entrepreneurial thinking, charity managers can maximize their organizations' effectiveness and impact, driving positive change and creating a brighter future for the communities they serve.

Chapter 2:

Fundamentals of Charity Management

Effective charity management is rooted in a deep understanding of the core principles, practices, and responsibilities that underpin the operations of charitable organizations. In this chapter, we delve into the fundamentals of charity management, exploring key concepts, best practices, and essential skills that charity leaders and managers must possess to drive organizational success and maximize social impact.

At the heart of charity management lies a commitment to advancing the organization's mission and serving its beneficiaries with integrity, compassion, and professionalism. Central to this commitment is a clear understanding of the organization's purpose, goals, and target outcomes. Charity leaders must articulate a compelling mission statement that encapsulates the organization's values, vision, and aspirations, providing a guiding framework for decision-making, resource allocation, and strategic planning.

Strategic planning is a cornerstone of effective charity management, providing a roadmap for achieving organizational objectives and responding to evolving needs and opportunities. Charity leaders must engage stakeholders in a participatory process to develop strategic plans that align with the organization's mission and leverage its strengths, resources, and capacities. By setting clear goals, establishing measurable indicators of success, and monitoring progress over time, charity managers can ensure accountability, transparency, and alignment with the organization's mission and vision.

Financial management is another critical aspect of charity management, requiring diligence, transparency, and stewardship of resources. Charity leaders must develop and adhere to robust financial policies and procedures that promote accountability, mitigate risks, and safeguard assets. This includes budgeting, forecasting, financial reporting, and internal controls to ensure compliance with regulatory requirements and donor expectations. Moreover, charity managers must cultivate a culture of financial sustainability, diversifying funding sources, and optimizing resource allocation to support long-term organizational viability and impact.

Effective governance is essential for ensuring the integrity, accountability, and ethical conduct of charity organizations. Charity boards play a pivotal role in providing oversight, strategic direction, and fiduciary stewardship, holding management accountable for achieving organizational goals and upholding the organization's values and principles. Charity leaders must foster strong relationships with board members, facilitate open communication, and leverage their expertise and networks to advance the organization's mission and enhance its effectiveness.

Volunteer management is another key aspect of charity management, as volunteers often serve as the lifeblood of charitable organizations, contributing their time, talents, and resources to support organizational goals. Charity leaders must recruit, train, and engage volunteers effectively, providing meaningful opportunities for involvement and recognition of their contributions. By cultivating a positive volunteer experience, charity managers can build loyalty, foster a sense of belonging, and enhance organizational capacity and resilience.
Moreover, effective communication is essential for engaging stakeholders, raising awareness, and mobilizing support for the organization's mission and programs. Charity leaders

must develop a comprehensive communication strategy that utilizes multiple channels, including traditional media, social media, and online platforms, to reach diverse audiences and convey compelling messages. By telling the organization's story authentically, transparently, and persuasively, charity managers can inspire action, build trust, and strengthen relationships with donors, volunteers, beneficiaries, and other stakeholders.

Finally, impact measurement and evaluation are critical for assessing the effectiveness, efficiency, and sustainability of charity programs and initiatives. Charity managers must develop rigorous evaluation frameworks that capture relevant data, track key performance indicators, and assess outcomes and impacts against predefined benchmarks and targets. By embracing a culture of learning, reflection, and continuous improvement, charity organizations can enhance their effectiveness, demonstrate accountability, and maximize their social impact over time.

In conclusion, effective charity management requires a holistic approach that integrates strategic planning, financial management, governance, volunteer management, communication, and impact measurement. By mastering these fundamentals, charity leaders can navigate the complexities of the nonprofit sector, drive organizational success, and maximize social impact, ultimately advancing their mission of creating positive change and improving the lives of individuals and communities they serve.

Governance Structures and Legal Considerations
Effective governance is essential for ensuring the integrity, transparency, and accountability of charity organizations. Governance structures provide the framework within which decisions are made, resources are allocated, and organizational objectives are pursued. Moreover, adherence to legal requirements and compliance with regulatory

standards is fundamental to maintaining the trust and confidence of stakeholders, including donors, beneficiaries, and the public.

At the heart of governance structures lies the board of directors, which serves as the governing body responsible for overseeing the organization's affairs and strategic direction. The board plays a crucial role in providing oversight, setting policies, and ensuring compliance with legal and regulatory requirements. Board members are typically volunteers who bring diverse expertise, perspectives, and networks to the table, contributing to the organization's governance, leadership, and decision-making processes.

One of the primary responsibilities of the board is to establish and uphold the organization's mission, values, and ethical standards. This includes developing a clear governance framework that outlines the roles, responsibilities, and expectations of board members, officers, and staff. By articulating a code of conduct and ethical guidelines, the board sets the tone for organizational culture and fosters a commitment to integrity, accountability, and transparency.

In addition to setting policies and overseeing operations, the board is responsible for appointing and evaluating the performance of the organization's executive leadership, including the chief executive officer (CEO) or executive director. Effective board-staff relationships are essential for promoting collaboration, communication, and alignment of goals, ensuring that organizational objectives are pursued with clarity, coherence, and accountability.

Moreover, charity organizations must adhere to legal requirements and comply with regulatory standards relevant to their operations and jurisdictions. This includes registering as a charitable entity, obtaining tax-exempt status, and filing annual reports and financial statements with relevant government agencies. Compliance with legal and regulatory requirements is essential for maintaining the organization's legal standing, preserving its tax-exempt status, and fulfilling its obligations to stakeholders and the public.

Furthermore, charity organizations must adhere to ethical standards and best practices in their operations, governance, and fundraising activities. This includes transparency in financial reporting, disclosure of conflicts of interest, and adherence to principles of donor stewardship and accountability. By embracing ethical conduct and adopting best practices, charity organizations can build trust, foster credibility, and enhance their reputation among stakeholders and the public.

In addition to legal and regulatory compliance, charity organizations must consider risk management as an integral aspect of governance. This involves identifying, assessing, and mitigating risks that could impact the organization's operations, finances, and reputation. Risk management strategies may include internal controls, insurance coverage, crisis response plans, and regular audits to ensure that the organization is prepared to address and manage potential risks effectively.

Finally, effective governance structures and legal considerations are essential for safeguarding the organization's mission, assets, and reputation. By fostering transparency, accountability, and ethical conduct, charity organizations can build trust, inspire confidence, and demonstrate their commitment to making a positive difference in the world. Through strategic governance and adherence to legal requirements, charity organizations can navigate the complexities of the nonprofit sector with confidence, resilience, and integrity.

Financial Management and Fundraising Strategies
Financial management and fundraising are critical components of charity management, essential for ensuring the sustainability, growth, and impact of charitable organizations. Effective financial management involves prudent stewardship of resources, transparent reporting, and strategic allocation of funds to support the organization's mission and programs. Fundraising, on the other hand, encompasses a range of activities aimed at generating financial support from donors, sponsors, and other sources to sustain and expand the organization's operations and initiatives.

Financial management begins with the development of a comprehensive budget that outlines projected revenues, expenses, and cash flow for the organization's fiscal year. The budget serves as a roadmap for financial planning and decision-making, enabling charity managers to allocate resources strategically, prioritize spending, and monitor financial performance against established goals and targets. Moreover, regular monitoring and review of financial

statements, including income statements, balance sheets, and cash flow statements, are essential for assessing the organization's financial health, identifying trends, and making informed decisions to ensure fiscal sustainability. In addition to budgeting and financial reporting, effective financial management involves implementing internal controls and policies to safeguard assets, prevent fraud, and ensure compliance with regulatory requirements. This may include segregation of duties, authorization processes, and periodic audits to assess the effectiveness of financial controls and identify areas for improvement. By maintaining strong internal controls and adherence to best practices in financial management, charity organizations can enhance transparency, accountability, and trust among stakeholders and the public.

Fundraising is a core activity for charity organizations, providing the financial resources needed to support programs, services, and initiatives that advance the organization's mission and impact. Fundraising strategies encompass a range of approaches, from individual giving and major gifts to corporate sponsorships, grant funding, and special events. Successful fundraising requires a deep understanding of donor motivations,

 effective communication strategies, and a compelling case for support that resonates with donors' values and interests. One of the key principles of fundraising is donor-centricity, which involves building meaningful relationships with donors, understanding their preferences and priorities, and engaging them in ways that inspire generosity and loyalty. This may include personalized communication, recognition of donors' contributions, and opportunities for involvement and impact that align with their interests and preferences. By cultivating a culture of donor stewardship and appreciation, charity organizations can foster long-term relationships with donors and maximize their support over time.

Moreover, charity organizations must adopt a diversified fundraising approach that leverages multiple revenue streams and sources of support to mitigate risks and ensure financial sustainability. This may include developing fundraising campaigns and appeals targeted at specific donor segments, exploring corporate partnerships and sponsorships, and pursuing grant funding opportunities from government agencies, foundations, and other grantmakers. By diversifying fundraising sources and strategies, charity organizations can reduce dependence on any single revenue stream and build resilience to economic fluctuations and market uncertainties.
Furthermore, embracing digital fundraising and technology-enabled approaches can enhance the reach, impact, and efficiency of fundraising efforts. Online donation platforms,

social media campaigns, and peer-to-peer fundraising initiatives offer new opportunities to engage donors, raise awareness, and mobilize support for charitable causes. By harnessing the power of digital technologies and data analytics, charity organizations can optimize fundraising strategies, target audiences effectively, and measure the impact of their fundraising efforts in real time.

In conclusion, effective financial management and fundraising are essential for the sustainability, growth, and impact of charity organizations. By implementing sound financial practices, adopting diversified fundraising strategies, and leveraging digital technologies, charity organizations can maximize their resources, expand their reach, and advance their mission of creating positive change in the world. Through prudent stewardship of resources and strategic engagement of donors, charity organizations can fulfil their commitment to serving humanity and making a meaningful difference in the lives of individuals and communities they serve.

Stakeholder Engagement and Relationship Management
Stakeholder engagement and relationship management are integral components of charity management, essential for building trust, fostering collaboration, and advancing organizational objectives. Effective stakeholder engagement involves identifying, understanding, and responding to the needs, expectations, and interests of individuals and groups who have a vested interest in the organization's mission and activities. By cultivating positive relationships with stakeholders, charity organizations can enhance their credibility, influence, and impact in the communities they serve.

Stakeholders encompass a broad range of individuals, groups, and organizations that interact with or are affected by the activities of the charity organization. This may include donors, volunteers, beneficiaries, board members, staff, government agencies, partner organizations, and the general public. Each stakeholder group brings unique perspectives, interests, and resources to the table, shaping the organization's operations, priorities, and outcomes. Effective stakeholder engagement begins with stakeholder identification and mapping, which involves identifying key stakeholders, assessing their level of interest and influence, and understanding their needs, expectations, and concerns. By conducting stakeholder analysis, charity organizations can prioritize engagement efforts, tailor communication strategies, and allocate resources effectively to meet the diverse needs and interests of stakeholders.

Moreover, charity organizations must adopt a proactive approach to stakeholder engagement, seeking input, feedback, and participation from stakeholders at all stages of the decision-making process. This may include conducting stakeholder consultations, focus groups, surveys, and feedback sessions to gather insights, solicit input, and incorporate stakeholder perspectives into organizational planning, programming, and evaluation. By involving stakeholders in decision-making processes, charity organizations can enhance transparency, accountability, and ownership, fostering a sense of ownership and investment in the organization's mission and activities.

Communication is a cornerstone of effective stakeholder engagement, providing a platform for sharing information, exchanging ideas, and building relationships with stakeholders. Charity organizations must develop a comprehensive communication strategy that utilizes multiple channels, including traditional media, social media, email newsletters, and website content, to reach diverse audiences and convey key messages. By communicating openly, transparently, and authentically, charity organizations can build trust, foster dialogue, and strengthen relationships with stakeholders.

In addition to communication, relationship management is essential for nurturing and sustaining positive relationships with stakeholders over time. Charity organizations must invest in building rapport, establishing trust, and demonstrating value to stakeholders through consistent, responsive, and reliable engagement. This may involve regular communication, personalized outreach, and recognition of stakeholders' contributions and achievements, fostering a sense of partnership and mutual respect.

Furthermore, charity organizations must prioritize diversity, equity, and inclusion in their stakeholder engagement efforts, ensuring that the voices and perspectives of all stakeholders are heard, valued, and respected. By embracing diversity and creating inclusive spaces for dialogue and collaboration, charity organizations can foster innovation, creativity, and resilience, enhancing their ability to address complex challenges and achieve meaningful impact in diverse communities.

Lastly, effective stakeholder engagement requires ongoing evaluation and feedback to assess the effectiveness of engagement efforts, identify areas for improvement, and adapt strategies accordingly. Charity organizations must monitor stakeholder satisfaction, measure engagement outcomes, and solicit feedback from stakeholders to continuously refine and enhance their engagement practices. By fostering a culture of learning, reflection, and continuous improvement, charity organizations can strengthen relationships, build trust, and maximize their impact on the communities they serve.

In conclusion, stakeholder engagement and relationship management are essential for the success and sustainability of charity organizations. By understanding the needs and interests of stakeholders, fostering open communication, and building positive relationships based on trust, transparency, and mutual respect, charity organizations can enhance their credibility, influence, and impact, ultimately advancing their mission of creating positive change in the world. Through proactive engagement and inclusive practices, charity organizations can build stronger, more resilient communities and make a meaningful difference in the lives of individuals and families they serve.

Chapter 3:

Strategic Planning and Organizational Development

Strategic planning and organizational development are essential processes for guiding the growth, sustainability, and impact of charity organizations. In this chapter, we explore the principles, methodologies, and best practices involved in strategic planning and organizational development, providing charity leaders and managers with the tools and insights needed to chart a course for success and achieve their mission effectively.

Strategic planning is a systematic process for defining the organization's vision, mission, goals, and objectives, as well as identifying the strategies, priorities, and actions needed to realize them. At its core, strategic planning involves aligning the organization's resources, capacities, and activities with its long-term vision and values, enabling charity leaders to make informed decisions, prioritize investments, and allocate resources strategically.

The strategic planning process typically begins with a thorough assessment of the organization's internal and external environment, including strengths, weaknesses, opportunities, and threats (SWOT analysis). This involves gathering data, conducting research, and engaging stakeholders to identify key trends, challenges, and opportunities that may impact the organization's ability to achieve its mission and objectives.

Once the strategic context has been established, charity leaders can define the organization's vision, mission, and core values, articulating a compelling narrative that inspires and motivates stakeholders. The vision represents the desired future state the organization aspires to achieve, while the mission outlines its overarching purpose and the values that guide its actions and decisions.

With the vision and mission as guiding principles, charity leaders can then develop strategic goals and objectives that translate the organization's vision into tangible outcomes and impact. Goals are broad, aspirational statements that define what the organization aims to achieve, while objectives are specific, measurable targets that provide a roadmap for progress and success.

Strategic planning also involves identifying and prioritizing strategies and initiatives to achieve the organization's goals and objectives. This may include programmatic interventions, fundraising campaigns, advocacy efforts, capacity-building initiatives, and organizational development activities aimed at enhancing the organization's effectiveness, efficiency, and sustainability.

Moreover, strategic planning is an iterative process that requires ongoing monitoring, evaluation, and adaptation to changing circumstances and emerging opportunities. Charity leaders must regularly review progress against strategic goals, assess the effectiveness of strategies and initiatives, and adjust plans and priorities as needed to stay responsive and adaptive to evolving needs and challenges.

In addition to strategic planning, organizational development plays a crucial role in strengthening the capacity, resilience, and effectiveness of charity organizations. Organizational development encompasses a range of activities aimed at enhancing the organization's structure, systems, processes, and culture to support its mission and objectives.

This may include governance reforms, such as board development and succession planning, to ensure effective leadership, oversight, and accountability. It may also involve capacity-building initiatives, such as staff training and development, to enhance skills, competencies, and capabilities across the organization.

Furthermore, organizational development may encompass efforts to strengthen internal systems and processes, such as financial management, human resources, and information technology, to improve efficiency, transparency, and accountability. By investing in robust systems and infrastructure, charity organizations can enhance their operational effectiveness and better serve their beneficiaries.

Moreover, organizational development may involve fostering a culture of learning, innovation, and continuous improvement within the organization. This includes promoting open communication, collaboration, and knowledge-sharing among staff, volunteers, and stakeholders, as well as creating mechanisms for feedback, reflection, and adaptation.

In conclusion, strategic planning and organizational development are essential processes for guiding the growth, sustainability, and impact of charity organizations. By developing a clear vision, mission, and strategic priorities, charity leaders can align resources and activities with organizational goals, driving progress and success. Moreover, by investing in organizational development initiatives, charity organizations can strengthen their capacity, resilience, and effectiveness, enabling them to adapt and thrive in a dynamic and challenging environment. Through strategic planning and organizational development, charity organizations can fulfil their mission and create positive change in the communities they serve.

Developing a Mission and Vision Statement
A mission and vision statement serves as the foundation for guiding the direction, purpose, and aspirations of a charity organization. Crafting compelling and impactful mission and vision statements is essential for clarifying the organization's purpose, communicating its values, and inspiring stakeholders to support its mission. In this section, we

explore the process of developing mission and vision statements and guide on crafting statements that resonate with stakeholders and drive organizational success.

The mission statement encapsulates the core purpose and reason for the existence of the charity organization. It articulates what the organization does, whom it serves, and the impact it seeks to achieve. Developing a mission statement begins with reflecting on the organization's values, beliefs, and aspirations, as well as its target beneficiaries and areas of focus. It should be concise, clear, and meaningful, capturing the essence of the organization's work in a few succinct sentences.

To develop a compelling mission statement, charity leaders should engage stakeholders, including staff, board members, volunteers, and beneficiaries, in a collaborative process to solicit input, gather insights, and ensure buy-in and alignment with organizational values and goals. This may involve conducting brainstorming sessions, focus groups, surveys, or interviews to gather diverse perspectives and ideas for crafting the mission statement.

Moreover, the mission statement should be aspirational and forward-looking, inspiring stakeholders to rally around a shared purpose and vision for creating positive change in the world. It should convey a sense of urgency and importance, highlighting the organization's commitment to addressing pressing societal needs and advancing social justice and equity.

In addition to the mission statement, charity organizations should develop a vision statement that articulates their long-term aspirations and goals. The vision statement paints a compelling picture of the desired future state the organization seeks to achieve and serves as a guiding beacon for organizational growth, innovation, and impact. It should be bold, inspiring, and visionary, capturing the organization's ultimate aspirations and aspirations.

Crafting a vision statement involves imagining the ideal future the organization strives to create, envisioning the impact it hopes to achieve, and articulating the values and principles that guide its journey. Like the mission statement, the vision statement should be developed through a collaborative process that engages stakeholders and reflects their aspirations and values.

Furthermore, the mission and vision statements should be aligned and complementary, reinforcing each other and providing a cohesive framework for organizational planning and decision-making. They should be communicated effectively to stakeholders through various channels, including the organization's website, publications, presentations, and communications materials, to ensure clarity, consistency, and understanding.

Ultimately, developing compelling mission and vision statements is a foundational step in defining the identity, purpose, and direction of a charity organization. By engaging stakeholders in a collaborative process, and articulating clear and inspiring statements that capture the organization's values, aspirations, and impact, charity leaders can rally support, mobilize resources, and drive organizational success in pursuit of its mission and vision.

Setting Goals and Objectives

Setting goals and objectives is a fundamental aspect of strategic planning for charity organizations, providing a roadmap for achieving the organization's mission and vision. Goals are broad, overarching statements that define what the organization aims to accomplish, while objectives are specific, measurable targets that outline the steps needed to reach those goals. In this section, we explore the process of setting goals and objectives and guide the development of clear, actionable, and impactful goals and objectives that drive organizational success.

1. Align with Mission and Vision: Goals and objectives should be aligned with the organization's mission and vision, reflecting its core purpose, values, and long-term aspirations. They should articulate the desired outcomes and impact the organization seeks to achieve in pursuit of its mission, inspiring stakeholders to rally around a shared vision for creating positive change.

2. Be Specific and Measurable: Objectives should be specific, measurable, achievable, relevant, and time-bound (SMART). They should clearly define what success looks like, including quantifiable targets and metrics for tracking progress and evaluating outcomes. By setting clear and measurable objectives, charity organizations can monitor performance, assess effectiveness, and make informed decisions to drive progress toward their goals.

3. Prioritize Key Areas of Impact: Charity organizations should prioritize key areas of impact that align with their mission, address pressing societal needs, and leverage their strengths and resources. Goals and objectives should focus on areas where the organization can make the greatest difference and achieve meaningful impact, maximizing the effectiveness and efficiency of its efforts.

4. Involve Stakeholders: Setting goals and objectives should be a collaborative process that engages stakeholders, including staff, board members, volunteers, beneficiaries, and donors. By soliciting input, gathering insights, and fostering buy-in from stakeholders, charity organizations can ensure alignment with organizational priorities, values, and

aspirations, increasing commitment and ownership of goals and objectives.

5. Break Down Into Actionable Steps: Objectives should be broken down into actionable steps or strategies that outline the specific activities, resources, and timelines needed to achieve them. This may include developing implementation plans, assigning responsibilities, and establishing milestones to track progress and ensure accountability. By breaking down objectives into manageable tasks, charity organizations can facilitate execution and monitor progress toward goal attainment.

6. Continuously Monitor and Evaluate: Setting goals and objectives is not a one-time event but an iterative process that requires ongoing monitoring, evaluation, and adjustment. Charity organizations should regularly review progress against objectives, assess performance against targets, and identify areas for improvement or course correction. By continuously monitoring and evaluating progress, charity organizations can adapt strategies, allocate resources, and optimize efforts to maximize impact and achieve their goals effectively.

In conclusion, setting goals and objectives is a critical step in strategic planning for charity organizations, providing a roadmap for achieving the organization's mission and vision. By aligning goals with the mission and vision, being specific and measurable, prioritizing key areas of impact, involving stakeholders, breaking down objectives into actionable steps, and continuously monitoring and evaluating progress, charity organizations can drive organizational success and create positive change in the communities they serve.

Crafting Strategies for Impactful Programs and Services
Crafting strategies for impactful programs and services is essential for charity organizations to achieve their mission and create meaningful change in the communities they serve. Effective strategies involve thoughtful planning, stakeholder engagement, and a focus on maximizing impact and outcomes. In this section, we explore the process of crafting strategies for programs and services and guide developing approaches that drive positive change and address pressing societal needs.

1. Conduct Needs Assessment: Begin by conducting a thorough needs assessment to identify the most pressing challenges, gaps, and opportunities in the communities you serve. This may involve gathering data, conducting surveys, and engaging stakeholders to understand their needs, preferences, and priorities. By identifying key areas of need, charity organizations can tailor their programs and services to address the most critical issues and have the greatest impact.

2. Define Program Objectives: Clearly define the objectives and goals of your programs and services, outlining the specific outcomes and impact you aim to achieve. Objectives should be specific, measurable, achievable, relevant, and time-bound (SMART), providing a clear roadmap for program implementation and evaluation. By setting clear objectives, charity organizations can ensure alignment with their mission and vision and focus efforts on achieving meaningful outcomes.

3. Design Evidence-Based Interventions: Develop evidence-based interventions and strategies that are informed by best practices, research, and data-

driven insights. This may involve drawing on existing evidence and research findings, conducting pilot studies or experiments, and collaborating with experts and stakeholders to design effective and innovative solutions. By basing interventions on evidence and research, charity organizations can increase the likelihood of success and maximize the impact of their programs and services.

4. Foster Collaboration and Partnerships: Collaboration and partnerships are essential for maximizing impact and leveraging resources and expertise. Charity organizations should seek opportunities to collaborate with other organizations, government agencies, community groups, and stakeholders to share resources, coordinate efforts, and amplify impact. By fostering collaboration and partnerships, charity organizations can leverage complementary strengths, avoid duplication of efforts, and achieve greater scale and sustainability.

5. Empower Beneficiaries and Foster Community Ownership: Empower beneficiaries and foster community ownership and engagement in program design, implementation, and evaluation. Involve beneficiaries in decision-making processes, solicit their feedback and input, and prioritize their needs and preferences. By empowering beneficiaries and fostering community ownership, charity organizations can ensure programs are relevant, responsive, and sustainable, leading to greater impact and long-term change.

6. Monitor and Evaluate Program Impact: Implement robust monitoring and evaluation systems to track program implementation, measure outcomes, and assess impact. This may involve collecting data,

conducting surveys, and using qualitative and quantitative methods to evaluate program effectiveness and inform decision-making. By regularly monitoring and evaluating program impact, charity organizations can identify successes, challenges, and opportunities for improvement, allowing them to refine strategies and maximize impact over time.

7. Adapt and Innovate: Finally, charity organizations should be flexible and adaptive, willing to experiment, learn, and innovate in response to changing needs and circumstances. Embrace a culture of continuous improvement, encourage creativity and innovation, and be open to feedback and new ideas. By adapting and innovating, charity organizations can stay responsive and relevant, effectively addressing emerging challenges and opportunities and driving positive change in the communities they serve.

In conclusion, crafting strategies for impactful programs and services is essential for charity organizations to achieve their mission and create meaningful change. By conducting needs assessments, defining clear objectives, designing evidence-based interventions, fostering collaboration and partnerships, empowering beneficiaries, monitoring and evaluating program impact, and adapting and innovating, charity organizations can develop programs and services that drive positive change, address pressing societal needs, and make a lasting difference in the lives of individuals and communities.

Chapter 4:

Leadership and Team Management

Leadership and team management are critical components of effective charity management, shaping the culture, performance, and impact of organizations within the sector. In this chapter, we delve into the principles, practices, and skills involved in leadership and team management, providing insights and guidance for charity leaders and managers to inspire, empower, and guide their teams toward organizational success.

1. Visionary Leadership: Effective charity leaders inspire and motivate their teams by articulating a compelling vision, fostering a sense of purpose, and setting a clear direction for the organization. Visionary leaders communicate their vision with passion and authenticity, inspiring commitment and buy-in from stakeholders and guiding the organization toward its long-term goals and aspirations.

2. Strategic Thinking: Charity leaders must possess strategic thinking skills to navigate complex challenges, identify opportunities, and make informed decisions that advance the organization's mission and objectives. Strategic thinking involves analyzing trends, assessing risks, and developing innovative strategies that leverage the organization's strengths and resources to maximize impact and achieve sustainable growth.

3. Effective Communication: Communication is essential for effective leadership and team management, enabling leaders to convey their vision, expectations, and goals clearly and inspire confidence and trust among team members. Charity leaders must communicate openly, transparently, and empathetically, fostering a culture of

collaboration, feedback, and continuous improvement.

4. Empowering and Developing Teams: Effective leaders empower and develop their teams by providing guidance, support, and opportunities for growth and development. They delegate responsibility, encourage autonomy, and foster a culture of accountability and ownership, enabling team members to take initiative, learn from their experiences, and contribute to organizational success.

5. Building a Positive Organizational Culture: Charity leaders play a pivotal role in shaping organizational culture, values, and norms that promote collaboration, innovation, and inclusivity. They foster a positive work environment that celebrates diversity, recognizes achievements, and prioritizes employee well-being and satisfaction, enhancing morale, engagement, and productivity.

6. Leading Through Change: Change is inevitable in the dynamic environment of charity organizations, and effective leaders must navigate change with resilience, adaptability, and empathy. They communicate change effectively, involve stakeholders in the process, and provide support and resources to help team members navigate transitions and overcome challenges.

7. Promoting Diversity, Equity, and Inclusion: Charity leaders must prioritize diversity, equity, and inclusion in their leadership practices and organizational policies, ensuring that all team members feel valued, respected, and included. They foster a culture of diversity and inclusivity that celebrates differences, challenges biases and promotes equity and fairness in decision-making and resource allocation.

8. Conflict Resolution and Team Building: Charity leaders must possess strong conflict resolution and

team-building skills to address conflicts, foster collaboration, and build cohesive and high-performing teams. They facilitate open dialogue, mediate conflicts constructively, and promote mutual respect and understanding among team members, fostering a culture of trust and collaboration.

9. Leading by Example: Effective charity leaders lead by example, demonstrating integrity, professionalism, and a commitment to ethical conduct in all aspects of their leadership and management practices. They model the organization's values and behaviours, inspire trust and confidence among stakeholders, and set a high standard of excellence for their teams to emulate.

10. Continuous Learning and Improvement: Charity leaders must embrace a mindset of continuous learning and improvement, seeking feedback, reflecting on their experiences, and investing in their own professional development and growth. They cultivate a culture of learning and innovation within the organization, encouraging curiosity, experimentation, and adaptation to drive organizational success and impact.

In conclusion, leadership and team management are essential for effective charity management, shaping organizational culture, performance, and impact. By embodying visionary leadership, strategic thinking, effective communication, and a commitment to empowering and developing teams, charity leaders can inspire, motivate, and guide their organizations toward achieving their mission and making a meaningful difference in the communities they serve. Through strong leadership and team management practices, charity organizations can maximize their effectiveness, resilience, and impact, ultimately advancing their mission of creating positive change in the world.

Effective Leadership Styles in Charity Management

Effective leadership styles in charity management play a crucial role in inspiring, guiding, and empowering teams to achieve organizational goals and fulfil the organization's mission. Charity leaders must adapt their leadership styles to the unique needs, challenges, and opportunities within the nonprofit sector, fostering a culture of collaboration, innovation, and social impact. In this section, we explore several effective leadership styles in charity management and their application in driving organizational success:

1. Transformational Leadership: Transformational leadership is characterized by vision, inspiration, and empowerment, with leaders inspiring and motivating their teams to achieve higher levels of performance and commitment. In charity management, transformational leaders inspire stakeholders to rally around a shared vision for creating positive change, fostering innovation, and empowering teams to tackle complex challenges and pursue ambitious goals.

2. Servant Leadership: Servant leadership emphasizes humility, empathy, and service to others, with leaders prioritizing the needs and well-being of their team members and stakeholders. In charity management, servant leaders focus on supporting and empowering staff, volunteers, and beneficiaries, fostering a culture of compassion, collaboration, and inclusivity, and leading by example through acts of service and selflessness.

3. Collaborative Leadership: Collaborative leadership involves engaging stakeholders in decision-making, problem-solving, and goal-setting processes, fostering a sense of ownership, accountability, and shared responsibility for organizational success. In charity management, collaborative leaders prioritize

collaboration and partnership-building, seeking input and feedback from diverse stakeholders, and fostering a culture of inclusivity and collective action to address complex social challenges.

4. Adaptive Leadership: Adaptive leadership is characterized by flexibility, resilience, and the ability to navigate change and uncertainty effectively. In charity management, adaptive leaders embrace change as an opportunity for growth and innovation, empower teams to adapt and respond to evolving needs and circumstances, and foster a culture of learning, experimentation, and continuous improvement to drive organizational resilience and effectiveness.

5. Ethical Leadership: Ethical leadership emphasizes integrity, transparency, and accountability, with leaders demonstrating a commitment to ethical conduct, fairness, and social responsibility in all aspects of their leadership and management practices. In charity management, ethical leaders prioritize ethical decision-making, uphold high standards of integrity and professionalism, and promote transparency and accountability in organizational governance and operations to build trust and credibility with stakeholders.

6. Inspirational Leadership: Inspirational leadership involves inspiring and motivating teams through vision, passion, and authenticity, with leaders communicating a compelling vision, articulating a clear sense of purpose, and inspiring commitment and buy-in from stakeholders. In charity management, inspirational leaders inspire others to believe in the organization's mission, vision, and values, fostering a sense of purpose and

commitment among staff, volunteers, donors, and beneficiaries, and mobilizing support and resources to achieve organizational goals and create positive change.

7. Adaptive Leadership: Adaptive leadership is characterized by the ability to navigate change, uncertainty, and complexity effectively, with leaders embracing change as an opportunity for growth and innovation, and empowering teams to adapt and respond to evolving needs and circumstances. In charity management, adaptive leaders demonstrate resilience, flexibility, and creativity in the face of challenges, and foster a culture of learning, experimentation, and continuous improvement to drive organizational effectiveness and impact.

In conclusion, effective leadership styles in charity management encompass a range of approaches, each with its own strengths and applications in driving organizational success and social impact. By understanding the unique needs, challenges, and opportunities within the nonprofit sector, charity leaders can adapt their leadership styles to foster collaboration, innovation, and empowerment, and inspire their teams to achieve meaningful change and make a positive difference in the communities they serve. Through effective leadership, charity organizations can maximize their effectiveness, resilience, and impact, ultimately advancing their mission of creating positive change in the world.

Building and Motivating High-Performing Teams
Building and motivating high-performing teams is essential for charity organizations to achieve their mission and maximize their impact in the communities they serve. Effective teams are characterized by collaboration, communication, and a shared commitment to organizational goals and values. In this section, we explore strategies for

building and motivating high-performing teams in charity management:

1. Clarify Roles and Expectations: Clearly define roles, responsibilities, and expectations for each team member, ensuring that everyone understands their contributions to the team and how their work aligns with organizational goals. Establishing clear expectations fosters accountability and empowers team members to take ownership of their tasks and deliverables.

2. Foster Collaboration and Communication: Create a culture of collaboration and open communication, where team members feel comfortable sharing ideas, asking questions, and providing feedback. Encourage regular team meetings, brainstorming sessions, and collaborative problem-solving to foster creativity, innovation, and shared decision-making.

3. Promote Diversity and Inclusion: Embrace diversity and inclusion within the team, valuing and respecting the unique perspectives, backgrounds, and experiences of each team member. Promote a culture of inclusivity where all voices are heard and valued, and where differences are celebrated as strengths that contribute to the team's success.

4. Provide Opportunities for Growth and Development: Invest in the professional development and growth of team members, providing opportunities for training, skill-building, and career advancement. Encourage continuous learning and improvement, and support team members in pursuing their goals and aspirations within the organization.

5. Recognize and Reward Achievements: Recognize and celebrate the achievements and contributions of team members, acknowledging their hard work, dedication, and impact. Provide regular feedback

and praise for a job well done, and offer rewards and incentives to motivate and incentivize high performance.

6. Foster a Positive Work Environment: Create a positive and supportive work environment where team members feel valued, respected, and appreciated. Encourage camaraderie and teamwork, and promote work-life balance by offering flexibility, support, and resources to help team members thrive both personally and professionally.

7. Lead by Example: Lead by example as a role model for the team, demonstrating professionalism, integrity, and a strong work ethic in all aspects of your leadership and management practices. Set high standards of performance and conduct, and inspire team members to uphold these values in their work.

8. Encourage Innovation and Risk-Taking: Foster a culture of innovation and risk-taking within the team, encouraging creativity, experimentation, and exploration of new ideas and approaches. Embrace failure as a learning opportunity, and encourage team members to take calculated risks in pursuit of organizational goals and innovation.

9. Build Trust and Psychological Safety: Cultivate trust and psychological safety within the team, creating an environment where team members feel comfortable taking risks, sharing feedback, and expressing their ideas and concerns openly. Foster a sense of trust and mutual respect among team members, and encourage vulnerability and authenticity in communication and collaboration.

10. Foster a Sense of Purpose and Meaning: Connect team members to the organization's mission and purpose, helping them understand the impact of their work and how it contributes to the greater good.

Inspire a sense of purpose and meaning in their work, and cultivate a shared commitment to making a positive difference in the lives of others.

In conclusion, building and motivating high-performing teams is essential for charity organizations to achieve their mission and maximize their impact. By fostering collaboration, communication, diversity, and inclusion, providing opportunities for growth and development, recognizing and rewarding achievements, and creating a positive work environment, charity leaders can inspire and empower their teams to achieve excellence and make a meaningful difference in the communities they serve. Through effective team building and motivation strategies, charity organizations can harness the collective talents, skills, and passion of their teams to drive positive change and create lasting impact.

Conflict Resolution and Decision-Making in Charity Organizations

Conflict resolution and decision-making are critical aspects of effective management within charity organizations, enabling leaders to navigate challenges, foster collaboration, and drive organizational success. In this section, we explore strategies for conflict resolution and decision-making in charity organizations:

1. Understand the Nature of Conflict: Conflict is a natural and inevitable part of organizational life, arising from differences in perspectives, goals, and priorities. Charity leaders must understand the underlying causes and dynamics of conflict within their organization, whether they stem from interpersonal issues, differences in values or priorities, or external pressures.

2. Foster Open Communication: Open and transparent communication is essential for resolving conflicts and making informed decisions within charity organizations. Leaders should create opportunities

for dialogue and discussion, encourage active listening, and provide a safe space for team members to express their concerns, opinions, and perspectives openly.

3. Practice Active Listening: Active listening is a key skill in conflict resolution, allowing leaders to understand the underlying interests, needs, and concerns of all parties involved. Leaders should listen attentively to what each party is saying, ask clarifying questions, and demonstrate empathy and understanding to build rapport and trust.

4. Seek Common Ground: In resolving conflicts, charity leaders should focus on identifying common ground and areas of agreement among the parties involved. By finding shared interests and goals, leaders can facilitate compromise and collaboration, leading to mutually beneficial outcomes and strengthening relationships within the organization.

5. Use Mediation and Facilitation Techniques: In cases where conflicts escalate or become entrenched, leaders may need to employ mediation or facilitation techniques to facilitate resolution. Mediation involves a neutral third party helping the parties find common ground and reach a mutually acceptable solution, while facilitation involves guiding discussions and decision-making processes to ensure fairness and inclusivity.

6. Encourage Collaborative Decision-Making: Charity leaders should promote collaborative decision-making processes that involve input from all relevant stakeholders. By involving team members, volunteers, and beneficiaries in decision-making, leaders can harness diverse perspectives, promote buy-in and ownership, and enhance the quality and effectiveness of decisions.

7. Use Data and Evidence: In making decisions within charity organizations, leaders should rely on data, evidence, and informed analysis to inform their choices. By gathering relevant information and considering the potential impact of different options, leaders can make well-informed decisions that are grounded in objective evidence and analysis.

8. Consider Ethical and Values-Based Principles: Charity leaders should consider ethical and values-based principles in decision-making, ensuring that choices align with the organization's mission, values, and ethical standards. Leaders should consider the potential social, environmental, and ethical implications of decisions and strive to act in the best interests of the organization and its stakeholders.

9. Evaluate and Learn from Decisions: After making decisions, charity leaders should evaluate the outcomes and impacts of their choices, reflecting on what worked well and what could be improved. By learning from past decisions and experiences, leaders can refine their decision-making processes, build institutional knowledge, and enhance organizational effectiveness over time.

10. Foster a Culture of Respect and Trust: Ultimately, charity leaders should foster a culture of respect, trust, and collaboration within their organizations, where conflicts are addressed constructively, and decisions are made with integrity and transparency. By nurturing a positive organizational culture, leaders can create an environment where team members feel valued, empowered, and motivated to contribute to organizational success.

In conclusion, conflict resolution and decision-making are essential skills for effective leadership within charity organizations. By fostering open communication, practising active listening, seeking common ground, using mediation and facilitation techniques, encouraging collaborative decision-making, using data and evidence, considering ethical and values-based principles, evaluating decisions, and fostering a culture of respect and trust, charity leaders can navigate conflicts and make informed decisions that drive organizational success and advance the organization's mission of creating positive change in the world. Through effective conflict resolution and decision-making processes, charity organizations can strengthen relationships, enhance teamwork, and maximize their impact on the communities they serve.

Chapter 5:

Marketing and Communications in Charity Management

Marketing and communications play a vital role in charity management, enabling organizations to raise awareness, engage stakeholders, and mobilize support for their mission and programs. In this chapter, we explore the principles, strategies, and best practices involved in marketing and communications within charity organizations:

1. Understanding the Target Audience: Effective marketing and communications begin with a clear understanding of the target audience, including donors, volunteers, beneficiaries, and other stakeholders. Charity organizations should conduct audience research to identify their demographics, preferences, interests, and communication preferences, enabling them to tailor their messages and strategies to resonate with their audience effectively.

2. Crafting Compelling Messages: Charity organizations should craft compelling messages that inspire action and resonate with their target audience. Messages should communicate the organization's mission, values, and impact in a clear, concise, and compelling manner, highlighting the urgency and importance of supporting their cause.

3. Utilizing Multi-Channel Marketing: Charity organizations should leverage multiple communication channels to reach their target audience effectively. This may include traditional

channels such as print media, direct mail, and events, as well as digital channels such as websites, social media, email marketing, and online advertising. By utilizing a mix of channels, organizations can maximize their reach and engagement with diverse audiences.

4. Storytelling and Impactful Content: Storytelling is a powerful tool for engaging emotions, building connections, and inspiring action. Charity organizations should tell stories that highlight the impact of their work, featuring real-life examples of beneficiaries, volunteers, and donors whose lives have been touched by the organization's programs and services. Impactful content, such as photos, videos, testimonials, and case studies, can help bring these stories to life and resonate with audiences on an emotional level.

5. Building Strong Brand Identity: Charity organizations should invest in building a strong brand identity that reflects their mission, values, and unique value proposition. A strong brand identity helps organizations stand out in a crowded marketplace, build credibility and trust with stakeholders, and foster a sense of loyalty and connection among supporters.

6. Engaging with Stakeholders: Charity organizations should actively engage with stakeholders through various communication channels, including social media, email newsletters, website updates, and in-person events. Engaging with stakeholders allows

organizations to build relationships, gather feedback, and mobilize support for their cause, fostering a sense of community and belonging among supporters.

7. Measuring and Evaluating Impact: Charity organizations should measure and evaluate the impact of their marketing and communications efforts to assess effectiveness and inform future strategies. Key performance indicators (KPIs) such as website traffic, social media engagement, email open rates, and donation conversion rates can help organizations track progress and identify areas for improvement.

8. Adapting to Emerging Trends: Charity organizations should stay informed about emerging trends and technologies in marketing and communications and adapt their strategies accordingly. This may include leveraging new platforms and technologies, such as mobile apps, virtual reality, and artificial intelligence, to enhance engagement and reach new audiences.

9. Cultivating Relationships with Donors and Supporters: Charity organizations should prioritize cultivating relationships with donors and supporters through personalized communication, stewardship, and recognition. By expressing gratitude, keeping donors informed about the impact of their contributions, and involving them in the organization's work, organizations can foster loyalty and long-term support.

10. Advocacy and Public Relations: Charity organizations should engage in advocacy and public relations efforts to raise awareness about their cause, influence public opinion and policy, and drive social change. This may include media outreach, public speaking engagements, grassroots organizing, and coalition-building to amplify the organization's message and impact.

In conclusion, marketing and communications are essential components of effective charity management, enabling organizations to raise awareness, engage stakeholders, and mobilize support for their mission and programs. By understanding their target audience, crafting compelling messages, utilizing multi-channel marketing, storytelling, and impactful content, building a strong brand identity, engaging with stakeholders, measuring impact, adapting to emerging trends, cultivating relationships with donors and supporters, and engaging in advocacy and public relations efforts, charity organizations can maximize their reach and impact, driving positive change in the communities they serve. Through strategic marketing and communications efforts, charity organizations can raise awareness, inspire action, and make a meaningful difference in the world.

Branding and Positioning for Charity Organizations

Branding and positioning are essential components of marketing strategy for charity organizations, helping them establish a strong identity, differentiate themselves from competitors, and build credibility and trust with stakeholders. In this section, we explore strategies for branding and positioning in charity management:

1. Define Your Brand Identity: Start by defining your organization's brand identity, including its mission, values, and unique value proposition. Your brand identity should reflect what sets your organization apart and why donors, volunteers, and beneficiaries should support your cause. Consider elements such as your organization's name, logo, colours, and messaging, and ensure consistency across all communication channels.

2. Identify Your Target Audience: Understand your target audience, including donors, volunteers, beneficiaries, and other stakeholders. Conduct audience research to identify their demographics, preferences, and communication habits, and tailor your branding and messaging to resonate with their interests and values. By understanding your audience, you can develop more effective branding and communication strategies that engage and inspire action.

3. Articulate Your Brand Story: Your brand story is a powerful tool for connecting with stakeholders and inspiring support for your cause. Tell the story of your organization's founding, mission, and impact compellingly and authentically, highlighting the lives you've touched and the difference you've made. Use storytelling techniques to evoke emotion, build empathy, and inspire action among your audience.

4. Differentiate Your Organization: Identify what sets your organization apart from others in the charity sector and highlight these unique qualities in your branding and positioning. Whether it's your innovative approach, your track record of success, or your commitment to transparency and accountability, emphasize what makes your organization special and why donors should choose to support you over other causes.

5. Build Trust and Credibility: Trust and credibility are essential for charity organizations to build lasting relationships with donors, volunteers, and other stakeholders. Be transparent about your organization's finances, operations, and impact, and demonstrate accountability and integrity in all aspects of your work. Highlight success stories, testimonials, and third-party endorsements to build credibility and reassure donors of the impact of their contributions.

6. Establish Your Positioning: Positioning refers to how your organization is perceived relative to competitors and other players in the charity sector. Identify your unique value proposition and the specific niche or area of focus where your organization excels. Position yourself as a leader in your field, whether it's through your expertise, innovation, or impact, and communicate this positioning consistently in your branding and messaging.

7. Engage Your Audience: Engage your audience through interactive and participatory branding

initiatives that invite them to be part of your organization's story. Encourage user-generated content, testimonials, and social media campaigns that allow supporters to share their experiences and spread the word about your cause. By empowering your audience to become advocates for your organization, you can amplify your reach and impact.

8. Measure and Adapt: Continuously monitor and evaluate the effectiveness of your branding and positioning efforts, using metrics such as brand awareness, engagement, and donor retention to assess impact. Solicit feedback from stakeholders and adapt your branding strategies based on insights and learnings. Stay agile and responsive to changes in the external environment and evolving audience preferences to ensure your brand remains relevant and impactful.

9. Foster Brand Ambassadors: Cultivate brand ambassadors among your supporters, volunteers, and beneficiaries who are passionate about your cause and willing to advocate on your behalf. Provide training, resources, and opportunities for supporters to get involved and spread the word about your organization. By harnessing the enthusiasm and advocacy of your supporters, you can extend the reach of your brand and attract new supporters to your cause.

10. Collaborate and Partner: Collaborate with like-minded organizations, businesses, and influencers to amplify your brand and reach new audiences.

Partnering with other organizations allows you to leverage their networks, resources, and expertise to increase your organization's visibility and impact. Seek out strategic partnerships that align with your mission and values and offer opportunities for mutual benefit and collaboration.

In conclusion, branding and positioning are essential for charity organizations to establish a strong identity, differentiate themselves from competitors, and build credibility and trust with stakeholders. By defining your brand identity, identifying your target audience, articulating your brand story, differentiating your organization, building trust and credibility, establishing your positioning, engaging your audience, measuring and adapting, fostering brand ambassadors, and collaborating and partnering, charity organizations can create a compelling and impactful brand that resonates with donors, volunteers, and beneficiaries, driving support and advancing their mission of creating positive change in the world. Through strategic branding and positioning initiatives, charity organizations can strengthen their impact and achieve their goals more effectively.

Utilizing Digital Marketing and Social Media for Outreach

Digital marketing and social media have revolutionized the way charity organizations engage with their audience, allowing them to reach a wider audience, amplify their message, and mobilize support for their cause. In this section, we explore strategies for utilizing digital marketing and social media for outreach in charity management:

1. Establish a Strong Online Presence: Start by establishing a strong online presence through a

website and social media profiles on platforms such as Facebook, Twitter, Instagram, LinkedIn, and YouTube. Your website serves as the central hub for information about your organization, while social media platforms provide opportunities for engagement, conversation, and community-building.

2. Create Compelling Content: Create compelling and shareable content that resonates with your audience and inspires them to take action. This may include stories of impact, testimonials from beneficiaries and volunteers, behind-the-scenes glimpses of your work, and updates on upcoming events and campaigns. Use a mix of text, images, videos, and infographics to keep your content diverse and engaging.

3. Utilize Targeted Advertising: Use targeted advertising on social media platforms to reach specific segments of your audience with tailored messages and calls to action. Targeted advertising allows you to reach people based on demographics, interests, behaviour, and other factors, maximizing the effectiveness of your outreach efforts and driving engagement and conversion.

4. Engage with Your Audience: Actively engage with your audience on social media by responding to comments, messages, and mentions promptly and thoughtfully. Encourage conversation, ask questions, and solicit feedback to foster a sense of community and connection with your followers. By engaging

authentically with your audience, you can build trust, loyalty, and advocacy for your cause.

5. Leverage Social Media Influencers: Partner with social media influencers and advocates who align with your organization's values and mission to amplify your message and reach new audiences. Influencers can help raise awareness about your cause, drive engagement and donations, and lend credibility and authenticity to your brand. Choose influencers whose followers align with your target audience and whose values align with your organization's mission.

6. Harness the Power of Video: Video content is highly engaging and shareable, making it a powerful tool for outreach on social media. Create impactful videos that tell compelling stories, showcase the impact of your work, and inspire action among your audience. Consider live-streaming events, interviews, and behind-the-scenes footage to provide a more authentic and immersive experience for your followers.

7. Optimize for Mobile: With a growing number of people accessing the internet and social media platforms via mobile devices, it's essential to optimize your digital marketing efforts for mobile users. Ensure that your website and content are mobile-friendly and responsive, and consider mobile-specific advertising formats and strategies to reach and engage mobile audiences effectively.

8. Encourage User-Generated Content: Encourage your audience to create and share content related to your organization and cause. User-generated content, such as photos, videos, testimonials, and personal stories, can be a powerful way to showcase the impact of your work and inspire others to get involved. Create campaigns and hashtags that encourage supporters to share their experiences and contributions, and feature user-generated content on your website and social media platforms.

9. Track and Measure Results: Use analytics and tracking tools to monitor the performance of your digital marketing and social media efforts. Track metrics such as website traffic, engagement, conversion rates, and return on investment to assess the effectiveness of your campaigns and identify areas for improvement. Use data-driven insights to optimize your strategies and allocate resources more effectively.

10. Collaborate with Partners and Supporters: Collaborate with partners, supporters, and influencers to amplify your digital marketing and social media efforts. Partner with other organizations, businesses, and individuals who share your values and mission to co-create content, cross-promote campaigns, and reach new audiences. By leveraging the networks and resources of your partners and supporters, you can extend the reach and impact of your outreach efforts and drive positive change more effectively.

In conclusion, digital marketing and social media offer powerful tools for charity organizations to engage with their audience, raise awareness about their cause, and mobilize support for their mission. By establishing a strong online presence, creating compelling content, utilizing targeted advertising, engaging with your audience, leveraging social media influencers, harnessing the power of video, optimizing for mobile, encouraging user-generated content, tracking and measuring results, and collaborating with partners and supporters, charity organizations can maximize the impact of their outreach efforts and drive positive change in the communities they serve. Through strategic digital marketing and social media initiatives, charity organizations can amplify their message, inspire action, and make a meaningful difference in the world.

Effective Communication Strategies for Donor Engagement

Effective communication is crucial for engaging donors and building lasting relationships that support the mission and sustainability of charity organizations. In this section, we explore strategies for communicating effectively with donors to inspire support and foster donor engagement:

1. Personalized Communication: Tailor your communication to the interests, preferences, and giving history of individual donors. Use personalized salutations, address donors by name, and reference their past contributions or involvement with the organization to demonstrate appreciation and recognition. Personalization shows donors that their support is valued and encourages continued engagement.

2. Share Impactful Stories: Use storytelling to illustrate the impact of donors' contributions and demonstrate the tangible difference their support makes in the lives of beneficiaries. Share stories of individuals or communities who have benefited from the organization's programs and services, highlighting specific examples of positive outcomes and transformation. Personal stories evoke emotion, build empathy, and inspire donors to continue supporting the organization's mission.

3. Provide Regular Updates: Keep donors informed about the organization's activities, achievements, and progress toward goals through regular updates and communications. Share success stories, project milestones, and outcomes of funded initiatives to demonstrate transparency and accountability. Regular updates help donors feel connected to the organization's work and informed about the impact of their support.

4. Express Gratitude Sincerely: Express gratitude sincerely and authentically to donors for their generosity and support. Thank donors promptly and personally for their contributions, whether through handwritten notes, phone calls, or personalized emails. Acknowledge the specific impact of their gifts and the difference they are making in the lives of others. Genuine appreciation strengthens relationships and encourages continued support from donors.

5. Engage Donors in Meaningful Ways: Engage donors in meaningful ways beyond financial contributions by offering opportunities for involvement and participation. Invite donors to volunteer, attend events, serve on committees, or participate in advocacy efforts related to the organization's mission. Engaging donors in hands-on activities fosters a sense of ownership and investment in the organization's success and strengthens their connection to the cause.

6. Provide Transparency and Accountability: Be transparent about the organization's financials, operations, and use of funds to demonstrate accountability to donors. Provide clear and accessible information about the organization's budget, expenses, and impact metrics, and communicate how donor contributions are allocated and utilized to support programs and services. Transparency builds trust and confidence in the organization's stewardship of donor funds.

7. Foster Two-Way Communication: Foster two-way communication with donors by inviting feedback, questions, and input on organizational initiatives and decisions. Create opportunities for donors to share their thoughts, suggestions, and concerns through surveys, focus groups, or donor advisory councils. Actively listen to donor feedback and demonstrate responsiveness to their input, demonstrating that their opinions are valued and considered in organizational decision-making.

8. Segment Donor Communication: Segment donor communication is based on factors such as giving history, interests, and communication preferences to deliver targeted and relevant messages. Customize communication channels, frequency, and content to align with the preferences of different donor segments, whether it's through direct mail, email newsletters, social media updates, or personal calls. Segmenting communication ensures that donors receive information that is most meaningful and relevant to them, increasing engagement and responsiveness.

9. Cultivate Long-Term Relationships: Focus on cultivating long-term relationships with donors based on trust, respect, and mutual benefit. Invest in stewardship efforts to nurture ongoing connections with donors beyond individual transactions or campaigns. Communicate consistently with donors throughout the year, not just during fundraising appeals, to maintain engagement and reinforce their commitment to the organization's mission over time.

10. Measure and Evaluate Impact: Measure and evaluate the impact of donor communication efforts to assess effectiveness and inform future strategies. Track key performance indicators such as donor retention rates, response rates to communications, and levels of donor engagement to gauge the success of communication initiatives. Use data and feedback to refine communication strategies and optimize engagement with donors over time.

In conclusion, effective communication strategies are essential for engaging donors and fostering meaningful relationships that support the mission and sustainability of charity organizations. By personalizing communication, sharing impactful stories, providing regular updates, expressing gratitude sincerely, engaging donors in meaningful ways, providing transparency and accountability, fostering two-way communication, segmenting donor communication, cultivating long-term relationships, and measuring and evaluating impact, charity organizations can build stronger connections with donors, inspire support, and advance their mission of creating positive change in the world. Through strategic donor communication efforts, charity organizations can cultivate a loyal and committed donor base that continues to champion their cause and make a lasting impact in the communities they serve.

Chapter 6:

Impact Measurement and Evaluation

Impact measurement and evaluation are essential components of effective charity management, enabling organizations to assess the outcomes and effectiveness of their programs, demonstrate accountability to stakeholders, and make data-driven decisions to maximize their impact. In this chapter, we explore the principles, methods, and best practices involved in impact measurement and evaluation within charity organizations:

1. Defining Impact: Start by defining what impact means for your organization and the specific outcomes you aim to achieve through your programs and initiatives. Impact may include changes in behavior, attitudes, knowledge, skills, or conditions among beneficiaries, as well as broader societal or systemic changes related to the organization's mission and goals.

2. Establishing Objectives and Indicators: Establish clear objectives and measurable indicators to track progress and evaluate the impact of your programs and initiatives. Objectives should be specific, measurable, achievable, relevant, and time-bound (SMART), and indicators should be selected based on their relevance, reliability, and feasibility for measuring progress toward desired outcomes.

3. Developing Monitoring and Evaluation Plans: Develop monitoring and evaluation plans to systematically

collect, analyze, and interpret data on program inputs, activities, outputs, outcomes, and impacts. Determine the data collection methods, tools, and protocols to be used, as well as the frequency and responsibilities for data collection, analysis, and reporting.

4. Using Mixed-Methods Approaches: Utilize mixed-methods approaches that combine quantitative and qualitative data collection and analysis techniques to provide a comprehensive understanding of program impact. Quantitative methods, such as surveys, questionnaires, and statistical analysis, can measure the prevalence and magnitude of outcomes, while qualitative methods, such as interviews, focus groups, and case studies, can explore the underlying processes, mechanisms, and contextual factors that contribute to impact.

5. Conducting Baseline and Endline Assessments: Conduct baseline assessments at the outset of program implementation to establish a benchmark for measuring change over time and identify areas for improvement. Follow up with online assessments after program activities to evaluate the extent to which objectives have been achieved and assess the overall impact of the intervention.

6. Engaging Stakeholders in Evaluation: Engage stakeholders, including beneficiaries, donors, staff, volunteers, and partner organizations, in the evaluation process to ensure their perspectives, insights, and feedback are incorporated into

decision-making. Involve stakeholders in defining evaluation criteria, interpreting findings, and using evaluation results to inform program planning, implementation, and improvement.

7. Ensuring Ethical and Responsible Evaluation: Conduct evaluations ethically and responsibly, respecting the rights, dignity, and confidentiality of participants and adhering to ethical guidelines and standards for research and evaluation. Ensure informed consent, privacy, and confidentiality are maintained throughout the evaluation process, and address any potential risks or unintended consequences of evaluation activities.

8. Communicating Findings and Lessons Learned: Communicate evaluation findings, lessons learned, and recommendations to internal and external stakeholders in a clear, transparent, and accessible manner. Prepare evaluation reports, summaries, presentations, and other communication materials that effectively convey key findings, insights, and implications for decision-making and learning.

9. Using Evaluation Results for Learning and Improvement: Use evaluation results to inform organizational learning and continuous improvement by identifying strengths, weaknesses, and areas for enhancement in program design, implementation, and management. Reflect on evaluation findings, adapt strategies and practices based on lessons learned, and incorporate feedback into future planning and decision-making processes.

10. Advocating for Change and Accountability: Use evaluation evidence to advocate for change, accountability, and resource allocation in support of the organization's mission and goals. Share evaluation findings with policymakers, funders, and other stakeholders to demonstrate the value and impact of your programs, advocate for supportive policies and investments, and contribute to broader social change and systemic improvement.

In conclusion, impact measurement and evaluation are essential processes for charity organizations to assess the effectiveness and outcomes of their programs, demonstrate accountability to stakeholders, and drive continuous improvement and learning. By defining impact, establishing objectives and indicators, developing monitoring and evaluation plans, using mixed-methods approaches, conducting baseline and end-line assessments, engaging stakeholders in evaluation, ensuring ethical and responsible evaluation, communicating findings and lessons learned, using evaluation results for learning and improvement, and advocating for change and accountability, charity organizations can enhance their capacity to create positive change and make a meaningful difference in the lives of beneficiaries and communities. Through rigorous and evidence-based evaluation practices, charity organizations can maximize their impact, promote transparency and accountability, and contribute to sustainable development and social justice.

Monitoring and Evaluation Frameworks for Charity Programs

Monitoring and evaluation (M&E) frameworks provide charity organizations with a structured approach to systematically track and assess the progress, effectiveness, and impact of their programs and initiatives. In this section, we explore the key components and considerations for developing M&E frameworks for charity programs:

1. Establish Clear Objectives and Outcomes: Begin by clearly defining the objectives and intended outcomes of your charity program. Objectives should be specific, measurable, achievable, relevant, and time-bound (SMART), and outcomes should be defined in terms of changes in behaviour, conditions, or circumstances among beneficiaries or target populations.

2. Identify Key Performance Indicators (KPIs): Identify key performance indicators (KPIs) that will be used to measure progress toward program objectives and outcomes. KPIs should be selected based on their relevance, reliability, and feasibility for measuring program impact. Examples of KPIs may include the number of beneficiaries reached, changes in knowledge or attitudes, or improvements in health or well-being indicators.

3. Define Data Collection Methods and Tools: Determine the data collection methods and tools that will be used to collect information on program inputs, activities, outputs, outcomes, and impacts. This may include surveys, interviews, focus groups, observation, document review, and administrative

data sources. Select data collection tools that are appropriate for the context, target population, and objectives of the program.

4. Establish Baselines and Targets: Establish baselines for each key performance indicator at the outset of the program to provide a benchmark for measuring change over time. Set targets or benchmarks for desired outcomes and indicators to guide program implementation and measure progress toward program goals. Targets should be ambitious yet achievable within the program's timeframe and resource constraints.

5. Develop Monitoring Plans: Develop monitoring plans that outline the procedures, responsibilities, and timelines for collecting, analyzing, and reporting data on program activities and outcomes. Specify the frequency and methods of data collection, as well as the roles and responsibilities of staff and partners involved in monitoring activities. Monitor progress regularly to track implementation, identify challenges, and make timely adjustments as needed.

6. Conduct Regular Data Collection and Analysis: Implement data collection activities according to the monitoring plan and collect data regularly to track progress and performance against program objectives and targets. Analyze data using appropriate quantitative and qualitative methods to assess the effectiveness and impact of program interventions. Use data analysis to identify trends,

patterns, and lessons learned that can inform program decision-making and improvement.

7. Ensure Data Quality and Reliability: Ensure the quality and reliability of data collected through rigorous data collection protocols, training of data collectors, and validation procedures. Establish data quality assurance mechanisms to verify the accuracy, completeness, and consistency of data collected, and address any data quality issues or discrepancies identified during the monitoring process.

8. Engage Stakeholders in Evaluation: Engage stakeholders, including beneficiaries, donors, staff, volunteers, and partner organizations, in the evaluation process to ensure their perspectives, insights, and feedback are incorporated into decision-making. Involve stakeholders in defining evaluation criteria, interpreting findings, and using evaluation results to inform program planning, implementation, and improvement.

9. Use Evaluation Findings for Learning and Improvement: Use evaluation findings to assess the effectiveness and impact of the program, identify strengths, weaknesses, and areas for improvement, and make evidence-based decisions to enhance program performance. Share evaluation results with stakeholders and use them to guide program adaptation, innovation, and scaling of successful approaches.

10. Communicate Results and Lessons Learned: Communicate monitoring and evaluation results, lessons learned, and recommendations to internal and external stakeholders in a clear, transparent, and accessible manner. Prepare evaluation reports, summaries, presentations, and other communication materials that effectively convey key findings, insights, and implications for decision-making and learning.

In conclusion, monitoring and evaluation frameworks are essential tools for charity organizations to systematically track and assess the progress, effectiveness, and impact of their programs and initiatives. By establishing clear objectives and outcomes, identifying key performance indicators, defining data collection methods and tools, establishing baselines and targets, developing monitoring plans, conducting regular data collection and analysis, ensuring data quality and reliability, engaging stakeholders in evaluation, using evaluation findings for learning and improvement, and communicating results and lessons learned, charity organizations can enhance their capacity to create positive change and make a meaningful difference in the lives of beneficiaries and communities. Through rigorous monitoring and evaluation practices, charity organizations can demonstrate accountability, promote transparency, and drive continuous improvement in their programs and operations.

Assessing Social Impact and Effectiveness

Assessing social impact and effectiveness is a critical aspect of charity management, enabling organizations to understand the outcomes and broader societal changes resulting from their programs and initiatives. In this section, we explore key considerations and methodologies for assessing social impact and effectiveness in charity organizations:

1. Define Social Impact: Begin by defining what social impact means for your organization and the specific outcomes you aim to achieve through your programs and initiatives. Social impact encompasses changes in behaviour, attitudes, conditions, or circumstances among beneficiaries or target populations, as well as broader systemic or societal changes related to the organization's mission and goals.

2. Identify Key Impact Indicators: Identify key impact indicators that will be used to measure the social impact and effectiveness of your programs and initiatives. These indicators should be relevant, measurable, and aligned with the organization's mission and objectives. Examples of impact indicators may include improvements in health, education, economic empowerment, social inclusion, environmental sustainability, or community resilience.

3. Use Theory of Change or Logic Models: Develop a theory of change or logic model that outlines the causal pathways through which your programs are expected to achieve desired outcomes and impacts. Identify the inputs, activities, outputs, outcomes, and impacts of your programs, as well as the assumptions and external factors that may influence

program success. Use the theory of change to guide the selection of impact indicators and evaluation methods.

4. Employ Mixed-Methods Approaches: Utilize mixed-methods approaches that combine quantitative and qualitative data collection and analysis techniques to assess social impact and effectiveness comprehensively. Quantitative methods, such as surveys, questionnaires, and statistical analysis, can measure the prevalence and magnitude of outcomes, while qualitative methods, such as interviews, focus groups, and case studies, can provide insights into the underlying processes, mechanisms, and contextual factors that contribute to impact.

5. Conduct Baseline and Endline Assessments: Conduct baseline assessments at the outset of program implementation to establish a benchmark for measuring change over time and identify areas for improvement. Follow up with online assessments after program activities to evaluate the extent to which objectives have been achieved and assess the overall impact of the intervention. Compare baseline and end-line data to measure changes in key impact indicators and assess program effectiveness.

6. Engage Beneficiaries and Stakeholders: Engage beneficiaries and stakeholders in the assessment process to ensure their perspectives, insights, and feedback are incorporated into evaluation activities. Involve beneficiaries in defining evaluation criteria,

participating in data collection, and interpreting findings to ensure that assessment efforts are relevant, meaningful, and culturally appropriate. Engage stakeholders, including donors, staff, volunteers, and partner organizations, to gather diverse perspectives and insights into program impact.

7. Use Participatory and Empowerment Approaches: Adopt participatory and empowerment approaches that involve beneficiaries in the design, implementation, and evaluation of programs, empowering them to take ownership of their own development and contribute to positive change in their communities. Provide opportunities for beneficiaries to participate in decision-making, problem-solving, and advocacy efforts related to program goals and objectives.

8. Measure Sustainable Outcomes: Assess the sustainability of program outcomes by evaluating the extent to which changes achieved during the program continue after the intervention has ended. Measure long-term outcomes and impacts to determine whether program benefits are sustained over time and whether interventions have contributed to lasting improvements in the well-being and resilience of beneficiaries and communities.

9. Consider Contextual Factors and Externalities: Consider contextual factors and externalities that may influence program outcomes and impact, such as social, economic, political, and environmental

conditions, as well as external shocks and crises. Assess the extent to which programs are sensitive and responsive to local context, adaptive to changing circumstances, and resilient to external challenges and uncertainties.

10. Use Evaluation Findings for Learning and Improvement: Use evaluation findings to inform organizational learning and continuous improvement by identifying strengths, weaknesses, and areas for enhancement in program design, implementation, and management. Reflect on evaluation findings, adapt strategies and practices based on lessons learned, and incorporate feedback into future planning and decision-making processes. Use evaluation evidence to advocate for change, inform policy and practice, and contribute to broader social change and systemic improvement.

In conclusion, assessing social impact and effectiveness is essential for charity organizations to understand the outcomes and broader societal changes resulting from their programs and initiatives. By defining social impact, identifying key impact indicators, using the theory of change or logic models, employing mixed-methods approaches, conducting baseline and end-line assessments, engaging beneficiaries and stakeholders, using participatory and empowerment approaches, measuring sustainable outcomes, considering contextual factors and externalities, and using evaluation findings for learning and improvement, charity organizations can enhance their capacity to create positive change and make a meaningful difference in the lives of beneficiaries and communities. Through rigorous assessment practices, charity organizations can demonstrate accountability, promote transparency, and drive continuous improvement in their programs and operations.

Using Data for Continuous Improvement

Data-driven decision-making is a powerful tool for charity organizations to continuously improve their programs, operations, and impact. In this section, we explore how charity organizations can effectively use data for continuous improvement:

1. Define Data Needs and Objectives: Start by defining the data needs and objectives of your organization, including the specific information you need to collect, analyze, and use to inform decision-making and improvement efforts. Identify key performance indicators (KPIs) and metrics that align with your organizational goals and priorities.

2. Establish Data Collection Systems: Establish robust data collection systems and processes to systematically collect, manage, and analyze data on program inputs, activities, outputs, outcomes, and impacts. Use a combination of quantitative and qualitative data collection methods, such as surveys, interviews, focus groups, observation, and document review, to gather relevant information from beneficiaries, staff, volunteers, and other stakeholders.

3. Ensure Data Quality and Integrity: Ensure the quality and integrity of data collected through rigorous data

collection protocols, training of data collectors, and validation procedures. Establish data quality assurance mechanisms to verify the accuracy, completeness, and consistency of data collected, and address any data quality issues or discrepancies identified during the data collection process.

4. Analyze Data for Insights and Trends: Analyze data collected from various sources to identify insights, trends, and patterns that can inform decision-making and improvement efforts. Use descriptive and inferential statistical analysis techniques to summarize and interpret data, identify correlations and relationships, and uncover actionable insights for program optimization and refinement.

5. Monitor Key Performance Indicators (KPIs): Monitor key performance indicators (KPIs) and metrics regularly to track progress and performance against organizational goals and targets. Use data dashboards, scorecards, and visualizations to present KPIs in a clear and accessible format, allowing stakeholders to monitor performance trends and make informed decisions in real-time.

6. Conduct Root Cause Analysis: Conduct root cause analysis to identify underlying factors contributing to performance gaps, challenges, or issues identified through data analysis. Use techniques such as fishbone diagrams, 5 Whys, or Pareto analysis to systematically explore the causes and drivers of problems or trends observed in the data and identify opportunities for improvement.

7. Solicit Feedback and Input: Solicit feedback and input from stakeholders, including beneficiaries, staff, volunteers, donors, and partner organizations, to gather diverse perspectives and insights into program performance and areas for improvement. Use surveys, focus groups, interviews, and feedback mechanisms to engage stakeholders in the evaluation process and incorporate their input into decision-making.

8. Benchmark and Compare Performance: Benchmark your organization's performance against industry standards, best practices, and peer organizations to assess relative performance and identify areas for improvement. Compare your organization's performance metrics, outcomes, and impact indicators with relevant benchmarks and benchmarks to identify gaps and opportunities for enhancement.

9. Implement Continuous Improvement Strategies: Implement continuous improvement strategies based on insights and findings from data analysis, stakeholder feedback, and benchmarking exercises. Develop action plans and initiatives to address performance gaps, capitalize on strengths, and capitalize on opportunities identified through data-driven decision-making.

10. Evaluate Impact and Effectiveness: Evaluate the impact and effectiveness of improvement efforts over time to assess the outcomes and changes resulting from interventions and initiatives. Monitor and

measure changes in key performance indicators, outcomes, and impact indicators to determine the success and effectiveness of improvement strategies and initiatives.

In conclusion, using data for continuous improvement is essential for charity organizations to optimize their programs, operations, and impact. By defining data needs and objectives, establishing data collection systems, ensuring data quality and integrity, analyzing data for insights and trends, monitoring key performance indicators (KPIs), conducting root cause analysis, soliciting feedback and input, benchmarking and comparing performance, implementing continuous improvement strategies, and evaluating impact and effectiveness, charity organizations can enhance their capacity to create positive change and make a meaningful difference in the lives of beneficiaries and communities. Through data-driven decision-making and continuous improvement efforts, charity organizations can demonstrate accountability, promote transparency, and drive innovation and excellence in their programs and operations.

Chapter 7:

Global Trends and Innovations in Charity Management

In the ever-evolving landscape of charity management, organizations must stay abreast of global trends and innovations to remain effective, efficient, and impactful. In this chapter, we explore some of the emerging trends and innovative practices shaping charity management worldwide:

1. Technology Integration: Embracing technology is no longer optional but essential for charity organizations to streamline operations, enhance communication, and maximize impact. From donor management systems and online fundraising platforms to data analytics and artificial intelligence, charities are leveraging technology to improve efficiency, reach new audiences, and innovate service delivery.

2. Data-driven Decision-making: Charity organizations are increasingly using data analytics and insights to inform decision-making, measure impact, and optimize program effectiveness. By collecting and analyzing data on donor behaviour, program outcomes, and organizational performance, charities can make informed decisions, identify areas for improvement, and allocate resources more effectively.

3. Collaboration and Partnerships: Collaboration and partnerships are becoming more prevalent in charity management as organizations recognize the value of pooling resources, expertise, and networks to tackle

complex social challenges. Strategic partnerships with other charities, businesses, government agencies, and community organizations enable charities to leverage complementary strengths, share best practices, and scale impact.

4. Impact Investing: Impact investing, which seeks to generate positive social and environmental impact alongside financial returns, is gaining traction in the charity sector. Charities are exploring innovative financing models, such as social impact bonds, impact investment funds, and pay-for-success contracts, to attract capital, scale programs, and achieve sustainable outcomes.

5. Diversity, Equity, and Inclusion (DEI): Charity organizations are prioritizing diversity, equity, and inclusion (DEI) in their leadership, staffing, and programmatic efforts to ensure that their work is responsive to the needs and perspectives of diverse communities. By fostering inclusive environments, addressing systemic barriers, and centring marginalized voices, charities can enhance their effectiveness and relevance in serving all populations.

6. Advocacy and Policy Change: Charity organizations are increasingly engaged in advocacy and policy change efforts to address root causes of social problems, influence public policy, and drive systemic change. By advocating for policy reforms, mobilizing grassroots support, and collaborating with policymakers and stakeholders, charities can amplify

their impact and create lasting change at the local, national, and global levels.

7. Environmental Sustainability: Recognizing the interconnectedness of social and environmental issues, charity organizations are integrating environmental sustainability into their mission, operations, and programs. From adopting green practices and reducing carbon footprints to promoting eco-friendly initiatives and addressing climate change impacts, charities are aligning their work with sustainable development goals and principles.

8. Remote Work and Virtual Engagement: The COVID-19 pandemic has accelerated the adoption of remote work and virtual engagement practices in charity management. Organizations are embracing remote work arrangements, virtual meetings, and online events to adapt to changing circumstances, maintain productivity, and engage stakeholders in a digital-first world.

9. Transparency and Accountability: Transparency and accountability are paramount in charity management to build trust, foster donor confidence, and demonstrate impact. Charities are prioritizing transparency in their financial reporting, governance structures, and programmatic activities, and implementing robust accountability mechanisms to ensure responsible stewardship of resources and adherence to ethical standards.

10. Resilience and Adaptability: In a rapidly changing and uncertain world, resilience and adaptability are essential qualities for charity organizations to thrive. Charities are investing in organizational resilience, contingency planning, and adaptive management practices to withstand shocks and disruptions, navigate challenges, and seize opportunities for innovation and growth.

In conclusion, staying informed about global trends and innovations in charity management is essential for organizations to remain relevant, responsive, and resilient in fulfilling their missions and driving positive change. By embracing technology, data-driven decision-making, collaboration and partnerships, impact investing, diversity, equity, and inclusion (DEI), advocacy and policy change, environmental sustainability, remote work and virtual engagement, transparency and accountability, and resilience and adaptability, charity organizations can enhance their capacity to address pressing social challenges, meet evolving community needs, and create a more just, equitable, and sustainable world. Through continuous learning, innovation, and collaboration, charity organizations can position themselves as leaders in driving positive social change and improving the well-being of individuals and communities worldwide.

Emerging Technologies in the Charity Sector

Technological advancements are revolutionizing the way charity organizations operate, innovate, and deliver impact. In this section, we explore some of the emerging technologies shaping the charity sector:

1. Blockchain Technology: Blockchain technology offers transparent, secure, and immutable transaction records, making it ideal for improving transparency and accountability in charity operations. Charities are leveraging blockchain for donation tracking, ensuring funds reach intended recipients, and reducing fraud and corruption.

2. Artificial Intelligence (AI): AI-powered solutions are enhancing efficiency and effectiveness in charity management. Charities are using AI for donor segmentation, personalized fundraising campaigns, predictive analytics for resource allocation, and chatbots for donor engagement and support.

3. Internet of Things (IoT): IoT devices are enabling charities to collect real-time data and monitor environmental conditions, resource usage, and program impact remotely. Charities are using IoT sensors for disaster response, environmental monitoring, and optimizing the delivery of services in remote or underserved areas.

4. Virtual Reality (VR) and Augmented Reality (AR): VR and AR technologies are transforming donor engagement, storytelling, and immersive experiences. Charities are using VR and AR to create

virtual tours of projects, immersive fundraising events, and educational experiences to connect donors with their impact compellingly and interactively.

5. Digital Payment Solutions: Digital payment solutions, such as mobile wallets, contactless payments, and cryptocurrency, are facilitating seamless and secure donation transactions. Charities are embracing digital payment technologies to offer donors convenient ways to contribute, particularly in cashless societies or during crises.

6. Data Analytics and Predictive Modeling: Data analytics and predictive modelling are empowering charities to gain actionable insights from large datasets, identify trends, and forecast future outcomes. Charities are using data analytics to optimize fundraising strategies, target outreach efforts, and measure the effectiveness of programs in real-time.

7. Remote Monitoring and Telemedicine: Remote monitoring and telemedicine technologies are improving access to healthcare and essential services in underserved communities. Charities are using telehealth platforms, remote diagnostics, and mobile clinics to deliver medical care, health education, and disease prevention initiatives to remote or vulnerable populations.

8. Social Media and Digital Marketing: Social media platforms and digital marketing tools are enabling charities to amplify their reach, engage supporters,

and mobilize communities for social good. Charities are leveraging social media campaigns, influencer partnerships, and viral content to raise awareness, drive donations, and advocate for causes.

9. 3D Printing and Digital Fabrication: 3D printing and digital fabrication technologies are revolutionizing disaster response, humanitarian aid, and sustainable development initiatives. Charities are using 3D printers to produce essential supplies, medical equipment, and infrastructure components in resource-constrained environments or emergencies.

10. Remote Work and Collaboration Tools: Remote work and collaboration tools facilitate seamless communication, collaboration, and coordination among charity staff, volunteers, and partners. Charities are adopting virtual meeting platforms, project management software, and cloud-based collaboration tools to support distributed teams, remote operations, and flexible work arrangements.

In conclusion, emerging technologies are offering unprecedented opportunities for charity organizations to innovate, optimize operations, and maximize impact. By embracing blockchain technology, artificial intelligence, the Internet of Things, virtual reality and augmented reality, digital payment solutions, data analytics and predictive modelling, remote monitoring and telemedicine, social media and digital marketing, 3D printing and digital fabrication, and remote work and collaboration tools, charities can harness the power of technology to address pressing social challenges, engage supporters, and create positive change in the world. Through strategic adoption and integration of emerging technologies, charity organizations can enhance their effectiveness, efficiency, and relevance in advancing their missions and improving the lives of individuals and communities worldwide.

Social Entrepreneurship and Sustainable Funding Models

Social entrepreneurship combines the innovative mindset of entrepreneurship with the social mission of creating a positive impact. In this section, we explore the concept of social entrepreneurship and sustainable funding models for charity organizations:

1. Definition of Social Entrepreneurship: Social entrepreneurship involves the pursuit of innovative solutions to address social, environmental, and economic challenges. Social entrepreneurs leverage entrepreneurial principles, creativity, and business acumen to develop sustainable ventures that generate both financial returns and positive social outcomes.

2. Triple Bottom Line Approach: Social entrepreneurs adopt a triple bottom line approach, focusing on people, the planet, and profit. They aim to create value for society, the environment, and stakeholders, while also generating financial sustainability to support their mission and growth.

3. Revenue Diversification: Social enterprises diversify their revenue streams to reduce dependency on traditional sources of funding, such as grants and donations. They generate income through a mix of

earned revenue, including product sales, service fees, licensing agreements, and social impact bonds.

4. Earned Income Ventures: Social enterprises develop earned income ventures that align with their mission and values while generating revenue to support their social initiatives. These ventures may include social enterprises, social businesses, or revenue-generating programs and services that address unmet needs in the market.

5. Impact Investment: Social enterprises attract impact investment from socially motivated investors, philanthropic foundations, and impact funds seeking both financial returns and measurable social impact. Impact investors provide patient capital, equity investments, or loans to support the growth and scalability of social ventures.

6. Corporate Partnerships: Social enterprises form strategic partnerships with corporations, businesses, and brands to leverage resources, expertise, and networks for mutual benefit. Corporate partnerships may include joint ventures, cause-related marketing campaigns, corporate social responsibility initiatives, or supply chain collaborations.

7. Crowdfunding and Peer-to-Peer Fundraising: Social enterprises engage their community of supporters through crowdfunding platforms and peer-to-peer fundraising campaigns to raise capital, generate awareness, and mobilize grassroots support. Crowdfunding enables social enterprises to access

funding directly from individual donors, supporters, and enthusiasts who share their vision and values.

8. Social Impact Bonds: Social enterprises leverage social impact bonds (SIBs) or pay-for-success contracts to finance innovative social programs and interventions. SIBs involve government agencies, investors, and service providers collaborating to achieve predefined outcomes and share financial risks and rewards based on performance.

9. Impact Measurement and Reporting: Social enterprises prioritize impact measurement and reporting to demonstrate accountability, transparency, and value to stakeholders. They use impact metrics, indicators, and evaluation frameworks to track progress, assess outcomes, and communicate the social and financial value created by their ventures.

10. Hybrid Models: Social enterprises may adopt hybrid business models that combine elements of nonprofit and for-profit structures to achieve their mission and sustainability goals. Hybrid models, such as benefit corporations, social purpose corporations, and cooperative enterprises, enable social entrepreneurs to balance financial sustainability with social impact and legal accountability.

In conclusion, social entrepreneurship offers a powerful approach to addressing social challenges and creating a sustainable impact. By adopting innovative business models, revenue diversification strategies, impact investment, corporate partnerships, crowdfunding, social impact bonds, impact measurement, and hybrid models, social enterprises can build resilient and sustainable ventures that drive positive change and contribute to a more equitable and sustainable future. Through the integration of entrepreneurial principles and social mission, social entrepreneurs can harness the power of business to create meaningful and lasting impact in the communities they serve.

Collaborations and Partnerships for Greater Impact

In today's interconnected world, collaboration and partnerships are essential strategies for charity organizations to amplify their impact, leverage resources, and address complex social challenges. In this section, we explore the importance of collaborations and partnerships for achieving greater impact:

1. Leveraging Complementary Strengths: Collaborations and partnerships enable charity organizations to leverage each other's complementary strengths, expertise, resources, and networks. By pooling together resources, skills, and knowledge, organizations can achieve outcomes that would be difficult or impossible to accomplish alone.

2. Enhancing Efficiency and Effectiveness: Collaborations and partnerships increase the efficiency and effectiveness of charity organizations by avoiding duplication of efforts, sharing best practices, and maximizing the use of limited resources. By working together, organizations can

streamline operations, reduce costs, and optimize the delivery of services and programs.

3. Catalyzing Innovation and Creativity: Collaborations and partnerships foster innovation and creativity by bringing together diverse perspectives, ideas, and approaches to problem-solving. By collaborating with external partners, charity organizations can gain fresh insights, access new technologies, and explore innovative solutions to address social challenges.

4. Scaling Impact and Reach: Collaborations and partnerships enable charity organizations to scale their impact and reach by expanding their geographic footprint, engaging new target audiences, and reaching underserved communities. By partnering with other organizations, charities can amplify their message, mobilize support, and extend the reach of their programs and initiatives.

5. Advocating for Systemic Change: Collaborations and partnerships empower charity organizations to advocate for systemic change, policy reforms, and structural solutions to address the root causes of social problems. By joining forces with like-minded organizations, charities can amplify their voice, influence decision-makers, and drive collective action for social justice and equity.

6. Strengthening Community Engagement: Collaborations and partnerships strengthen community engagement and ownership by involving stakeholders, beneficiaries, and grassroots organizations in the design, implementation, and

evaluation of programs and initiatives. By collaborating with local partners, charities can build trust, foster empowerment, and ensure the relevance and sustainability of interventions.

7. Expanding Funding Opportunities: Collaborations and partnerships open up new funding opportunities for charity organizations by attracting support from diverse sources, including government agencies, private foundations, corporations, and individual donors. By partnering with other organizations, charities can access larger grants, secure multi-year funding, and diversify their revenue streams.

8. Building Resilience and Sustainability: Collaborations and partnerships build resilience and sustainability by creating networks, alliances, and ecosystems of support that can withstand shocks, adapt to changing circumstances, and sustain impact over the long term. By collaborating with strategic partners, charities can navigate challenges, seize opportunities, and build capacity for growth and innovation.

9. Fostering Trust and Mutual Respect: Collaborations and partnerships foster trust, mutual respect, and shared values among participating organizations, laying the foundation for long-term relationships and collaboration. By cultivating strong partnerships based on transparency, accountability, and integrity, charities can navigate differences, resolve conflicts, and achieve common goals effectively.

10. Promoting Collective Impact: Collaborations and partnerships promote collective impact by aligning diverse stakeholders around a shared vision, goals, and metrics for success. By mobilizing cross-sectoral partnerships, charities can address complex social problems holistically, coordinate efforts across multiple stakeholders, and achieve greater impact than any single organization could accomplish alone.

In conclusion, collaborations and partnerships are essential strategies for charity organizations to achieve greater impact, scale their efforts, and address complex social challenges effectively. By leveraging complementary strengths, enhancing efficiency and effectiveness, catalyzing innovation and creativity, scaling impact and reach, advocating for systemic change, strengthening community engagement, expanding funding opportunities, building resilience and sustainability, fostering trust and mutual respect, and promoting collective impact, charities can harness the power of collaboration to create positive change and improve the well-being of individuals and communities worldwide. Through strategic partnerships and collective action, charity organizations can amplify their impact, drive systemic change, and contribute to a more just, equitable, and sustainable world.

Chapter 8:

Ethics and Governance in Charity Management

Ethics and governance are foundational principles that guide the operations, decision-making, and accountability of charity organizations. In this chapter, we delve into the importance of ethics and governance in charity management:

1. Upholding Ethical Standards: Charity organizations are entrusted with the responsibility of serving the public good and advancing social causes. Upholding ethical standards is paramount to maintaining trust, credibility, and integrity with stakeholders, including donors, beneficiaries, staff, volunteers, and the broader community. Charity leaders and stakeholders must adhere to ethical principles such as honesty, transparency, fairness, accountability, and respect for human dignity in all aspects of their operations and interactions.

2. Ensuring Legal Compliance: Charity organizations must comply with applicable laws, regulations, and standards governing their operations, fundraising activities, financial management, and governance structures. Legal compliance helps charities mitigate risks, avoid legal liabilities, and uphold their legal obligations to stakeholders, including regulatory authorities, donors, and beneficiaries. Charity leaders must stay informed about relevant legal requirements and ensure that their organizations operate in accordance with the law.

3. Implementing Robust Governance Structures: Charity organizations should establish robust governance structures and processes to oversee and guide their operations effectively. Governance mechanisms, such as boards of directors, advisory councils, and governance committees, provide oversight, strategic direction, and accountability for organizational decision-making and management. Charity boards play a critical role in setting policies, monitoring performance, managing risks, and ensuring compliance with ethical and legal standards.

4. Promoting Transparency and Accountability: Transparency and accountability are essential principles for charity organizations to demonstrate their commitment to responsible stewardship and good governance. Charity organizations should disclose relevant information about their mission, programs, finances, and impact to stakeholders in a clear, accurate, and accessible manner. Transparent reporting helps build trust, foster donor confidence, and enable stakeholders to make informed decisions about supporting and engaging with charities.

5. Managing Conflicts of Interest: Charity organizations must effectively manage conflicts of interest to avoid potential conflicts or perceptions of impropriety that could undermine trust and integrity. Charity leaders, board members, and staff should disclose any conflicts of interest and recuse themselves from decisions where their personal interests may conflict with the best interests of the organization.

Establishing conflict of interest policies, procedures, and disclosure requirements helps mitigate risks and ensure ethical decision-making.

6. Safeguarding Financial Integrity: Charity organizations should maintain financial integrity and accountability by implementing sound financial management practices, internal controls, and fiscal oversight mechanisms. Financial transparency, accountability, and integrity are critical for building donor trust, ensuring proper use of funds, and achieving financial sustainability. Charity leaders should adopt financial policies, procedures, and reporting practices that promote transparency, accuracy, and accountability in financial management.

7. Ensuring Responsible Fundraising Practices: Charity organizations should adhere to responsible fundraising practices that prioritize donor trust, donor privacy, and donor rights. Charity leaders should ensure that fundraising activities are conducted ethically, transparently, and in compliance with relevant fundraising regulations and standards. Organizations should provide accurate information to donors, use funds responsibly, and respect donor wishes regarding the use of their contributions.

8. Fostering a Culture of Ethical Conduct: Charity organizations should foster a culture of ethical conduct and integrity among staff, volunteers, and stakeholders. Ethical leadership, training, and

communication are essential for promoting ethical behaviour, decision-making, and accountability throughout the organization. Charity leaders should lead by example, communicate clear expectations about ethical conduct, and provide training and resources to support ethical decision-making and behaviour.

9. Engaging Stakeholders in Governance: Charity organizations should engage stakeholders, including donors, beneficiaries, staff, volunteers, and the community, in governance processes to ensure accountability, transparency, and responsiveness to stakeholder needs and interests. Meaningful stakeholder engagement promotes inclusivity, diversity, and representation in decision-making, enhances organizational legitimacy, and fosters trust and collaboration.

10. Continuous Improvement and Learning: Charity organizations should continuously monitor, evaluate, and improve their ethical and governance practices to adapt to changing circumstances, emerging risks, and evolving stakeholder expectations. By embracing a culture of continuous improvement and learning, charities can strengthen their governance structures, enhance their ethical performance, and uphold their commitment to serving the public good effectively.

In conclusion, ethics and governance are essential principles for charity organizations to uphold in fulfilling their mission, serving their beneficiaries, and earning the trust and support of stakeholders. By prioritizing ethical conduct, legal compliance, robust governance structures, transparency, accountability, conflict management, financial integrity, responsible fundraising practices, stakeholder engagement, and continuous improvement, charity organizations can strengthen their capacity to create positive change and make a meaningful difference in the world. Through ethical leadership, responsible stewardship, and good governance practices, charity organizations can uphold their commitment to ethical values, fulfil their social responsibilities, and contribute to a more just, equitable, and sustainable society.

Ethical Considerations in Fundraising and Resource Allocation

Fundraising and resource allocation are critical aspects of charity management, requiring careful consideration of ethical principles to ensure responsible stewardship of funds and alignment with organizational values and mission. In this section, we explore key ethical considerations in fundraising and resource allocation:

1. Donor Relationships and Trust: Charity organizations have a responsibility to build and maintain trust with donors by upholding ethical standards in fundraising practices. Organizations should be transparent about how donated funds will be used, provide accurate information about their mission and impact, and honour donor preferences regarding the use of their contributions. Building strong donor relationships based on trust, transparency, and integrity is essential for long-term fundraising success.

2. Donor Privacy and Confidentiality: Charity organizations should respect donor privacy and confidentiality by safeguarding donor information and using it only for legitimate fundraising purposes. Organizations should have clear policies and procedures in place to protect donor data from unauthorized access, use, or disclosure and comply with relevant privacy laws and regulations. Respecting donor privacy and confidentiality helps maintain donor trust and confidence in the organization.

3. Truthfulness and Accuracy in Fundraising Appeals: Charity organizations should ensure that fundraising appeals are truthful, accurate, and not misleading to donors. Organizations should avoid using exaggerated or sensational language, emotional manipulation, or false promises to solicit donations. Fundraising communications should provide clear and factual information about the organization's mission, programs, impact, and financial needs to enable donors to make informed decisions about supporting the organization.

4. Ethical Considerations in Gift Acceptance: Charity organizations should establish clear policies and guidelines for accepting gifts, donations, and grants to ensure alignment with the organization's mission, values, and ethical principles. Organizations should assess the ethical implications of accepting funds from sources with conflicting interests, questionable reputations, or conditions that may compromise the organization's independence, integrity, or

effectiveness. Organizations should exercise discretion and due diligence in evaluating potential donors and gifts to maintain ethical standards and preserve organizational integrity.

5. Equitable Resource Allocation: Charity organizations should allocate resources equitably and responsibly to maximize their impact and address the most pressing needs of their beneficiaries and communities. Organizations should prioritize programs and initiatives that demonstrate effectiveness, efficiency, and alignment with organizational goals and values. Resource allocation decisions should be guided by ethical principles such as fairness, impartiality, and consideration of the needs and preferences of diverse stakeholders.

6. Avoidance of Waste and Excessive Overhead: Charity organizations should strive to minimize waste and excessive overhead costs to maximize the impact of donor contributions and ensure efficient use of resources. Organizations should maintain cost-effectiveness in their operations, avoid unnecessary expenses, and allocate funds directly to programmatic activities that deliver tangible benefits to beneficiaries. Transparency and accountability in financial management help donors trust that their contributions are being used responsibly and effectively to support the organization's mission.

7. Ethical Considerations in Emergency Fundraising: In times of crisis or emergency, charity organizations may engage in urgent fundraising appeals to respond

to immediate needs and provide assistance to affected communities. Organizations should ensure that emergency fundraising appeals are conducted ethically and responsibly, without exploiting the vulnerability or suffering of affected individuals. Fundraising efforts should prioritize meeting basic needs, providing essential services, and supporting long-term recovery and resilience efforts in affected areas.

8. Accountability to Stakeholders: Charity organizations must be accountable to their stakeholders, including donors, beneficiaries, staff, volunteers, and the broader community. Organizations should maintain transparency in their fundraising and resource allocation practices, provide regular updates on the use and impact of donor funds, and solicit feedback from stakeholders to inform decision-making and improve organizational performance. Accountability mechanisms, such as financial reporting, impact assessments, and independent audits, help ensure that organizations uphold ethical standards and fulfil their obligations to stakeholders.

9. Conflict of Interest Management: Charity organizations should establish policies and procedures for managing conflicts of interest in fundraising and resource allocation decisions. Organizations should identify and disclose potential conflicts of interest among board members, staff, volunteers, and other stakeholders involved in fundraising activities or resource allocation decisions. Effective conflict of interest management

ensures that decisions are made impartially, without bias or undue influence, and in the best interests of the organization and its mission.

10. Ethical Oversight and Governance: Charity organizations should establish robust oversight and governance structures to ensure ethical fundraising and resource allocation practices are upheld throughout the organization. Boards of directors, governance committees, and internal controls play a critical role in setting ethical standards, monitoring compliance, and holding the organization accountable for ethical conduct. Ethical oversight and governance mechanisms help maintain organizational integrity, protect against ethical lapses, and build trust with stakeholders.

In conclusion, ethical considerations are fundamental to fundraising and resource allocation in charity management, guiding organizations to uphold principles of trust, transparency, fairness, and accountability in their interactions with donors, beneficiaries, and the broader community. By adhering to ethical standards in fundraising appeals, gift acceptance, resource allocation decisions, and conflict of interest management, charity organizations can maintain donor trust, ensure responsible stewardship of funds, and advance their mission with integrity and impact. Through ethical leadership, governance, and oversight, charity organizations can uphold the highest standards of ethical conduct and contribute to positive social change and the well-being of individuals and communities worldwide.

Transparency and Accountability Practices

Transparency and accountability are essential principles for charity organizations to uphold in their operations, decision-making, and interactions with stakeholders. In this section, we explore key transparency and accountability practices that charity organizations should adopt to build trust, foster donor confidence, and demonstrate responsible stewardship:

1. Clear Communication of Mission and Impact: Charity organizations should communicate their mission, goals, values, and impact to stakeholders in a clear, compelling, and accessible manner. Organizations should articulate their vision for social change, describe the programs and initiatives they support, and highlight the positive outcomes and benefits achieved for beneficiaries and communities. Clear communication helps stakeholders understand the organization's purpose, activities, and contributions to the public good.

2. Transparent Financial Reporting: Charity organizations should maintain transparency in their financial reporting practices by providing accurate, timely, and comprehensive information about their financial performance, revenue sources, and expenses. Organizations should publish annual financial statements, including balance sheets, income statements, and cash flow statements, following generally accepted accounting principles (GAAP) or other relevant accounting standards. Transparent financial reporting helps donors and

stakeholders assess the organization's financial health, sustainability, and stewardship of resources.

3. Open Access to Governance Information: Charity organizations should provide stakeholders with open access to governance information, including information about their board of directors, governance structure, policies, and decision-making processes. Organizations should publish their bylaws, articles of incorporation, conflict of interest policies, and board meeting minutes to demonstrate transparency and accountability in governance. Open access to governance information promotes transparency, accountability, and stakeholder engagement in organizational decision-making.

4. Donor Privacy and Consent: Charity organizations should respect donor privacy and obtain informed consent for the collection, use, and disclosure of donor information. Organizations should have clear policies and procedures in place to protect donor privacy, safeguard donor data, and comply with applicable privacy laws and regulations. Donors should have the option to opt out of communications or requests for personal information and have confidence that their privacy rights will be respected.

5. Independent Financial Audits and Reviews: Charity organizations should undergo independent financial audits and reviews conducted by qualified auditors or accounting firms to verify the accuracy and integrity of their financial statements and internal controls. Audits provide an objective assessment of

the organization's financial performance, compliance with legal and regulatory requirements, and adherence to best practices in financial management. Independent audits enhance transparency, credibility, and confidence in the organization's financial reporting and governance practices.

6. Impact Measurement and Reporting: Charity organizations should measure and report on their social, environmental, and economic impact to demonstrate accountability and effectiveness in achieving their mission and goals. Organizations should develop impact metrics, indicators, and evaluation frameworks to assess the outcomes and long-term effects of their programs and initiatives on beneficiaries and communities. Impact reporting should be transparent, evidence-based, and aligned with organizational objectives to inform decision-making and promote continuous improvement.

7. Stakeholder Engagement and Feedback Mechanisms: Charity organizations should actively engage stakeholders, including donors, beneficiaries, staff, volunteers, and the community, in organizational decision-making and feedback processes. Organizations should solicit input, feedback, and perspectives from stakeholders through surveys, focus groups, town hall meetings, and other engagement mechanisms to inform strategic planning, program design, and performance evaluation. Effective stakeholder engagement fosters

trust, inclusivity, and collaboration in organizational governance and decision-making.

8. Conflict of Interest Disclosure and Management: Charity organizations should establish policies and procedures for disclosing and managing conflicts of interest among board members, staff, volunteers, and other stakeholders involved in organizational activities. Organizations should require individuals to disclose potential conflicts of interest and recuse themselves from decisions where their personal interests may conflict with the best interests of the organization. Transparent conflict of interest management helps mitigate risks, ensure impartiality, and maintain trust in organizational decision-making.

9. Whistleblower Protection and Reporting Mechanisms: Charity organizations should establish whistleblower protection policies and reporting mechanisms to encourage the reporting of suspected misconduct, unethical behaviour, or violations of organizational policies and procedures. Organizations should provide avenues for individuals to report concerns confidentially, anonymously, and without fear of retaliation. Whistleblower protection promotes transparency, accountability, and integrity in organizational operations by enabling the identification and resolution of issues that may compromise organizational effectiveness and reputation.

10. Continuous Improvement and Learning: Charity organizations should commit to continuous improvement and learning by regularly evaluating and enhancing their transparency and accountability practices based on feedback, lessons learned, and best practices. Organizations should conduct internal assessments, external reviews, and benchmarking exercises to identify areas for improvement and innovation in transparency, accountability, and governance. Continuous improvement fosters organizational resilience, adaptability, and effectiveness in fulfilling the organization's mission and serving its stakeholders.

In conclusion, transparency and accountability practices are foundational to the credibility, integrity, and effectiveness of charity organizations in fulfilling their mission, serving their stakeholders, and achieving positive social impact. By adopting clear communication practices, transparent financial reporting, open access to governance information, donor privacy and consent policies, independent financial audits, impact measurement and reporting, stakeholder engagement mechanisms, conflict of interest disclosure and management policies, whistleblower protection measures, and a commitment to continuous improvement and learning, charity organizations can build trust, inspire confidence, and demonstrate responsible stewardship of resources. Through transparency, accountability, and ethical governance practices, charity organizations can uphold their commitment to serving the public good and making a meaningful difference in the world.

Ensuring Compliance with Legal and Regulatory Requirements

Compliance with legal and regulatory requirements is essential for charity organizations to maintain their integrity, credibility, and legal standing. In this section, we explore key considerations and best practices for ensuring compliance with applicable laws, regulations, and standards:

1. Understanding Applicable Laws and Regulations: Charity organizations should have a thorough understanding of the legal and regulatory framework governing their operations, including nonprofit laws, tax regulations, fundraising regulations, employment laws, and reporting requirements. Organizations should stay informed about changes in relevant laws and regulations that may impact their activities and compliance obligations.

2. Obtaining Legal Recognition and Tax Exemption: Charity organizations should obtain legal recognition as a nonprofit entity and seek tax-exempt status from relevant government authorities, such as the Internal Revenue Service (IRS) in the United States or the Charity Commission in the United Kingdom. Legal recognition and tax exemption status confer certain privileges, such as eligibility for tax-deductible donations and exemption from certain taxes, but also come with compliance obligations and reporting requirements.

3. Establishing Governance Policies and Procedures: Charity organizations should establish governance policies and procedures to ensure compliance with legal and regulatory requirements, promote ethical

conduct, and mitigate risks. Organizations should develop and maintain governing documents, such as bylaws, articles of incorporation, and conflict of interest policies, that comply with legal requirements and best practices in nonprofit governance.

4. Maintaining Financial Transparency and Accountability: Charity organizations should maintain transparency and accountability in their financial management practices to comply with legal and regulatory requirements and meet stakeholder expectations. Organizations should keep accurate financial records, prepare annual financial statements, and undergo independent audits or reviews conducted by qualified professionals to verify compliance with accounting standards and regulatory requirements.

5. Registering and Reporting for Fundraising Activities: Charity organizations should register with relevant regulatory authorities and comply with fundraising regulations in jurisdictions where they solicit donations or conduct fundraising activities. Organizations should obtain permits, licenses, or registrations as required by law, and report on fundraising activities, financial disclosures, and use of funds following regulatory requirements and reporting deadlines.

6. Ensuring Compliance with Employment Laws: Charity organizations should comply with applicable employment laws and regulations governing recruitment, hiring, compensation, benefits, working

conditions, and employee relations. Organizations should provide a safe and inclusive work environment, respect employee rights and protections, and adhere to employment laws related to wages, hours, discrimination, harassment, and labour standards.

7. Safeguarding Donor Privacy and Data Protection: Charity organizations should comply with laws and regulations governing data protection, privacy, and security, particularly in handling donor information and personal data. Organizations should have policies and procedures in place to safeguard donor privacy, obtain consent for the collection and use of personal data, and comply with data protection laws, such as the General Data Protection Regulation (GDPR) in the European Union or the Health Insurance Portability and Accountability Act (HIPAA) in the United States.

8. Adhering to Reporting and Compliance Obligations: Charity organizations should adhere to reporting and compliance obligations imposed by regulatory authorities, including filing annual reports, tax returns, and other regulatory filings in a timely and accurate manner. Organizations should maintain records of regulatory filings, track compliance deadlines, and ensure that reporting requirements are met to avoid penalties, fines, or loss of legal status.

9. Implementing Risk Management and Compliance Controls: Charity organizations should implement

risk management and compliance controls to identify, assess, and mitigate legal and regulatory risks that may impact their operations and reputation. Organizations should conduct periodic risk assessments, monitor regulatory developments, and establish internal controls, policies, and procedures to prevent legal violations, detect compliance gaps, and address non-compliance issues proactively.

10. Seeking Legal Counsel and Professional Advice: Charity organizations should seek legal counsel and professional advice from qualified attorneys, accountants, consultants, or advisors with expertise in nonprofit law, governance, and compliance. Legal counsel can guide interpreting and complying with complex legal and regulatory requirements, resolving compliance issues, and mitigating legal risks to ensure the organization's continued compliance and success.

In conclusion, ensuring compliance with legal and regulatory requirements is essential for charity organizations to fulfil their mission, maintain their legal standing, and build trust with stakeholders. By understanding applicable laws and regulations, establishing governance policies and procedures, maintaining financial transparency and accountability, registering and reporting for fundraising activities, complying with employment laws, safeguarding donor privacy and data protection, adhering to reporting and compliance obligations, implementing risk management and compliance controls, and seeking legal counsel and professional advice, charity organizations can navigate the legal and regulatory landscape effectively and operate with integrity, credibility, and confidence. Through proactive compliance efforts and a commitment to ethical conduct, charity organizations can uphold their legal obligations, mitigate risks, and advance their mission of serving the public good and making a positive impact in the communities they serve.

Chapter 9:

Career Development and Professional Growth

Career development and professional growth are essential aspects of success and fulfilment for individuals working in the charity sector. In this chapter, we explore strategies, opportunities, and considerations for advancing careers and fostering personal growth within charity organizations:

1. Setting Career Goals and Objectives: Individuals in the charity sector should begin by setting clear and achievable career goals and objectives aligned with their personal values, interests, and aspirations. Setting specific, measurable, attainable, relevant, and time-bound (SMART) goals helps individuals clarify their career direction, identify areas for development, and track progress over time.

2. Identifying Skills and Competencies: Charity professionals should assess their skills, knowledge, and competencies to identify strengths and areas for growth. Individuals should cultivate a diverse set of skills, including leadership, communication, fundraising, project management, strategic planning, financial management, advocacy, and program evaluation, to succeed in various roles within the charity sector.

3. Pursuing Continuous Learning and Development: Individuals in the charity sector should prioritize continuous learning and professional development to stay current with industry trends, best practices, and emerging issues. Professionals can participate in

training programs, workshops, seminars, conferences, and online courses offered by professional associations, academic institutions, and nonprofit organizations to enhance their skills and expand their knowledge base.

4. Seeking Mentorship and Networking Opportunities: Charity professionals should seek mentorship and networking opportunities to connect with experienced professionals, seek guidance and advice, and expand their professional network. Mentors can provide valuable insights, support, and mentorship to help individuals navigate their career paths, overcome challenges, and achieve their goals. Networking events, conferences, and industry associations provide opportunities for individuals to build relationships, exchange ideas, and explore career opportunities within the charity sector.

5. Exploring Career Pathways and Opportunities: Charity professionals should explore diverse career pathways and opportunities within the sector, including roles in program management, fundraising, marketing and communications, advocacy, policy analysis, research and evaluation, governance, and leadership. Individuals should consider their interests, strengths, and career goals when exploring different roles and opportunities for career advancement and growth.

6. Building a Strong Professional Brand: Charity professionals should build a strong professional brand by showcasing their skills, experience, and

contributions within the sector. Individuals can create professional profiles on networking platforms, such as LinkedIn, and participate in industry discussions, conferences, and events to raise their visibility, build credibility, and attract career opportunities within the charity sector.

7. Seizing Leadership Opportunities: Charity professionals should seize leadership opportunities to demonstrate their leadership potential, initiative, and impact within their organizations and the broader sector. Individuals can take on leadership roles in projects, committees, task forces, and volunteer initiatives to develop leadership skills, build relationships, and contribute to organizational success.

8. Embracing Diversity, Equity, and Inclusion: Charity professionals should embrace diversity, equity, and inclusion (DEI) principles in their career development and professional growth efforts. Individuals should seek opportunities to promote DEI within their organizations, advocate for inclusive policies and practices, and support initiatives that advance equity and social justice in the charity sector.

9. Balancing Work-Life Integration: Charity professionals should prioritize work-life integration to maintain a healthy balance between their professional and personal lives. Individuals should set boundaries, manage their time effectively, and prioritize self-care to avoid burnout and sustain long-term career success and well-being within the

demanding and rewarding environment of the charity sector.

10. Reflecting and Reassessing Career Goals: Charity professionals should regularly reflect on their career goals, experiences, and achievements to reassess their career direction and aspirations. Individuals should seek feedback from mentors, colleagues, and supervisors, evaluate their progress against their goals, and adjust their career plans as needed to align with evolving interests, priorities, and opportunities within the dynamic landscape of the charity sector.

In conclusion, career development and professional growth are ongoing processes that require dedication, self-awareness, and proactive planning within the charity sector. By setting clear career goals, identifying skills and competencies, pursuing continuous learning and development, seeking mentorship and networking opportunities, exploring diverse career pathways, building a strong professional brand, seizing leadership opportunities, embracing diversity and inclusion, balancing work-life integration, and reflecting on career goals regularly, charity professionals can advance their careers, fulfil their potential, and make meaningful contributions to the mission and impact of charity organizations. Through intentional career development efforts and a commitment to lifelong learning and growth, individuals can navigate their career paths with purpose, resilience, and fulfilment within the dynamic and rewarding field of the charity sector.

Pathways to Becoming a Charity Management Consultant, Practitioner, Director

Becoming a charity management consultant, practitioner, or director involves a combination of education, experience, skills development, and networking within the charity sector. In this section, we outline pathways and strategies for individuals aspiring to pursue careers in charity management consultancy, practice, or leadership:

1. Education and Qualifications: Individuals interested in charity management roles should consider pursuing relevant education and qualifications to develop the knowledge, skills, and credentials needed for success. Academic degrees in fields such as nonprofit management, social work, business administration, public administration, or philanthropy can provide a strong foundation for a career in charity management. Additionally, professional certifications, such as Certified Fund Raising Executive (CFRE), Certified Nonprofit Professional (CNP), or Certified Association Executive (CAE), can enhance credibility and demonstrate expertise in specific areas of charity management. (check your own country or region)

2. Gain Practical Experience: Practical experience is essential for individuals aspiring to pursue careers in charity management consultancy, practice, or leadership. Individuals can gain experience through internships, volunteer opportunities, part-time or full-time employment, and project-based work within charity organizations, consulting firms, nonprofit

agencies, or philanthropic institutions. Hands-on experience allows individuals to develop practical skills, gain exposure to different aspects of charity management, and build a professional network within the sector.

3. Develop Key Skills and Competencies: Charity management professionals should develop a diverse set of skills and competencies to succeed in their roles. Key skills and competencies include leadership, communication, fundraising, strategic planning, financial management, program development and evaluation, stakeholder engagement, advocacy, project management, and organizational development. Individuals can enhance their skills through training programs, workshops, seminars, online courses, and professional development opportunities tailored to the charity sector.

4. Specialize in a Niche Area: Charity management professionals can differentiate themselves by specializing in a niche area or expertise within the sector. Specializations may include fundraising and development, grant writing, donor relations, marketing and communications, program evaluation, policy analysis, advocacy and lobbying, governance and board development, social entrepreneurship, impact investing, or international development. Specializing in a niche area allows professionals to deepen their knowledge, demonstrate expertise, and pursue career opportunities aligned with their interests and strengths.

5. Build a Professional Network: Networking is crucial for individuals seeking to advance their careers in charity management consultancy, practice, or leadership. Professionals can build a professional network by attending industry conferences, workshops, seminars, and networking events; joining professional associations, such as the Association of Fundraising Professionals (AFP), Council on Foundations, or Nonprofit Leadership Alliance; participating in online forums and discussion groups; and connecting with peers, mentors, colleagues, and industry leaders through social media platforms, such as LinkedIn. Building a strong professional network provides opportunities for learning, collaboration, mentorship, and career advancement within the charity sector.

6. Pursue Further Education and Training: Charity management professionals should pursue further education and training to stay current with industry trends, best practices, and emerging issues. Professionals can enrol in continuing education programs, executive education courses, advanced degrees, or specialized training programs offered by universities, colleges, professional associations, or nonprofit organizations. Lifelong learning and professional development help professionals expand their knowledge, skills, and expertise and remain competitive in the evolving landscape of charity management.

7. Gain Consulting Experience: Individuals interested in charity management consultancy roles should gain

consulting experience to develop expertise in advising charity organizations on strategic planning, organizational development, fundraising strategies, program evaluation, governance, and other areas of management. Consulting experience can be gained through employment with consulting firms specializing in nonprofit or philanthropic consulting, freelance consulting projects, or partnerships with charity organizations seeking external expertise and support.

8. Demonstrate Leadership and Impact: Charity management professionals should demonstrate leadership and impact in their roles to advance their careers and build credibility within the sector. Professionals can demonstrate leadership by taking on leadership roles within their organizations, leading initiatives or projects, contributing to industry publications, presenting at conferences or workshops, volunteering on nonprofit boards or committees, or advocating for policy changes or social causes. Demonstrating tangible impact and outcomes in their work helps professionals build a reputation as effective leaders and trusted experts in charity management.

9. Stay Informed and Engaged: Charity management professionals should stay informed and engaged with developments, trends, and issues shaping the charity sector locally, nationally, and globally. Professionals can stay informed by reading industry publications, newsletters, reports, and blogs; following relevant organizations, thought leaders, and influencers on

social media; attending conferences, webinars, or seminars; participating in professional development programs; and engaging in ongoing dialogue and exchange with peers and colleagues within the sector. Staying informed and engaged allows professionals to anticipate changes, seize opportunities, and contribute to positive change and innovation within the charity sector.

10. Seek Mentorship and Guidance: Charity management professionals can benefit from mentorship and guidance from experienced professionals who can provide advice, support, and perspective on career development and advancement within the sector. Professionals can seek mentorship from senior leaders, colleagues, industry experts, or professional mentors through formal mentoring programs, networking relationships, or informal mentorship arrangements. Mentorship provides opportunities for learning, growth, and career guidance tailored to the individual's goals, aspirations, and challenges in charity management.

In conclusion, pursuing a career in charity management consultancy, practice, or leadership requires a combination of education, experience, skills development, networking, and professional growth within the sector. By gaining practical experience, developing key skills and competencies, specializing in a niche area, building a professional network, pursuing further education and training, gaining consulting experience, demonstrating leadership and impact, staying informed and engaged, seeking mentorship and guidance, and seizing opportunities for career advancement and growth, individuals can build successful and fulfilling careers in charity management and make a positive impact in the communities they serve. Through dedication, passion, and commitment to excellence, charity management professionals can contribute to the success and sustainability of charity organizations, advance social change, and improve the well-being of individuals and communities worldwide.

Developing Skills and Competencies for Success

Success in charity management requires a diverse set of skills and competencies that enable professionals to effectively lead, manage, and support charitable organizations in achieving their mission and impact. In this section, we explore key skills and competencies essential for success in charity management and strategies for developing and enhancing them:

1. Leadership Skills:
   - Effective leadership is crucial for guiding and inspiring teams, mobilizing resources, and driving organizational success.
   - Develop skills in strategic thinking, decision-making, problem-solving, and vision-setting to provide direction and steer the organization toward its goals.
   - Cultivate emotional intelligence, empathy, and interpersonal skills to build trust, motivate teams, and foster a positive organizational culture.
   - Seek leadership opportunities within the organization, such as leading projects,

initiatives, or teams, to develop and demonstrate leadership abilities.
2. Communication Skills:
    - Strong communication skills are essential for conveying ideas, building relationships, and engaging stakeholders effectively.
    - Develop clear and concise written and verbal communication skills to articulate the organization's mission, goals, and impact to diverse audiences.
    - Practice active listening and empathy to understand stakeholders' perspectives, concerns, and needs, and tailor communication messages accordingly.
    - Utilize storytelling techniques to convey the organization's impact and connect with donors, supporters, and beneficiaries on an emotional level.
3. Financial Management Skills:
    - Financial management skills are critical for overseeing budgets, allocating resources, and ensuring fiscal responsibility.
    - Develop proficiency in financial analysis, budgeting, forecasting, and financial reporting to monitor and manage the organization's financial health and sustainability.
    - Gain knowledge of relevant financial regulations, accounting principles, and compliance requirements to ensure adherence to legal and regulatory standards.
    - Collaborate with finance professionals or seek training in financial management to enhance financial literacy and competency.
4. Fundraising and Development Skills:
    - Fundraising and development skills are essential for securing funding, cultivating

donor relationships, and diversifying revenue streams.
- Develop skills in donor prospecting, solicitation, stewardship, and donor relationship management to cultivate long-term partnerships and support.
- Learn fundraising techniques, such as grant writing, major gift solicitation, corporate partnerships, and online fundraising, to leverage different fundraising channels effectively.
- Stay informed about fundraising trends, best practices, and emerging technologies to adapt strategies and approaches to changing donor preferences and market dynamics.

5. Program Management Skills:
- Program management skills are necessary for designing, implementing, and evaluating effective programs and services that address community needs.
- Develop skills in project planning, implementation, monitoring, and evaluation to ensure program quality, efficiency, and impact.
- Learn program evaluation methodologies, data collection and analysis techniques, and performance measurement frameworks to assess program effectiveness and outcomes.
- Collaborate with program staff, partners, and stakeholders to design and deliver programs that meet the needs of beneficiaries and achieve desired outcomes.

6. Strategic Planning and Organizational Development Skills:
- Strategic planning and organizational development skills are vital for setting

direction, aligning resources, and driving organizational change and growth.
- Develop skills in strategic thinking, goal setting, SWOT analysis, and scenario planning to develop and implement strategic plans that guide the organization's direction and priorities.
- Learn change management principles, organizational design concepts, and capacity-building strategies to strengthen the organization's internal capabilities and resilience.
- Engage board members, staff, and stakeholders in the strategic planning process to ensure buy-in, alignment, and ownership of organizational goals and priorities.

7. Stakeholder Engagement and Relationship Management Skills:
- Stakeholder engagement and relationship management skills are essential for building trust, collaboration, and support among diverse stakeholders.
- Develop skills in stakeholder mapping, engagement planning, and relationship-building to identify and prioritize key stakeholders and foster meaningful partnerships.
- Cultivate networking skills, negotiation skills, and conflict resolution skills to navigate complex stakeholder dynamics and resolve conflicts effectively.
- Communicate transparently, authentically, and consistently with stakeholders to build and maintain trust, manage expectations, and address concerns.

8. Advocacy and Public Relations Skills:

- Advocacy and public relations skills are important for raising awareness, influencing public opinion, and advocating for policy change and social impact.
- Develop skills in message development, media relations, public speaking, and storytelling to effectively communicate the organization's mission, values, and impact to external audiences.
- Learn advocacy strategies, lobbying techniques, and grassroots organizing tactics to mobilize supporters, engage policymakers, and drive legislative or policy change.
- Collaborate with communications professionals or seek training in public relations to enhance messaging, branding, and media outreach efforts.

9. Ethical Leadership and Decision-Making Skills:
- Ethical leadership and decision-making skills are fundamental for upholding integrity, transparency, and accountability in charity management.
- Develop a strong ethical framework, values-driven decision-making approach, and commitment to ethical conduct and compliance with legal and regulatory standards.
- Practice ethical reasoning, critical thinking, and moral courage to navigate ethical dilemmas and make principled decisions that serve the best interests of stakeholders and the organization.
- Lead by example, promote a culture of ethics and accountability within the organization, and hold yourself and others accountable for upholding ethical standards and integrity.

10. Lifelong Learning and Professional Development:

- Lifelong learning and professional development are essential for staying current with industry trends, expanding knowledge, and adapting to evolving challenges and opportunities.
- Commit to continuous learning and skill-building through formal education, professional development programs, workshops, seminars, conferences, and self-directed learning.
- Seek feedback, mentorship, and coaching from peers, supervisors, and mentors to identify areas for growth, receive guidance, and accelerate professional development.
- Stay curious, open-minded, and proactive in exploring new ideas, perspectives, and approaches to charity management, and embrace opportunities for personal and professional growth.

In conclusion, developing skills and competencies for success in charity management requires a commitment to continuous learning, practice, and growth. By focusing on leadership skills, communication skills, financial management skills, fundraising and development skills, program management skills, strategic planning and organizational development skills, stakeholder engagement and relationship management skills, advocacy and public relations skills, ethical leadership and decision-making skills, and lifelong learning and professional development, charity management professionals can enhance their effectiveness, advance their careers, and make a meaningful impact in the communities they serve. Through intentional skill development and a dedication to excellence, individuals can contribute to the success and sustainability of charity organizations and advance social change and well-being worldwide.

Networking and Building a Professional Reputation

Networking and building a professional reputation are essential for success and advancement in charity management. In this section, we explore strategies and best practices for effectively networking and establishing a strong professional reputation within the charity sector:

1. Define Your Goals and Objectives:
   - Clarify your networking goals and objectives to guide your networking efforts and focus your time and energy on activities that align with your professional aspirations.
   - Determine what you hope to achieve through networking, such as expanding your professional network, seeking mentorship or career opportunities, or gaining insights and knowledge from industry experts.

2. Identify Key Contacts and Organizations:
   - Identify key individuals, organizations, and professional associations within the charity sector that align with your interests, expertise, and career goals.
   - Research potential contacts and organizations through online platforms, industry directories, conferences, and networking events to identify opportunities for connection and collaboration.

3. Attend Networking Events and Conferences:
   - Attend charity sector networking events, conferences, workshops, and seminars to meet and connect with industry professionals, thought leaders, and peers.
   - Participate in panel discussions, breakout sessions, and networking receptions to engage in conversations, exchange ideas, and build relationships with fellow attendees.

4. Join Professional Associations and Groups:

- Join professional associations, networking groups, and online communities focused on charity management, nonprofit leadership, fundraising, and related fields.
- Participate in association meetings, webinars, and networking events to connect with peers, access resources and professional development opportunities, and stay informed about industry trends and best practices.

5. Utilize Online Networking Platforms:
   - Leverage online networking platforms, such as LinkedIn, to connect with charity professionals, leaders, and influencers, and expand your professional network.
   - Customize your LinkedIn profile to highlight your skills, experience, and accomplishments, and actively engage with connections through messaging, commenting, and sharing relevant content.

6. Build Genuine Relationships:
   - Focus on building genuine, mutually beneficial relationships with contacts by showing interest, listening attentively, and offering support and assistance where possible.
   - Seek opportunities to add value to your network by sharing knowledge, resources, and connections, and offering assistance or expertise to others in need.

7. Follow Up and Stay Connected:
   - Follow up with new contacts after networking events or meetings to express appreciation for the conversation and continue the relationship.
   - Stay connected with your network through regular communication, updates, and

interactions, such as sending personalized messages, sharing relevant articles or resources, and congratulating contacts on their achievements.

8. Seek Mentorship and Guidance:
    - Seek mentorship and guidance from experienced professionals within your network who can offer advice, support, and insights based on their own experiences and expertise.
    - Be proactive in reaching out to potential mentors, expressing your interest in learning from them, and requesting opportunities for mentorship or informational interviews.

9. Showcase Your Expertise and Contributions:
    - Showcase your expertise, thought leadership, and contributions to the charity sector through speaking engagements, panel discussions, articles, blog posts, or social media content.
    - Share your insights, experiences, and best practices with your network and the broader industry community to establish yourself as a credible and respected professional.

10. Maintain Professionalism and Integrity:
- Maintain professionalism, integrity, and ethical conduct in all your networking interactions and communications.
- Respect confidentiality, honour commitments, and follow through on promises to build trust and credibility with your network and uphold your professional reputation.

In conclusion, networking and building a professional reputation are essential for advancing your career, fostering connections, and accessing opportunities within the charity sector. By defining your networking goals, identifying key contacts and organizations, attending networking events, joining professional associations, utilizing online networking platforms, building genuine relationships, following up and staying connected, seeking mentorship and guidance, showcasing your expertise and contributions, and maintaining professionalism and integrity, you can effectively network and establish a strong professional reputation within the charity sector. Through intentional networking efforts and a commitment to building authentic relationships, you can expand your professional network, enhance your visibility and credibility, and advance your career in charity management.

Chapter 10:

Future Directions in Charity Management

As charity management evolves in response to shifting societal needs, technological advancements, and emerging trends, it is crucial to anticipate future directions and prepare for the challenges and opportunities ahead. In this chapter, we explore potential trends and developments shaping the future of charity management:

1. Embracing Technological Innovation:
   - The integration of technology into charity management processes will continue to accelerate, offering new tools and solutions to enhance efficiency, transparency, and impact.
   - Artificial intelligence, machine learning, blockchain technology, and data analytics will play increasingly significant roles in fundraising, donor engagement, program delivery, and impact measurement.
   - Charity organizations must adapt to technological advancements by investing in digital infrastructure, data management systems, and staff training to harness the full potential of technology for social good.

2. Leveraging Data for Decision-Making:
   - Data-driven decision-making will become increasingly prevalent in charity management, as organizations seek to measure and maximize their social impact.
   - Charity organizations will leverage data analytics, performance metrics, and outcome indicators to assess program effectiveness, optimize resource allocation, and demonstrate accountability to stakeholders.

- Data-driven insights will inform strategic planning, program design, fundraising strategies, and advocacy efforts, enabling charities to make evidence-based decisions and achieve greater results.
3. Enhancing Collaboration and Partnerships:
    - Collaboration and partnerships will be essential for addressing complex social challenges and maximizing collective impact in the charity sector.
    - Charity organizations will increasingly collaborate with government agencies, corporations, academia, and other nonprofits to leverage resources, expertise, and networks for greater effectiveness and scale.
    - Cross-sector partnerships, collective impact initiatives, and collaborative networks will facilitate knowledge sharing, innovation, and coordinated action to tackle systemic issues and drive sustainable change.
4. Fostering Diversity, Equity, and Inclusion:
    - Diversity, equity, and inclusion (DEI) will be prioritized in charity management, as organizations recognize the importance of representing and serving diverse communities.
    - Charity organizations will implement DEI strategies and practices to ensure equitable access to resources, opportunities, and services for all individuals, regardless of race, gender, ethnicity, or socioeconomic status.
    - DEI considerations will be integrated into organizational policies, hiring practices, program design, and decision-making processes to promote fairness, inclusivity, and social justice within the sector.
5. Adapting to Changing Donor Preferences:

- Donor preferences and expectations will continue to evolve, influencing fundraising strategies, communication methods, and engagement tactics employed by charity organizations.
- Donors will increasingly seek personalized and meaningful experiences, transparency, and impact measurement from the charities they support.
- Charity organizations will need to adopt donor-centric approaches, tailor communication strategies to diverse donor segments, and demonstrate tangible outcomes and stories of impact to engage and retain supporters effectively.

6. Navigating Regulatory and Legal Challenges:
   - Charity organizations will face evolving regulatory and legal landscapes, as governments introduce new regulations, compliance requirements, and reporting standards.
   - Increased scrutiny and accountability measures may necessitate greater transparency, governance, and risk management practices within the sector.
   - Charity organizations must stay informed about regulatory changes, ensure compliance with legal requirements, and uphold ethical standards and best practices to maintain public trust and credibility.

7. Addressing Environmental and Global Challenges:
   - Charity organizations will increasingly engage with environmental and global challenges, such as climate change, environmental degradation, poverty, inequality, and humanitarian crises.

- Climate resilience, sustainable development, and social justice will become central priorities for charity management, as organizations seek to address interconnected environmental and social issues.
- Charity organizations will collaborate across sectors and borders to promote sustainability, resilience, and equitable access to resources and opportunities for vulnerable populations worldwide.

8. Promoting Innovation and Entrepreneurship:
   - Innovation and entrepreneurship will drive creative solutions and disruptive approaches to addressing social problems and driving positive change in charity management.
   - Social entrepreneurs, impact investors, and philanthropic innovators will play a key role in catalyzing innovation, scaling promising initiatives, and driving systemic transformation within the sector.
   - Charity organizations will embrace experimentation, risk-taking, and agile methodologies to foster innovation, iterate on solutions, and adapt to evolving needs and challenges.

9. Cultivating Leadership and Talent:
   - Developing strong leadership and talent pipelines will be critical for ensuring the future success and sustainability of charity organizations.
   - Charity organizations will invest in leadership development, mentorship programs, and succession planning to nurture the next generation of leaders and empower staff to drive organizational growth and impact.
   - Emphasis will be placed on cultivating diverse leadership teams, fostering inclusive

workplace cultures, and empowering staff to contribute their skills, ideas, and perspectives to advance the organization's mission and vision.

10. Embracing Change and Adaptation:
- Charity organizations must embrace change and adaptability as core principles in navigating the evolving landscape of charity management.
- Agility, resilience, and innovation will be essential for responding effectively to shifting priorities, emerging challenges, and disruptive forces shaping the sector.
- Charity leaders must foster a culture of continuous learning, experimentation, and adaptation within their organizations to thrive in an uncertain and dynamic environment.

In conclusion, the future of charity management will be shaped by technological innovation, data-driven decision-making, collaboration and partnerships, diversity and inclusion, changing donor preferences, regulatory challenges, global issues, innovation and entrepreneurship, leadership development, and adaptability. Charity organizations must anticipate and embrace these trends, positioning themselves to leverage opportunities, address challenges, and drive positive social impact in a rapidly evolving world. By staying informed, proactive, and agile, charity organizations can navigate the complexities of the future landscape and continue to fulfil their mission of making a difference in the lives of individuals and communities worldwide.

Anticipating and Adapting to Changing Trends

In the dynamic landscape of charity management, organizations must remain vigilant and proactive in anticipating and adapting to changing trends to ensure relevance, effectiveness, and sustainability. Here are strategies for charities to anticipate and adapt to evolving trends:

1. Environmental Scanning:
   - Regularly scan the external environment to identify emerging trends, shifts in public sentiment, technological advancements, regulatory changes, and socioeconomic developments that may impact charity management.
   - Monitor industry publications, news sources, research reports, social media discussions, and stakeholder feedback to stay informed about relevant trends and issues affecting the charity sector.

2. Scenario Planning:
   - Engage in scenario planning exercises to anticipate alternative futures and assess the potential implications of different trends and scenarios on charity operations, programs, and stakeholders.
   - Consider best-case, worst-case, and most likely scenarios to develop contingency plans, mitigation strategies, and adaptive responses to potential disruptions or opportunities arising from changing trends.

3. Stakeholder Engagement:
   - Engage with stakeholders, including donors, beneficiaries, staff, volunteers, board members, partners, and community members, to solicit input, gather insights, and understand their perspectives on emerging trends and priorities.
   - Foster open dialogue, feedback mechanisms, and collaborative decision-making processes to ensure that charity strategies, programs,

and initiatives are responsive to the needs
and expectations of key stakeholders.

4. Continuous Learning and Development:
   - Cultivate a culture of continuous learning and development within the organization to empower staff, volunteers, and leaders to stay informed, adaptable, and innovative in response to changing trends.
   - Provide training, professional development opportunities, and resources to build staff capacity, enhance skills, and foster agility in navigating evolving challenges and opportunities.

5. Strategic Planning and Agility:
   - Develop flexible and adaptive strategic plans that allow for iterative adjustments, course corrections, and real-time responses to changing trends and external dynamics.
   - Embrace agile methodologies, rapid prototyping, and experimentation to test new ideas, innovate solutions, and pivot strategies based on emerging insights and feedback from stakeholders.

6. Collaboration and Partnerships:
   - Collaborate with other charities, nonprofits, government agencies, businesses, academia, and community organizations to leverage complementary strengths, resources, and expertise in addressing shared challenges and opportunities.
   - Form strategic partnerships, consortia, and networks to pool resources, share knowledge, and scale impact in response to complex and multifaceted trends affecting the charity sector.

7. Technology Adoption and Innovation:

- Embrace technology adoption and innovation as enablers for enhancing operational efficiency, improving service delivery, and engaging stakeholders in new and meaningful ways.
- Invest in digital infrastructure, data analytics, cloud computing, collaboration tools, and digital marketing platforms to leverage technology for fundraising, donor engagement, program management, and impact measurement.

8. Diversity, Equity, and Inclusion:
- Prioritize diversity, equity, and inclusion (DEI) considerations in charity management practices to ensure that organizational policies, programs, and services are inclusive, equitable, and responsive to the needs of diverse communities.
- Foster a culture of inclusion, belonging, and respect within the organization, and actively address systemic barriers, biases, and inequalities that may hinder equitable access and participation.

9. Risk Management and Resilience:
- Proactively identify, assess, and mitigate risks associated with changing trends, disruptive events, and external shocks that may impact charity operations, finances, reputation, and mission delivery.
- Develop robust risk management plans, crisis response protocols, and business continuity strategies to build organizational resilience and ensure continuity of critical services and operations in the face of uncertainty and adversity.

10. Monitoring and Evaluation:

- Establish monitoring and evaluation mechanisms to track progress, measure outcomes, and assess the effectiveness of strategies, programs, and initiatives in response to changing trends and priorities.
- Regularly review performance metrics, key performance indicators (KPIs), and impact indicators to identify successes, challenges, and areas for improvement, and adjust strategies accordingly to maximize impact and relevance.

In conclusion, by adopting proactive strategies for anticipating and adapting to changing trends, charities can position themselves to navigate uncertainty, seize opportunities, and drive positive social change in an ever-evolving environment. By staying informed, agile, and responsive to emerging trends and stakeholder needs, charities can remain resilient, relevant, and impactful in fulfilling their mission and advancing their vision for a better world.

Innovations in Philanthropy and Social Impact Investing

As the landscape of philanthropy and social impact investing continues to evolve, innovative approaches and models are emerging to address complex social and environmental challenges. In this section, we explore key innovations in philanthropy and social impact investing:

1. Venture Philanthropy:
   - Venture philanthropy applies principles from venture capital and entrepreneurship to philanthropic giving, focusing on strategic investments in nonprofits and social enterprises with high potential for scalable impact.
   - Venture philanthropists provide not only financial support but also strategic guidance, capacity-building resources, and

performance measurement tools to help organizations achieve sustainable growth and maximize social return on investment.

2. Impact Bonds:
   - Social impact bonds (SIBs) and development impact bonds (DIBs) are innovative financing mechanisms that leverage private capital to fund social programs and interventions with measurable outcomes.
   - Investors provide upfront capital to service providers to deliver interventions, and governments or other outcome funders repay investors based on predetermined performance metrics and achieved results, thereby shifting financial risk from taxpayers to investors.

3. Pay for Success:
   - Pay for Success (PFS) initiatives align financial incentives with social outcomes by linking payments for social services to the achievement of predetermined outcomes and performance targets.
   - Governments or other outcome funders pay service providers based on the demonstrated success of interventions in achieving agreed-upon outcomes, incentivizing innovation, efficiency, and accountability in service delivery.

4. Impact Investing:
   - Impact investing involves deploying capital to generate measurable social or environmental impact alongside financial returns, seeking to address social and environmental challenges through market-based approaches.
   - Impact investors allocate capital to businesses, funds, or projects that generate positive social or environmental outcomes,

such as affordable housing, renewable energy, healthcare, education, and sustainable agriculture while delivering competitive financial returns.

5. Blended Finance:
   - Blended finance structures combine public, private, philanthropic, and development finance to address market failures, leverage additional investment capital, and mobilize resources for sustainable development initiatives.
   - Blended finance mechanisms, such as guarantees, concessional loans, equity investments, and risk-sharing instruments, help de-risk investments, catalyze private sector participation, and unlock capital for projects with social or environmental impact.

6. Impact Measurement and Management:
   - Impact measurement and management (IMM) frameworks and tools are essential for assessing, quantifying, and optimizing social and environmental impact across philanthropic and investment portfolios.
   - IMM methodologies, such as the Impact Management Project (IMP), Global Impact Investing Network (GIIN) Standards, and Social Return on Investment (SROI) analysis, enable investors and philanthropists to track outcomes, monitor progress, and make informed decisions to maximize impact.

7. ESG Integration:
   - Environmental, social, and governance (ESG) integration involves incorporating ESG factors into investment decision-making processes to assess and manage risks, enhance performance, and promote responsible investing practices.

- Investors consider ESG criteria, such as climate change mitigation, human rights, diversity and inclusion, labour practices, and corporate governance, to align investment portfolios with sustainability goals and values.

8. Catalytic Philanthropy:
    - Catalytic philanthropy focuses on catalyzing systemic change and addressing the root causes of social problems by investing in innovative solutions, policy advocacy, and capacity-building initiatives.
    - Catalytic philanthropists leverage their resources, networks, and influence to drive transformative impact, amplify the voices of marginalized communities, and advocate for systemic reforms to address structural inequities and injustices.

9. Collaborative Funding Models:
    - Collaborative funding models, such as pooled funds, collective impact initiatives, and collaborative grantmaking platforms, bring together multiple funders to pool resources, share risks, and coordinate efforts to address complex social issues.
    - Collaborative funding models promote synergy, alignment, and coordination among diverse stakeholders, maximizing the collective impact of philanthropic investments and fostering innovation and learning within the sector.

10. Philanthropy 2.0:
- Philanthropy 2.0 encompasses a shift toward more participatory, democratized, and inclusive approaches to philanthropy, engaging donors, beneficiaries, and communities as co-creators and

partners in shaping philanthropic strategies and solutions.
- Philanthropy 2.0 leverages technology, social media, crowdfunding platforms, and online giving tools to democratize access to philanthropic giving, amplify the voices of grassroots organizations and empower individuals to contribute to social change initiatives.

In conclusion, innovations in philanthropy and social impact investing are transforming the way we address social and environmental challenges, driving greater collaboration, accountability, and effectiveness in achieving positive change. By embracing innovative approaches, leveraging new financing mechanisms, and integrating impact measurement and management practices, philanthropists, investors, and social entrepreneurs can unlock new opportunities for creating lasting impact and advancing sustainable development goals worldwide.

Building Resilient and Sustainable Charity Organizations

In the face of evolving challenges and uncertainties, building resilient and sustainable charity organizations is essential to ensure long-term effectiveness, impact, and relevance. Here are key strategies for fostering resilience and sustainability within charity organizations:

1. Mission Clarity and Alignment:
    - Define a clear and compelling mission statement that articulates the organization's purpose, values, and goals, providing a guiding framework for decision-making, resource allocation, and strategic direction.
    - Ensure alignment between the organization's mission, programs, activities, and stakeholder needs, regularly evaluating and adjusting strategies to stay true to the

mission while responding to changing external conditions.

2. Diversified Funding Streams:
   - Cultivate diversified funding streams to reduce reliance on any single source of revenue and mitigate financial risks associated with fluctuations in donor support, economic downturns, or funding uncertainties.
   - Explore diverse revenue sources, such as individual donations, corporate partnerships, foundation grants, earned income ventures, social enterprises, and government contracts, to create a sustainable funding mix that supports organizational resilience and growth.

3. Financial Stewardship and Transparency:
   - Practice sound financial stewardship and accountability, maintaining robust financial management practices, internal controls, and transparency measures to ensure the responsible use of resources and build trust with stakeholders.
   - Adhere to ethical fundraising standards, financial reporting requirements, and regulatory compliance obligations, providing donors, supporters, and beneficiaries with clear and accurate information about the organization's financial health and impact.

4. Strategic Planning and Adaptive Management:
   - Engage in strategic planning processes that involve stakeholders in setting goals, identifying priorities, and developing adaptive strategies to address emerging challenges, seize opportunities, and achieve long-term impact.

- Embrace adaptive management practices that enable the organization to monitor progress, learn from feedback, and adjust strategies in real time, fostering agility, resilience, and responsiveness to changing dynamics and stakeholder needs.

5. Talent Development and Leadership Succession:
   - Invest in talent development, leadership training, and succession planning to cultivate a pipeline of skilled and empowered staff, volunteers, and leaders capable of driving organizational growth, innovation, and sustainability.
   - Provide opportunities for professional growth, mentorship, and leadership development, fostering a culture of learning, collaboration, and continuous improvement within the organization.

6. Collaboration and Partnerships:
   - Foster collaborative partnerships and networks with other charities, nonprofits, government agencies, businesses, academia, and community organizations to leverage resources, expertise, and networks for greater collective impact.
   - Seek opportunities for strategic alliances, consortia, and shared services arrangements that enhance operational efficiency, scale programmatic impact, and address systemic challenges more effectively through collective action.

7. Organizational Resilience and Risk Management:
   - Build organizational resilience by identifying, assessing, and mitigating risks associated with external threats, internal vulnerabilities, and operational disruptions that may impact

the organization's mission, programs, or sustainability.

- Develop risk management plans, crisis response protocols, and business continuity strategies to prepare for and respond to emergencies, disasters, or unexpected events with agility, effectiveness, and resilience.

8. Innovation and Adaptation:
   - Foster a culture of innovation, experimentation, and learning within the organization, encouraging staff, volunteers, and stakeholders to explore new ideas, test innovative solutions, and adapt to changing circumstances.
   - Embrace technology adoption, data-driven decision-making, and agile methodologies to enhance organizational effectiveness, improve service delivery, and capitalize on emerging opportunities for innovation and impact.

9. Community Engagement and Empowerment:
   - Engage with beneficiaries, communities, and stakeholders as partners in the organization's mission and programs, seeking their input, participation, and feedback to ensure programs are relevant, responsive, and inclusive.
   - Empower individuals and communities to take ownership of their own development, fostering participatory approaches, community-led solutions, and grassroots initiatives that build local capacity and resilience.

10. Continuous Learning and Improvement:
- Commit to continuous learning, evaluation, and improvement processes that enable the organization

to assess performance, measure outcomes, and adapt strategies based on evidence and feedback.
- Invest in monitoring and evaluation systems, impact assessment tools, and learning mechanisms that promote accountability, transparency, and organizational learning, driving greater effectiveness and sustainability over time.

In conclusion, building resilient and sustainable charity organizations requires a holistic approach that encompasses strategic planning, financial stewardship, talent development, collaboration, risk management, innovation, community engagement, and continuous learning. By adopting these strategies and fostering a culture of resilience, adaptability, and innovation, charity organizations can navigate challenges, seize opportunities, and achieve lasting impact in the communities they serve, ensuring their sustainability and relevance for generations to come.

Chapter 11:

Charity Scams and Frauds

Charity scams and frauds pose significant risks to the integrity, reputation, and effectiveness of charitable organizations, undermining public trust and diverting resources away from legitimate charitable activities. In this chapter, we examine common types of charity scams and frauds, explore strategies for preventing and detecting fraudulent activities, and discuss the importance of transparency, accountability, and ethical conduct in charity management.

1. Understanding Charity Scams and Frauds:
    - Charity scams and frauds involve deceptive or dishonest practices aimed at exploiting donors, beneficiaries, or the public for personal gain or fraudulent purposes.
    - Common types of charity scams include fake charities, fraudulent fundraising appeals, misrepresentation of charitable activities or impact, diversion of funds for personal use, and embezzlement or financial fraud by staff or volunteers.

2. Red Flags and Warning Signs:
    - Recognizing red flags and warning signs of charity scams is essential for donors, volunteers, and stakeholders to avoid falling victim to fraudulent schemes.
    - Red flags may include high-pressure fundraising tactics, vague or misleading mission statements, requests for cash or wire transfers, lack of transparency or financial accountability, and refusal to provide detailed information about the organization's programs or finances.

3. Due Diligence and Research:

- Conducting due diligence and research before donating to a charity is critical for donors to verify the legitimacy, credibility, and impact of the organization.
- Donors should research the charity's mission, programs, governance structure, financial health, and regulatory compliance status through reputable sources, such as charity watchdogs, government databases, and independent evaluations.

4. Transparency and Accountability:
   - Promoting transparency and accountability in charity management is essential for preventing fraud and maintaining public trust.
   - Charity organizations should disclose detailed information about their mission, programs, finances, governance structure, and impact to donors, regulators, and stakeholders, fostering transparency and accountability in their operations.

5. Ethical Fundraising Practices:
   - Adhering to ethical fundraising practices and standards is crucial for charity organizations to uphold their integrity and reputation.
   - Charity fundraisers should operate with honesty, integrity, and respect for donor rights, avoiding misleading or deceptive tactics, providing accurate information about the charity's activities and impact, and honouring donor preferences and privacy rights.

6. Internal Controls and Oversight:
   - Implementing robust internal controls and oversight mechanisms is essential for preventing and detecting fraud within charity organizations.

- Charity boards and management should establish clear policies, procedures, and safeguards to prevent conflicts of interest, ensure segregation of duties, conduct regular financial audits, and monitor compliance with ethical and legal standards.

7. Whistleblower Protections:
   - Establishing whistleblower protections and reporting mechanisms encourages staff, volunteers, and stakeholders to report suspected fraud, misconduct, or unethical behaviour without fear of retaliation.
   - Charity organizations should maintain confidential whistleblower hotlines, anonymous reporting channels, and whistleblower protection policies to promote accountability and transparency in addressing fraud and misconduct.

8. Collaboration and Information Sharing:
   - Collaborating with other charities, regulatory agencies, law enforcement authorities, and industry stakeholders fosters collective efforts to combat charity scams and frauds.
   - Charity organizations should share best practices, resources, and information about fraudulent schemes and emerging threats, collaborating to raise awareness, strengthen regulatory enforcement, and protect donors and beneficiaries from harm.

9. Legal and Regulatory Compliance:
   - Ensuring compliance with relevant laws, regulations, and reporting requirements is essential for charity organizations to operate ethically and transparently.
   - Charity boards and management should stay informed about applicable legal and regulatory frameworks governing charitable

activities, fundraising practices, financial reporting, and tax-exempt status, maintaining compliance to uphold the organization's integrity and credibility.

10. Education and Awareness:

- Educating donors, volunteers, and stakeholders about charity scams and frauds empowers them to make informed decisions and protect themselves against fraudulent schemes.
- Charity organizations should provide outreach, education, and awareness campaigns to raise awareness about common types of charity scams, warning signs, and best practices for safe giving, empowering individuals to support legitimate charities and avoid fraudulent schemes.

In the charitable sector, the overwhelming majority of organizations operate with integrity, transparency, and a genuine commitment to making a positive difference in the world. However, it is crucial to be aware of the existence of charity scams and frauds that exploit goodwill and deceive donors, volunteers, and beneficiaries. In this chapter, we delve into the various types of charity scams and frauds, their impact, and strategies for prevention and detection:

Types of Charity Scams:

Fake Charities: Fraudulent entities masquerade as legitimate charities, often using names similar to well-known organizations, to deceive donors into contributing funds that are misappropriated for personal gain rather than charitable purposes.

Donation Fraud: Scammers exploit natural disasters, humanitarian crises, or high-profile events to solicit donations for fake relief efforts or nonexistent causes, diverting funds away from genuine relief efforts and victims.

Overhead Exaggeration: Some charities mislead donors by inflating administrative and fundraising costs, diverting a disproportionate amount of funds away from programmatic activities and direct services to beneficiaries.

Embezzlement and Mismanagement: Internal fraud may occur within charities through the misappropriation of funds, fraudulent accounting practices, or misuse of assets by staff, board members, or executives for personal enrichment.

High-Pressure Tactics: Dishonest fundraisers or telemarketers may use aggressive or manipulative tactics to pressure individuals into making donations, often targeting vulnerable populations such as the elderly or individuals with cognitive impairments.

Impact of Charity Scams:

Financial Losses: Charity scams result in significant financial losses for donors who contribute funds under false pretences, diminishing trust in charitable giving and diverting resources away from legitimate causes and organizations.

Diminished Trust: Charity scams erode public trust and confidence in the charitable sector, undermining the credibility of genuine charities and hindering their ability to fulfil their missions and serve communities effectively.

Harm to Beneficiaries: Funds diverted through charity scams deprive intended beneficiaries of essential services, support, and resources, exacerbating social problems, and perpetuating cycles of poverty and inequality.

Reputational Damage: Charities implicated in scams or frauds may suffer reputational damage, negative publicity, and loss of donor support, jeopardizing their sustainability, partnerships, and ability to attract funding and volunteers.

Prevention and Detection Strategies:

Due Diligence: Conduct thorough research and due diligence before donating to a charity, verifying its legitimacy, mission, impact, and financial accountability through reputable sources such as charity watchdog organizations, regulatory agencies, and independent audits.

Transparency and Accountability: Support charities that demonstrate transparency, accountability, and responsible stewardship of resources by providing clear information about their programs, finances, governance, and impact on donors and stakeholders.

Watchdog Oversight: Consult charity watchdog organizations such as Charity Navigator, GuideStar, and the Better Business Bureau Wise Giving Alliance to evaluate charities' performance, governance practices, and adherence to ethical standards and best practices.

Reporting Suspected Fraud: Report suspected charity scams or fraudulent activities to relevant authorities, such as state attorneys general, consumer protection agencies, or law enforcement agencies, to investigate and take appropriate legal action against perpetrators.

Donor Education: Educate donors about common charity scams, warning signs of fraudulent solicitations, and best practices for making informed, responsible giving decisions to protect themselves and support reputable organizations making a genuine impact.

Internal Controls and Oversight: Implement strong internal controls, financial management policies, and oversight mechanisms within charities to prevent fraud, detect irregularities, and ensure compliance with legal and ethical standards.

Whistleblower Protection: Establish whistleblower policies and mechanisms to encourage staff, volunteers, and stakeholders to report suspected fraud, misconduct, or unethical behaviour without fear of retaliation, facilitating early detection and intervention.

In conclusion, charity scams and frauds pose significant risks to donors, beneficiaries, and the charitable sector as a whole, undermining trust, integrity, and impact. By raising awareness, practising due diligence, promoting transparency, and implementing robust safeguards, stakeholders can work together to prevent and detect charity scams, protect vulnerable populations, and uphold the values of accountability, trustworthiness, and ethical conduct in charitable giving and philanthropy.

Combating charity scams and frauds requires vigilance, transparency, accountability, and collaboration among charity organizations, donors, regulators, and stakeholders. By implementing due diligence practices, promoting transparency and ethical conduct, establishing internal controls and oversight mechanisms, fostering whistleblower protections, collaborating with industry partners, complying with legal and regulatory requirements, and educating stakeholders about fraud prevention, charity organizations can safeguard their integrity, protect the public trust, and fulfil their mission of making a positive difference in the world.

Identifying Common Charity Scams and Fraudulent Practices

Recognizing common charity scams and fraudulent practices is essential for protecting donors, volunteers, and beneficiaries from exploitation and financial harm. In this section, we highlight key signs and red flags that may indicate fraudulent activities within charitable organizations:

1. High-Pressure Solicitations:
   - Beware of charities that use aggressive or high-pressure tactics to solicit donations, such as persistent phone calls, unsolicited emails, or door-to-door fundraising, often targeting vulnerable individuals who may be more susceptible to manipulation.
2. Lack of Transparency:

- Exercise caution when charities refuse to provide detailed information about their mission, programs, finances, or governance structure, as transparency is essential for building trust and accountability with donors and stakeholders.
3. Overhead Exaggeration:
    - Scrutinize charities that claim unusually high percentages of donations are allocated to administrative expenses or fundraising costs, diverting a disproportionate amount of funds away from programmatic activities and direct services to beneficiaries.
4. Name Similarity to Established Charities:
    - Be cautious of charities with names similar to well-known, reputable organizations, as scammers may intentionally use misleading or deceptive names to capitalize on the goodwill and brand recognition of established charities.
5. Lack of Documentation or Accountability:
    - Request documentation and financial reports from charities to verify their legitimacy, impact, and accountability, including annual reports, audited financial statements, IRS Form 990 filings, and evidence of program outcomes and achievements.
6. Suspicious Financial Practices:
    - Investigate charities that exhibit irregular financial practices, such as commingling of funds, inadequate record-keeping, frequent cash transactions, or unexplained discrepancies in financial statements, which may indicate potential embezzlement or mismanagement.
7. False Claims of Endorsement or Accreditation:

- Be sceptical of charities that falsely claim endorsements or accreditations from reputable organizations, regulatory agencies, or government entities, as these claims may be fabricated or misleading to deceive donors and enhance credibility.

8. Lack of Impact or Results:
   - Evaluate charities based on their demonstrated impact, results, and outcomes achieved through their programs and services, as well as their ability to measure, evaluate, and communicate the effectiveness of their interventions in addressing social needs and achieving stated goals.

9. Failure to Provide Documentation or Follow-Up:
   - Avoid charities that fail to provide documentation, receipts, or acknowledgements for donations, as well as those that do not follow up with donors to provide updates on how their contributions were used or the impact they helped to achieve.

10. Refusal to Answer Questions or Provide Information:
    - Be wary of charities that evade or refuse to answer questions about their activities, governance, finances, or impact, as transparency, openness, and accountability are essential principles of ethical and responsible charitable practices.

By being vigilant, informed, and discerning, donors and stakeholders can identify and avoid common charity scams and fraudulent practices, safeguarding their contributions, trust, and support for legitimate charitable organizations and making a positive difference in the world.

Strategies for Preventing and Combatting Fraud in Charity Organizations

Preventing and combatting fraud is paramount for maintaining the integrity, trustworthiness, and effectiveness of charity organizations. By implementing robust safeguards, oversight mechanisms, and proactive measures, charities can mitigate the risk of fraud and protect their donors, beneficiaries, and stakeholders. Here are key strategies for preventing and combatting fraud in charity organizations:

1. Establish a Culture of Integrity and Ethical Conduct:
    - Foster a culture of integrity, transparency, and ethical conduct within the organization, emphasizing the importance of honesty, accountability, and adherence to ethical standards and best practices at all levels of the organization.

2. Implement Strong Internal Controls and Oversight:
    - Establish and enforce internal controls, financial management policies, and oversight mechanisms to prevent and detect fraud, including segregation of duties, dual authorization requirements, regular reconciliations, and independent audits.

3. Conduct Risk Assessments:
    - Conduct regular risk assessments to identify potential vulnerabilities, fraud risks, and areas of exposure within the organization's operations, finances, governance, and programs, prioritizing areas for enhanced scrutiny and mitigation measures.

4. Educate Staff, Volunteers, and Board Members:
    - Provide comprehensive training and awareness programs for staff, volunteers, and board members on fraud prevention, detection, reporting, and response protocols, empowering them to recognize red flags,

adhere to policies, and report suspected fraud promptly.

5. Implement Whistleblower Policies and Reporting Mechanisms:
    - Establish whistleblower policies, anonymous reporting channels, and confidential hotlines to encourage staff, volunteers, and stakeholders to report suspected fraud, misconduct, or unethical behaviour without fear of retaliation, ensuring timely intervention and investigation.

6. Strengthen Financial Management and Oversight:
    - Implement rigorous financial management practices, including budgetary controls, expenditure authorization processes, cash handling procedures, and internal audit functions to ensure accountability, accuracy, and transparency in financial transactions and reporting.

7. Conduct Due Diligence on Partners and Vendors:
    - Conduct due diligence and background checks on potential partners, vendors, contractors, and service providers to verify their legitimacy, credibility, and reputation before entering into agreements or engaging in collaborative ventures to minimize the risk of fraud or corruption.

8. Monitor and Review Financial Transactions:
    - Monitor financial transactions, expenditures, and revenue streams regularly through internal audits, reviews, and reconciliations to detect irregularities, discrepancies, or unauthorized activities that may indicate potential fraud or misuse of funds.

9. Segregate Duties and Responsibilities:
    - Segregate duties and responsibilities among staff and volunteers to prevent conflicts of

interest, collusion, or opportunities for fraud, ensuring that no single individual has control over all aspects of a transaction or financial process.

10. Stay Informed about Emerging Fraud Risks and Trends:
    - Stay informed about emerging fraud risks, trends, and schemes within the charitable sector by monitoring industry publications, regulatory updates, and alerts from law enforcement agencies and fraud prevention organizations to proactively adapt and strengthen anti-fraud measures.

11. Collaborate with External Partners and Regulators:
    - Collaborate with external partners, regulators, law enforcement agencies, and industry associations to share information, resources, and best practices for preventing and combatting fraud, fostering a collective response to fraud prevention and enforcement efforts.

12. Review and Update Policies and Procedures Regularly:
    - Review and update organizational policies, procedures, and controls regularly to adapt to changing risks, regulations, and operating environments, ensuring that anti-fraud measures remain effective, relevant, and aligned with industry standards and best practices.

By implementing these strategies and fostering a culture of vigilance, accountability, and ethical conduct, charity organizations can strengthen their resilience, protect their assets, and uphold their commitment to integrity, transparency, and accountability in serving their mission and beneficiaries.

Legal and Ethical Considerations in Charity Fundraising

Charity fundraising plays a vital role in generating financial support for philanthropic causes and advancing the mission of nonprofit organizations. However, charities need to adhere to legal and ethical standards to maintain trust, integrity, and compliance with regulatory requirements. Here are key legal and ethical considerations in charity fundraising:

1. Compliance with Regulatory Requirements:
   - Understand and comply with applicable laws, regulations, and guidelines governing charitable fundraising activities, including registration and reporting requirements imposed by federal, state, and local authorities, such as the Internal Revenue Service (IRS-USA), (check your local/national authority of Registrations and Tax department) state attorney general's offices, and fundraising regulatory agencies.

2. Transparency and Accountability:
   - Maintain transparency and accountability in fundraising practices by providing clear, accurate, and accessible information to donors about the organization's mission, programs, finances, impact, and use of funds, as well as any associated risks, restrictions, or disclosures relevant to charitable contributions.

3. Truthful and Accurate Representation:
   - Ensure that all fundraising communications, solicitations, and promotional materials accurately represent the organization's activities, achievements, and financial needs without exaggeration, misleading statements, or false promises to donors.

4. Donor Privacy and Data Protection:
   - Safeguard donor privacy and personal information following applicable privacy laws

and regulations, implementing data protection policies, procedures, and security measures to prevent unauthorized access, misuse, or disclosure of donor data.

5. Consent and Permission-Based Fundraising:
    - Obtain consent and permission from donors before soliciting their support, using their personal information, or communicating with them for fundraising purposes, respecting their preferences, privacy rights, and autonomy in decision-making.

6. Avoidance of Coercive or Manipulative Tactics:
    - Avoid using coercive, manipulative, or high-pressure tactics to solicit donations, respecting donors' autonomy, free will, and right to make informed decisions about charitable giving without undue influence or intimidation.

7. Donor Stewardship and Recognition:
    - Practice donor stewardship by expressing gratitude, appreciation, and recognition to donors for their generosity, acknowledging their contributions, and providing regular updates on how their support is making a difference in advancing the organization's mission and serving beneficiaries.

8. Conflict of Interest Disclosure:
    - Disclose and manage conflicts of interest that may arise in fundraising activities, such as relationships with major donors, corporate sponsors, or vendors, ensuring transparency, fairness, and impartiality in decision-making processes and resource allocation.

9. Ethical Use of Fundraising Techniques:
    - Exercise ethical judgment and discretion in the use of fundraising techniques, such as direct mail, telephone solicitation, online

crowdfunding, special events, and cause-related marketing, avoiding tactics that may exploit donor emotions, vulnerability, or sympathy for personal gain.

10. Professionalism and Integrity:
- Uphold professional standards of conduct, integrity, and ethical behaviour in all fundraising activities, adhering to codes of ethics, standards of practice, and guidelines established by professional associations, such as the Association of Fundraising Professionals (AFP) or the Council for Advancement and Support of Education (CASE).

11. Compliance with Donor Restrictions and Designations:
- Honour donor restrictions, designations, and intentions regarding the use of their contributions, ensuring that funds are allocated and utilized following donors' wishes and specified purposes, and providing accurate reporting and accountability for how donations are allocated and spent.

12. Continuous Monitoring and Improvement:
- Regularly review, evaluate, and improve fundraising practices, policies, and procedures to address emerging ethical challenges, mitigate risks, and enhance accountability, transparency, and donor trust in the organization's fundraising efforts.

By adhering to these legal and ethical considerations, charity organizations can demonstrate their commitment to integrity, accountability, and responsible stewardship of donor support, fostering trust, credibility, and long-term sustainability in advancing their charitable mission and serving their beneficiaries.

Chapter 12:

Dealing with Fake Charities and Misrepresentation

In the charitable sector, the proliferation of fake charities and misrepresentation poses significant risks to donors, beneficiaries, and the integrity of philanthropic efforts. Deceptive practices and fraudulent entities undermine public trust, divert resources from legitimate causes, and hinder the ability of genuine charities to fulfil their missions. In this chapter, we explore strategies for identifying, addressing, and combating fake charities and misrepresentation:

1. Awareness and Education:
    - Raise awareness among donors, volunteers, and the general public about the prevalence of fake charities and the tactics used by scammers to deceive individuals into making fraudulent donations.
    - Provide educational resources, guidance, and training on how to recognize red flags, conduct due diligence, and verify the legitimacy of charitable organizations before making contributions.
2. Conduct Due Diligence:
    - Conduct thorough due diligence and research before donating to a charity, verifying its legitimacy, credibility, and effectiveness through reputable sources such as charity watchdog organizations, regulatory agencies, and independent evaluations.
    - Verify the charity's registration status, mission statement, programs, financial transparency, governance structure, and track record of impact to ensure alignment with your philanthropic goals and values.
3. Verify Accreditation and Endorsements:

- Check whether the charity is accredited by reputable organizations such as the Better Business Bureau Wise Giving Alliance, Charity Navigator, GuideStar, or other independent evaluators that assess charities' performance, accountability, and adherence to ethical standards.
- Be cautious of charities that falsely claim endorsements, affiliations, or partnerships with well-known individuals, organizations, or celebrities to enhance credibility and solicit donations through misleading or deceptive means.

4. Scrutinize Fundraising Appeals:
- Scrutinize fundraising appeals, solicitations, and promotional materials for signs of misrepresentation, exaggeration, or false claims regarding the charity's programs, impact, achievements, or financial needs.
- Be wary of high-pressure tactics, emotional manipulation, or guilt-inducing appeals used by scammers to exploit donors' generosity and sympathy for fraudulent purposes.

5. Report Suspected Fraud:
- Report suspected fake charities, fraudulent solicitations, or misrepresentation to relevant authorities, such as state attorneys general, consumer protection agencies, law enforcement agencies, or regulatory bodies responsible for overseeing charitable activities.
- Provide detailed information, evidence, and documentation to facilitate investigations and enforcement actions against perpetrators engaged in deceptive practices or fraudulent conduct.

6. Support Regulatory Oversight and Enforcement:

- Advocate for stronger regulatory oversight, enforcement measures, and penalties to deter fraudulent activities, hold accountable those engaged in deceptive practices, and protect donors, beneficiaries, and the integrity of the charitable sector.
- Support legislative efforts to strengthen consumer protection laws, enhance transparency requirements, and improve regulatory frameworks for registering, monitoring, and regulating charitable organizations to prevent abuse and exploitation.

7. Promote Transparency and Accountability:
   - Promote transparency and accountability in charitable fundraising by encouraging charities to disclose relevant information about their activities, finances, governance, and impact to donors, regulators, and the public.
   - Support initiatives that promote best practices, ethical standards, and self-regulatory mechanisms within the charitable sector to foster trust, integrity, and responsible stewardship of charitable resources.

8. Engage in Due Diligence on Third-Party Fundraisers:
   - Exercise caution when donating to charities using third-party fundraisers, commercial solicitors, professional telemarketers, or online platforms, conducting due diligence on both the charity and the fundraising entity to ensure legitimacy, compliance, and transparency in fundraising practices.

By adopting these strategies and working collaboratively with stakeholders, regulators, and enforcement agencies, individuals and organizations can help detect, address, and prevent the proliferation of fake charities and misrepresentation, safeguarding the integrity of charitable giving and ensuring that resources are directed to genuine causes that make a positive impact on society.

Recognizing Red Flags of Fake Charities
Identifying red flags as indicative of fake charities is crucial for donors to avoid falling victim to fraudulent schemes and ensure that their contributions support legitimate charitable causes. Here are key indicators that may signal the presence of a fake charity:

1. Lack of Transparency:
    - Fake charities often lack transparency regarding their mission, programs, finances, and governance structure, making it difficult for donors to assess their credibility, effectiveness, and impact.
2. High-Pressure Tactics:
    - Be wary of charities that use aggressive or high-pressure tactics to solicit donations, such as incessant phone calls, urgent appeals, or emotional manipulation, aiming to exploit donors' goodwill and generosity for fraudulent purposes.
3. Unverified Endorsements or Affiliations:
    - Verify claims of endorsements, affiliations, or partnerships with well-known individuals, organizations, or celebrities, as fake charities may falsely claim support from reputable entities to enhance credibility and solicit donations under false pretenses.
4. Lack of Accreditation or Evaluation:
    - Check whether the charity is accredited by reputable watchdog organizations, such as the Better Business Bureau Wise Giving Alliance, Charity Navigator, or GuideStar, that assess charities' performance,

accountability, and adherence to ethical standards.

5. Vague or Misleading Mission Statements:
   - Scrutinize the charity's mission statement and objectives for clarity, specificity, and alignment with its purported charitable activities, as fake charities may use vague or misleading language to obscure their true intentions or activities.

6. Suspicious Financial Practices:
   - Investigate the charity's financial practices, including how donations are collected, managed, and disbursed, as well as the allocation of funds to programmatic activities versus administrative expenses, to ensure transparency and accountability in financial management.

7. Lack of Documentation or Impact Reporting:
   - Request documentation, reports, or evidence of the charity's impact, achievements, and outcomes achieved through its programs and services, as well as how donor contributions are used to support charitable activities, to verify legitimacy and effectiveness.

8. Unverified Contact Information or Address:
   - Verify the charity's contact information, address, phone number, and website for authenticity and legitimacy, as fake charities may use untraceable or fictitious contact details to evade detection or disguise their fraudulent activities.

9. No History or Track Record:
   - Research the charity's history, track record, and reputation within the charitable sector, including its registration status, regulatory compliance, and any past allegations or

complaints of fraud, mismanagement, or
unethical conduct.
10. Lack of Independent Verification or Oversight:
- Look for evidence of independent verification,
oversight, or validation of the charity's
activities, impact, and governance practices
by reputable third parties, regulatory
agencies, or industry associations to
corroborate claims and ensure credibility.

By remaining vigilant, informed, and discerning, donors can
recognize red flags of fake charities and make informed,
responsible giving decisions that support genuine charitable
causes, maximize impact, and avoid contributing to
fraudulent schemes that exploit goodwill and trust for
personal gain.

Reporting Suspected Fraudulent Activities

Reporting suspected fraudulent activities is essential for
safeguarding donors, beneficiaries, and the integrity of the
charitable sector. If you suspect that a charity is engaged in
fraudulent or deceptive practices, taking prompt action to
report your concerns to the appropriate authorities can help
prevent further harm and hold accountable those
responsible for misconduct. Here are steps for reporting
suspected fraudulent activities involving charities:

1. Gather Information:
- Document any evidence, documentation, or
observations that support your suspicion of
fraudulent activities, including emails, letters,
advertisements, financial records, or
interactions with the charity's
representatives.
2. Contact Regulatory Authorities:
- Report your concerns to relevant regulatory
authorities responsible for overseeing
charitable organizations and fundraising
activities, such as state attorneys general,

consumer protection agencies, or the IRS's Tax Exempt and Government Entities division.
- Provide detailed information, including the name and contact information of the charity, a description of the suspected fraudulent activities, and any supporting documentation or evidence you have gathered.

3. File a Complaint:
- File a formal complaint or report with the appropriate regulatory agency or enforcement authority through their designated channels, online complaint forms, or hotline numbers, following their specific procedures and requirements for reporting suspected fraud.
- Be prepared to provide your contact information, as well as any additional details, witnesses, or corroborating evidence that may assist investigators in their inquiry into the alleged fraudulent activities.

4. Seek Legal Advice:
- Consider seeking legal advice or consulting with an attorney specializing in nonprofit law, fraud prevention, or consumer protection if you have concerns about potential legal implications, liabilities, or remedies associated with reporting suspected fraudulent activities.
- Understand your rights and responsibilities as a whistleblower or complainant, including protections against retaliation or reprisal for reporting suspected fraud under applicable whistleblower laws or regulations.

5. Collaborate with Watchdog Organizations:
- Collaborate with watchdog organizations, consumer advocacy groups, or charity watchdogs that specialize in monitoring,

evaluating, and exposing fraudulent or unethical practices within the charitable sector.

- Share your findings, concerns, and evidence with reputable watchdog organizations or media outlets that investigate and report on charitable fraud, misconduct, or mismanagement to raise awareness and prompt action.

6. Follow Up and Stay Informed:
   - Follow up with regulatory authorities or enforcement agencies periodically to inquire about the status of your complaint, investigation, or any actions taken in response to your report of suspected fraudulent activities.
   - Stay informed about developments, outcomes, or resolutions related to your complaint or report through updates from regulatory agencies, media coverage, or official announcements to ensure that appropriate measures are taken to address the alleged fraud.

By reporting suspected fraudulent activities promptly and responsibly, you can help protect donors, beneficiaries, and the public from exploitation, hold fraudulent actors accountable for their actions, and uphold the integrity, transparency, and trustworthiness of the charitable sector.

Building Trust and Credibility in the Charity Sector

Establishing and maintaining trust and credibility is essential for charity organizations to attract donors, engage stakeholders, and fulfil their missions effectively. By adopting transparent, accountable, and ethical practices, charities can build confidence, inspire support, and demonstrate their commitment to making a positive impact. Here are key strategies for building trust and credibility in the charity sector:

1. Transparency and Accountability:
    - Embrace transparency by openly sharing information about the organization's mission, programs, finances, governance structure, and impact with donors, stakeholders, and the public.
    - Provide clear, accurate, and accessible reports, disclosures, and financial statements that demonstrate how donations are used, the results achieved, and the effectiveness of the charity's programs and services.

2. Ethical Conduct and Integrity:
    - Uphold high standards of ethical conduct, integrity, and honesty in all interactions, decisions, and operations, adhering to ethical codes, principles, and guidelines established by professional associations and regulatory bodies.
    - Demonstrate integrity by honouring commitments, fulfilling promises, and acting in the best interests of beneficiaries, donors, and the community, even in challenging or uncertain circumstances.

3. Mission Alignment and Impact:
    - Align organizational activities, initiatives, and resource allocation with the charity's mission, vision, and core values, ensuring that programs and services address genuine social needs, achieve meaningful outcomes, and make a tangible difference in the lives of beneficiaries.
    - Communicate the organization's impact, results, and success stories through compelling narratives, testimonials, and

evidence-based data that illustrate the positive change and transformative impact facilitated by donor support and philanthropic investments.
4. Donor Stewardship and Engagement:
   - Cultivate strong relationships with donors through personalized communication, engagement opportunities, and stewardship practices that express appreciation, recognition, and gratitude for their generosity and support.
   - Involve donors in the organization's decision-making processes, programmatic planning, and strategic initiatives, seeking their input, feedback, and collaboration to enhance transparency, accountability, and donor satisfaction.
5. Compliance with Regulatory Standards:
   - Adhere to applicable laws, regulations, and guidelines governing charitable activities, fundraising practices, and financial management, ensuring compliance with regulatory requirements, reporting obligations, and ethical standards.
   - Maintain up-to-date registration, licensure, and accreditation with relevant authorities, regulatory agencies, and oversight bodies to demonstrate credibility, legitimacy, and adherence to industry standards.
6. Independent Evaluation and Validation:
   - Seek independent evaluation, assessment, and validation of the organization's programs, operations, and impact by reputable third-party evaluators, auditors, or accreditation agencies that provide impartial scrutiny and assurance of effectiveness and accountability.

Participate in voluntary accreditation programs, certification processes, or peer-reviewed assessments offered by recognized accrediting bodies or industry associations to benchmark performance, improve practices, and enhance credibility.

7. Continuous Improvement and Learning:
Commit to continuous improvement, learning, and innovation by soliciting feedback, evaluating performance, and implementing best practices, lessons learned, and feedback mechanisms to enhance organizational effectiveness, efficiency, and impact.

Foster a culture of learning, adaptation, and innovation that encourages experimentation, risk-taking, and collaboration to address emerging challenges, seize opportunities, and drive positive change within the organization and the broader charitable sector.

8. Engage in Collaboration and Partnerships:
Collaborate with other charities, nonprofit organizations, government agencies, businesses, and community stakeholders to leverage resources, expertise, and collective impact in addressing complex social issues, maximizing efficiency, and achieving shared goals.

Forge strategic partnerships, alliances, and coalitions that amplify the organization's reach, influence, and effectiveness, fostering collaboration, trust, and mutual support among stakeholders and beneficiaries.
By prioritizing transparency, accountability, integrity, and stakeholder engagement, charity organizations can build trust and credibility with donors, beneficiaries, and the public, ensuring sustained support, a positive reputation, and a lasting impact in advancing their charitable mission and serving the common good.

Chapter 13:

Donation Collection and Marketing Plans

Effective donation collection and marketing plans are essential for charity organizations to attract support, raise funds, and advance their mission. By leveraging strategic marketing techniques and employing innovative fundraising strategies, charities can engage donors, cultivate relationships, and maximize donations to support their programs and initiatives. In this chapter, we explore key components and strategies for developing successful donation collection and marketing plans:

1. Understanding Donor Behavior and Preferences:

   - Conduct research and analysis to understand donor demographics, motivations, preferences, and giving patterns, allowing charities to tailor their fundraising appeals and marketing strategies to resonate with target audiences effectively.

2. Setting Clear Objectives and Goals:

   - Define specific, measurable, achievable, relevant, and time-bound (SMART) objectives and goals for donation collection and fundraising efforts, aligning them with the organization's mission, strategic priorities, and financial needs.

3. Segmenting Donor Base:

- Segment donors into distinct groups based on factors such as giving history, donation frequency, donation amount, interests, and engagement level, enabling charities to customize their marketing messages, appeals, and engagement tactics to each segment's preferences and needs.

4. Developing Compelling Messaging and Appeals:

- Craft compelling, emotive, and persuasive messaging and appeals that resonate with donors' values, emotions, and aspirations, emphasizing the impact of their contributions in addressing critical social needs and making a difference in the lives of beneficiaries.

5. Leveraging Multiple Channels and Platforms:

- Utilize a multi-channel approach to reach donors through various platforms and channels, including direct mail, email marketing, social media, website donations, crowdfunding platforms, peer-to-peer fundraising, special events, and corporate partnerships.

- Tailor marketing messages and fundraising appeals to the unique characteristics and audience demographics of each channel, optimizing engagement, conversion, and donor retention rates across different communication platforms.

6. Implementing Data-Driven Strategies:

   - Harness data analytics, donor management systems, and fundraising software to track, analyze, and segment donor data, enabling charities to personalize communications, target high-value donors, and optimize fundraising campaigns based on actionable insights and metrics.

   - Utilize A/B testing, experimentation, and iterative improvements to refine marketing strategies, donation appeals, and fundraising tactics, continuously optimizing performance, conversion rates, and return on investment (ROI) over time.

7. Cultivating Donor Relationships:

   - Prioritize donor stewardship, cultivation, and engagement through personalized communication, gratitude, and recognition initiatives that foster strong relationships, loyalty, and long-term support from donors.

   - Implement donor-centric practices such as timely acknowledgements, updates on program impact, exclusive opportunities for engagement, and opportunities for donor involvement in decision-making processes to enhance donor satisfaction and retention.

8. Incorporating Storytelling and Impact Narrative:

- Harness the power of storytelling and impact narrative to convey the organization's mission, values, and achievements compellingly and memorably, using real-life stories, testimonials, and case studies to illustrate the tangible impact of donor contributions.

- Highlight success stories, testimonials, and testimonials that showcase the transformative power of philanthropy, inspiring empathy, connection, and action among donors and reinforcing their sense of purpose and connection to the organization's mission.

9. Measuring and Evaluating Performance:

- Establish key performance indicators (KPIs), benchmarks, and metrics to track and evaluate the effectiveness of donation collection and marketing efforts, including donation conversion rates, donor retention rates, average donation value, and return on investment (ROI).

- Conduct regular performance reviews, post-campaign evaluations, and data analysis to assess the impact, effectiveness, and ROI of fundraising campaigns, identifying areas for improvement, optimization, and innovation in future initiatives.

10. Ensuring Compliance and Ethical Practices:

- Adhere to ethical fundraising practices, regulatory requirements, and industry standards governing donation collection, marketing communications, and donor stewardship, ensuring transparency, integrity, and accountability in all fundraising activities.

- Comply with data protection laws, privacy regulations, and fundraising codes of conduct to safeguard donor privacy, prevent misuse of donor information, and maintain trust and confidence in the organization's fundraising practices.

By developing comprehensive donation collection and marketing plans that prioritize donor engagement, storytelling, data-driven strategies, and ethical practices, charity organizations can maximize their fundraising effectiveness, inspire support, and advance their mission to create positive change in the world.

Developing Effective Donation Collection Strategies

Effective donation collection strategies are essential for charity organizations to generate financial support, sustain operations, and fulfil their mission. By employing strategic approaches and leveraging diverse channels, charities can engage donors, encourage giving, and maximize donations. Here are key steps for developing effective donation collection strategies:

1. Define Clear Objectives:

   - Clearly define the objectives of the donation collection strategy, including fundraising goals, target audiences, and desired outcomes. Set specific, measurable, achievable, relevant, and time-bound (SMART) targets to guide the strategy's implementation and evaluation.

2. Segment Donor Base:

   - Segment donors into distinct groups based on factors such as giving history, donation frequency, demographics, and interests. Customize donation collection strategies and messaging to resonate with the preferences and characteristics of each donor segment.

3. Diversify Fundraising Channels:

   - Utilize a diverse range of fundraising channels and methods to appeal to different donor preferences and behaviours. Explore options such as online donations, direct mail campaigns, peer-to-peer fundraising, special events, corporate partnerships, and major donor solicitations.

4. Optimize Online Donation Platforms:

   - Optimize the organization's website and online donation platform to make it easy, convenient, and secure for donors to contribute. Streamline the donation process, minimize barriers to giving, and provide multiple payment options to accommodate donor preferences.

5. Leverage Social Media and Digital Marketing:

   - Harness the power of social media and digital marketing to expand the organization's reach, raise awareness, and solicit donations. Create engaging content, storytelling campaigns, and fundraising appeals on social media platforms to inspire action and encourage sharing.

6. Encourage Recurring Donations:

   - Promote recurring donation programs that allow donors to make regular, ongoing contributions on a monthly, quarterly, or annual basis. Highlight the impact of recurring donations in providing sustained support for the organization's programs and initiatives.

7. Cultivate Major Donors and Partnerships:

   - Cultivate relationships with major donors, philanthropic foundations, corporations, and high-net-worth individuals who can make significant contributions. Develop personalized cultivation strategies and stewardship plans to engage major donors and secure large gifts.

8. Provide Incentives and Matching Gifts:

   - Offer incentives or matching gift opportunities to motivate donors to give. Examples include challenge grants, matching gift programs, donor recognition benefits, and exclusive opportunities for engagement or involvement with the organization.

9. Foster a Culture of Philanthropy:

   - Foster a culture of philanthropy within the organization and among staff, volunteers, and board members. Encourage participation in fundraising efforts, promote a shared commitment to fundraising goals, and recognize and celebrate fundraising successes.

10. Monitor and Evaluate Performance:

    - Monitor key performance indicators (KPIs), metrics, and benchmarks to assess the effectiveness of donation collection strategies. Track donation trends, conversion rates, donor retention rates, and fundraising ROI to identify areas for improvement and optimization.

11. Engage Donors in Impact Reporting:

    - Communicate the impact and outcomes of donor contributions through regular updates, impact reports, success stories, and testimonials. Demonstrate the tangible difference donors' support makes in advancing the organization's mission and benefiting its beneficiaries.

12. Adapt and Iterate:

- Continuously adapt and refine donation collection strategies based on feedback, data analysis, and changing donor preferences. Experiment with new approaches, test fundraising tactics and iterate on successful initiatives to optimize fundraising performance over time.

By developing and implementing effective donation collection strategies that prioritize donor engagement, diversification of fundraising channels, and strategic cultivation of major donors and partnerships, charity organizations can enhance their fundraising effectiveness, maximize donations, and achieve their philanthropic goals.

Crafting Compelling Marketing Campaigns to Increase Donor Engagement

Crafting compelling marketing campaigns is essential for charity organizations to increase donor engagement, raise awareness about their mission, and inspire support for their cause. By leveraging storytelling, emotional appeal, and strategic messaging, charities can capture the attention of donors, cultivate relationships, and drive meaningful action. Here are key steps for crafting compelling marketing campaigns to increase donor engagement:

1. Define Campaign Objectives:
   - Clearly define the objectives of the marketing campaign, such as raising funds for a specific program, increasing donor acquisition or retention, or promoting awareness about a

particular issue. Align campaign objectives with the organization's overall fundraising and strategic goals.

2. Identify Target Audience:

    - Identify the target audience for the marketing campaign based on factors such as demographics, interests, giving behaviour, and affinity with the organization's mission. Tailor messaging, content, and communication channels to resonate with the preferences and characteristics of the target audience.

3. Develop a Compelling Narrative:

    - Develop a compelling narrative or storytelling angle that highlights the organization's mission, impact, and beneficiaries. Use real-life stories, testimonials, and case studies to evoke empathy, emotion, and connection with donors, illustrating the tangible difference their support makes.

4. Create Engaging Content:

    - Create engaging and visually appealing content that captures the attention of donors and communicates the organization's message effectively. Utilize multimedia formats such as videos, infographics, photos, and interactive storytelling to convey information and evoke emotion.

5. Leverage Emotional Appeal:

   - Tap into the emotional appeal of the organization's mission and beneficiaries to evoke empathy, compassion, and motivation among donors. Highlight the human stories behind the statistics, illustrating the personal struggles, triumphs, and aspirations of those served by the charity.

6. Use Clear Calls to Action:

   - Include clear and compelling calls to action (CTAs) in marketing materials that prompt donors to take specific actions, such as making a donation, signing up for a newsletter, volunteering, or sharing the campaign with their network. Use persuasive language and urgency to motivate immediate action.

7. Utilize Multi-Channel Approach:

   - Utilize a multi-channel approach to reach donors through various communication channels, including email marketing, social media, website content, direct mail, events, and traditional media. Tailor messaging and content to each channel's format and audience demographics.

8. Personalize Communication:

   - Personalize communication with donors by addressing them by name, acknowledging their past support or involvement, and segmenting them into targeted groups based on their interests, preferences, or giving history. Customize messaging and content to resonate with each donor segment.

9. Engage Donors Through Storytelling:

  - Engage donors through storytelling by sharing compelling stories, testimonials, and impact narratives that illustrate the organization's mission and the transformative power of philanthropy. Use storytelling as a powerful tool to create empathy, connection, and inspiration.

10. Foster Two-Way Communication:

  - Foster two-way communication with donors by soliciting feedback, inviting dialogue, and responding to inquiries, comments, or concerns promptly. Encourage donor participation and engagement through interactive features, surveys, and Q&A sessions.

11. Measure and Analyze Results:

  - Measure the effectiveness of the marketing campaign by tracking key performance indicators (KPIs), such as donation conversion rates, engagement metrics, website traffic, and social media interactions. Analyze campaign data to assess impact, identify trends, and inform future marketing strategies.

12. Iterate and Optimize:

- Iterate and optimize marketing campaigns based on insights gained from data analysis, donor feedback, and performance evaluation. Test different messaging, content formats, and communication channels to identify what resonates most effectively with donors and drive better results.

By following these steps and crafting compelling marketing campaigns that leverage storytelling, emotional appeal, and strategic messaging, charity organizations can increase donor engagement, raise awareness, and inspire support for their mission, ultimately driving positive change and making a meaningful impact in the community.

Leveraging Technology for Streamlined Donation Processes

In today's digital age, charity organizations can harness technology to streamline donation processes, enhance donor experience, and maximize fundraising efficiency. By adopting innovative fundraising platforms, donor management systems, and digital payment solutions, charities can simplify donation collection, increase donor engagement, and optimize fundraising outcomes. Here are key strategies for leveraging technology to streamline donation processes:

1. Online Donation Platforms:

- Implement user-friendly online donation platforms that enable donors to make secure and convenient contributions through the organization's website or dedicated donation portal. Provide multiple payment options, such as credit/debit cards, PayPal, and mobile payment methods, to accommodate donor preferences.

2. Mobile Giving Apps:

- Develop or integrate mobile giving apps that allow donors to make donations conveniently from their smartphones or mobile devices. Mobile apps can streamline the donation process, facilitate one-click donations, and provide instant confirmation, enhancing donor convenience and accessibility.

3. Peer-to-Peer Fundraising:

- Utilize peer-to-peer fundraising platforms that empower supporters to create personalized fundraising pages, share their stories, and solicit donations from their networks on behalf of the organization. Peer-to-peer fundraising leverages the power of social networks to amplify fundraising efforts and reach new donors.

4. Text-to-Give Campaigns:

- Launch text-to-give campaigns that enable donors to make donations quickly and easily by sending a text message with a designated keyword or shortcode. Text-to-give technology simplifies the donation process, eliminates barriers to giving, and leverages the widespread use of mobile devices.

5. Donor Management Systems:

   - Implement donor management software or customer relationship management (CRM) systems to streamline donor data collection, tracking, and communication. Donor management systems enable charities to maintain accurate donor records, track donation history, and segment donors for targeted outreach and stewardship.

6. Automated Email Marketing:

   - Use email marketing automation tools to send personalized donation appeals, acknowledgements, and updates to donors based on their preferences, behaviour, and engagement level. Automated email campaigns can nurture donor relationships, drive engagement, and prompt recurring giving.

7. Donation Tracking and Reporting:

   - Implement systems for tracking and reporting donations in real-time, providing donors with instant confirmation and acknowledgement of their contributions. Transparency and accountability in donation tracking build trust and confidence among donors and demonstrate the impact of their support.

8. Social Media Fundraising Tools:

    - Take advantage of social media fundraising tools and features offered by platforms such as Facebook, Instagram, and Twitter to launch fundraising campaigns, collect donations directly from social media posts, and engage supporters through peer-to-peer sharing and promotion.

9. Virtual Fundraising Events:

    - Host virtual fundraising events, such as online auctions, virtual galas, and live-streaming fundraisers, using video conferencing platforms and event management software. Virtual events leverage technology to reach donors globally, reduce overhead costs, and facilitate interactive engagement.

10. Integration with Payment Gateways:

    - Integrate donation platforms with secure payment gateways and financial processing services to ensure PCI compliance, data security, and seamless transaction processing. Integration with reputable payment gateways enhances donor trust and confidence in the donation process.

11. Donor Recognition and Stewardship:

- Implement automated donor recognition and stewardship programs that acknowledge donors promptly, express gratitude for their support, and provide personalized updates on the impact of their contributions. Automated stewardship tools strengthen donor relationships and encourage continued engagement and support.

12. Data Analytics and Insights:

- Leverage data analytics and reporting tools to analyze donation trends, track campaign performance, and gain insights into donor behaviour and preferences. Data-driven insights enable charities to refine fundraising strategies, optimize messaging, and target resources effectively to maximize fundraising results.

By embracing technology and leveraging innovative tools and platforms, charity organizations can streamline donation processes, enhance donor engagement, and drive fundraising success. By providing donors with convenient, secure, and personalized giving experiences, charities can inspire greater generosity, build lasting relationships, and achieve their philanthropic goals.

Chapter 14:

Digital Charity Management

Digital charity management encompasses the use of technology and digital tools to streamline operations, enhance efficiency, and maximize impact within charitable organizations. In today's digital era, leveraging digital solutions is essential for charities to effectively manage programs, engage stakeholders, and drive fundraising efforts. This chapter explores key aspects of digital charity management and strategies for harnessing technology to optimize organizational performance:

1. Digital Fundraising Platforms:

   - Implement digital fundraising platforms and online donation portals to facilitate seamless and secure donation collection. These platforms enable donors to contribute conveniently through various payment methods while providing charities with real-time tracking and reporting of donations.

2. Donor Relationship Management Systems:

   - Utilize donor relationship management (CRM) systems to maintain comprehensive donor databases, track donor interactions, and personalize communication. CRM systems enable charities to cultivate donor relationships, segment donor lists, and tailor fundraising appeals based on donor preferences and giving history.

3. Volunteer Management Software:

   - Adopt volunteer management software to recruit, schedule, and coordinate volunteers effectively. These digital tools streamline volunteer registration, assignment, and communication, ensuring smooth operations and maximizing volunteer engagement and impact.

4. Program Management Platforms:

   - Implement program management platforms to oversee and track program activities, participant engagement, and outcomes. These platforms enable charities to efficiently manage program logistics, monitor progress, and measure impact, leading to more effective program delivery and evaluation.

5. Digital Marketing and Outreach:

   - Leverage digital marketing strategies, including social media marketing, email campaigns, and content marketing, to raise awareness, engage stakeholders, and amplify the organization's message. Digital marketing tools enable charities to reach wider audiences, drive website traffic, and cultivate donor relationships online.

6. Cloud-Based Collaboration Tools:

   - Embrace cloud-based collaboration tools, such as project management software, document-sharing platforms, and virtual communication tools, to facilitate remote teamwork and collaboration. These tools enable staff and volunteers to collaborate effectively, regardless of geographical location, enhancing productivity and efficiency.

7. Online Learning and Training:

- Offer online learning and training programs for staff, volunteers, and beneficiaries to build skills, knowledge, and capacity. Digital learning platforms provide flexible and accessible training opportunities, empowering individuals to learn at their own pace and acquire essential skills for personal and professional development.

8. Data Analytics and Insights:

- Harness data analytics tools and dashboards to analyze organizational data, track performance metrics, and gain actionable insights. Data analytics enable charities to make data-driven decisions, optimize strategies, and measure the effectiveness of programs and fundraising efforts.

9. Cybersecurity and Data Protection:

- Prioritize cybersecurity measures and data protection protocols to safeguard sensitive information and donor data. Implement robust cybersecurity practices, encryption technologies, and data privacy policies to protect against cyber threats and ensure compliance with data protection regulations.

10. Continuous Innovation and Adaptation:

- Foster a culture of continuous innovation and adaptation to stay abreast of emerging technologies and digital trends. Encourage experimentation, feedback, and learning within the organization to drive innovation, improve processes, and remain agile in a rapidly evolving digital landscape.

By embracing digital charity management practices and leveraging technology effectively, charitable organizations can enhance operational efficiency, strengthen stakeholder engagement, and maximize their impact in advancing their mission and serving their communities. Digital transformation enables charities to thrive in an increasingly digital world, driving positive change and making a meaningful difference in the lives of others.

Implementing Digital Solutions for Efficient Charity Operations

In today's digital age, implementing digital solutions is essential for charity organizations to streamline operations, improve efficiency, and maximize impact. By leveraging technology effectively, charities can optimize resource management, enhance communication, and deliver services more effectively. Here are key steps for implementing digital solutions to enhance charity operations:

1. Assess Organizational Needs:

   - Conduct a comprehensive assessment of organizational needs, challenges, and opportunities to identify areas where digital solutions can make the most significant impact. Engage stakeholders, including staff, volunteers, donors, and beneficiaries, to gather insights and prioritize technology investments.

2. Define Clear Objectives:

   - Define clear objectives and goals for implementing digital solutions, aligning them with the organization's strategic priorities and mission. Establish measurable targets and timelines to track progress and evaluate the success of digital initiatives.

3. Research and Select Appropriate Technologies:

   - Research and evaluate digital technologies and solutions that address identified needs and objectives. Consider factors such as functionality, scalability, cost-effectiveness, user-friendliness, and compatibility with existing systems when selecting technology vendors or platforms.

4. Invest in Digital Infrastructure:

- Invest in the necessary digital infrastructure, including hardware, software, and networking resources, to support the implementation and operation of digital solutions. Ensure that the organization has adequate IT resources, support, and cybersecurity measures in place to safeguard data and systems.

5. Adopt Cloud-Based Solutions:

- Embrace cloud-based solutions and software-as-a-service (SaaS) platforms to reduce IT infrastructure costs, improve accessibility, and facilitate remote access to organizational data and applications. Cloud-based solutions offer scalability, flexibility, and ease of integration with existing systems.

6. Streamline Administrative Processes:

- Implement digital tools and automation solutions to streamline administrative processes, such as donor management, volunteer scheduling, event planning, and financial management. Digital solutions can automate repetitive tasks, reduce paperwork, and increase operational efficiency.

7. Enhance Communication and Collaboration:

- Implement digital communication and collaboration tools, such as email, instant messaging, video conferencing, and project management platforms, to facilitate seamless communication and collaboration among staff, volunteers, and stakeholders. Digital communication tools enable real-time collaboration, file sharing, and decision-making.

8. Digitize Fundraising and Donor Engagement:

   - Digitize fundraising efforts and donor engagement activities through online donation platforms, peer-to-peer fundraising campaigns, and social media outreach. Leverage digital marketing strategies, email campaigns, and social media channels to expand reach, cultivate donor relationships, and drive donations.

9. Provide Digital Training and Support:

   - Provide training and support to staff, volunteers, and stakeholders on the use of digital tools and technologies. Offer workshops, tutorials, and resources to build digital literacy skills and ensure that users are proficient in leveraging digital solutions effectively.

10. Monitor Performance and Iterate:

    - Monitor the performance and impact of digital solutions through regular evaluation, feedback, and data analysis. Track key performance indicators (KPIs) related to efficiency, effectiveness, and user satisfaction to identify areas for improvement and optimization.

- Iterate on digital initiatives based on feedback and insights gained from monitoring and evaluation processes. Continuously adapt and refine digital solutions to better meet the evolving needs and expectations of the organization and its stakeholders.

By implementing digital solutions for efficient charity operations, organizations can enhance productivity, improve service delivery, and achieve greater impact in advancing their mission and serving their communities. Digital transformation enables charities to adapt to changing environments, leverage emerging opportunities, and drive positive change in the world.

Online Fundraising Platforms and Tools

Online fundraising platforms and tools play a crucial role in enabling charities to raise funds, engage donors, and support their mission effectively in today's digital landscape. By leveraging online fundraising platforms and tools, charities can reach wider audiences, simplify donation processes, and maximize fundraising efforts. Here are some key online fundraising platforms and tools commonly used by charities:

1. Donation Processing Platforms:

   - Donation processing platforms, such as PayPal, Stripe, and Donorbox, facilitate secure online transactions and payment processing for donations. These platforms offer flexible payment options, seamless integration with websites, and robust security features to ensure donor trust and confidentiality.

2. Crowdfunding Platforms:

    *   Crowdfunding platforms, such as GoFundMe, Kickstarter, and Indiegogo, enable charities to launch fundraising campaigns and solicit donations from a large pool of supporters. These platforms provide tools for creating compelling campaign pages, setting fundraising goals, and sharing campaign updates to engage donors effectively.

3. Peer-to-Peer Fundraising Software:

    *   Peer-to-peer fundraising software, such as Classy, Fundly, and JustGiving, empowers supporters to create personal fundraising pages and solicit donations from their networks on behalf of the charity. These platforms facilitate social sharing, donor tracking, and campaign management to amplify fundraising efforts and reach new donors.

4. Online Auction Platforms:

    *   Online auction platforms, such as BiddingForGood, 32auctions, and GiveSmart, enable charities to host virtual fundraising events and auctions to raise funds for specific programs or initiatives. These platforms provide tools for managing auction

items, bidding processes, and donor engagement in a virtual environment.

5. Event Management Software:

    - Event management software, such as Eventbrite, Cvent, and Attendify, facilitates the planning, promotion, and execution of fundraising events, such as galas, charity runs, and benefit concerts. These platforms offer features for online registration, ticketing, attendee management, and event promotion to streamline event logistics and maximize attendance.

6. Online Giving Days Platforms:

    - Online giving days platforms, such as GiveMN, GiveGab, and Network for Good, facilitate collaborative fundraising campaigns involving multiple charities and donors within a specific timeframe. These platforms provide centralized donation portals, leaderboard tracking, and social sharing tools to drive collective giving and community engagement.

7. Matching Gift Platforms:

    - Matching gift platforms, such as Double the Donation, Benevity, and YourCause, help charities maximize donations by enabling donors to leverage corporate matching gift programs. These platforms provide tools for identifying eligible matching gift opportunities, submitting matching gift requests, and tracking matching gift contributions.

8. Donor Management Systems (DMS):

    *   Donor management systems (DMS), such as Salesforce Nonprofit Cloud, Bloomerang, and NeonCRM, centralize donor data, track donation history, and automate communication with donors. These platforms offer features for donor segmentation, personalized outreach, and fundraising analytics to enhance donor engagement and retention.

9. Social Media Fundraising Tools:

    *   Social media fundraising tools, such as Facebook Fundraisers, Instagram Donation Stickers, and Twitter Fundraising Cards, enable charities to leverage social networks for fundraising campaigns and donor engagement. These platforms integrate seamlessly with social media platforms, allowing supporters to donate directly from their feeds and share campaigns with their networks.

10. Email Marketing Platforms:

    *   Email marketing platforms, such as Mailchimp, Constant Contact, and Campaign Monitor, enable charities to create and send targeted email campaigns to donors and supporters. These platforms offer features for

email segmentation, automated workflows, and performance tracking to optimize engagement and conversion rates.

By leveraging online fundraising platforms and tools, charities can expand their reach, increase donor engagement, and raise more funds to support their mission and programs. Whether through crowdfunding campaigns, peer-to-peer fundraising, virtual events, or social media outreach, online fundraising platforms offer charities versatile and effective ways to connect with donors and inspire support for their cause.

Data Security and Privacy Considerations in Digital Charity Management

In the digital age, data security and privacy are paramount concerns for charity organizations managing donor information, financial records, and sensitive operational data. Safeguarding donor trust and protecting personal information is essential for maintaining compliance with data protection regulations and ensuring the integrity of digital charity management practices. Here are key considerations for addressing data security and privacy in digital charity management:

1. Compliance with Data Protection Regulations:

    - Ensure compliance with data protection regulations, such as the General Data Protection Regulation (GDPR) in the European Union or the California Consumer Privacy Act (CCPA) in the United States. Familiarize yourself with relevant laws and regulations governing data privacy and security in your jurisdiction and implement measures to comply with legal requirements.

2. Secure Data Storage and Transmission:

   - Implement robust security measures to protect data stored on digital platforms and during transmission. Use encryption protocols, secure sockets layer (SSL) certificates, and multi-factor authentication to safeguard sensitive information from unauthorized access, interception, or tampering.

3. Access Control and Authentication:

   - Implement access control mechanisms to restrict access to sensitive data and systems based on user roles, permissions, and authentication credentials. Implement strong password policies, role-based access controls (RBAC), and user authentication protocols to prevent unauthorized access to critical resources.

4. Data Encryption and Anonymization:

   - Encrypt sensitive data at rest and in transit to protect it from unauthorized disclosure or interception. Utilize encryption algorithms and cryptographic protocols to encrypt data stored on servers, databases, and backup systems. Additionally, anonymize or pseudonymize personal data where possible to minimize the risk of data breaches or misuse.

5. Regular Security Audits and Vulnerability Assessments:

   - Conduct regular security audits and vulnerability assessments to identify and remediate security vulnerabilities and weaknesses in digital systems and infrastructure. Perform penetration testing, code reviews, and security scans to proactively detect and address potential threats or vulnerabilities before they can be exploited by malicious actors.

6. Data Minimization and Retention Policies:

   - Adhere to data minimization principles by collecting and retaining only the minimum amount of personal data necessary for legitimate purposes. Implement data retention policies and procedures to define the length of time data is retained and establish guidelines for secure data disposal or deletion when no longer needed.

7. Employee Training and Awareness:

   - Provide comprehensive training and awareness programs to educate staff, volunteers, and stakeholders about data security best practices and their responsibilities for safeguarding sensitive information. Promote a culture of security awareness and accountability throughout the organization to mitigate the risk of insider threats or human error.

8. Third-Party Risk Management:

   • Assess and manage the security risks associated with third-party vendors, service providers, and contractors that have access to or process organizational data. Conduct due diligence assessments, review vendor security practices, and include contractual provisions to ensure third-party compliance with data security and privacy requirements.

9. Incident Response and Data Breach Management:

   • Develop and implement incident response plans and procedures to effectively respond to and mitigate data security incidents, such as unauthorized access, data breaches, or cyberattacks. Establish protocols for reporting security incidents, notifying affected individuals or authorities, and implementing remediation measures promptly.

10. Transparency and Accountability:

    • Maintain transparency and accountability in data handling practices by clearly communicating to donors and stakeholders how their data is collected, used, and protected. Provide privacy notices, data protection policies, and consent mechanisms to inform individuals about their rights and choices regarding the use of their personal information.

By prioritizing data security and privacy considerations in digital charity management, organizations can build trust with donors, protect sensitive information, and mitigate the risk of data breaches or regulatory violations. By implementing robust security measures, fostering a culture of compliance, and staying vigilant against emerging threats, charities can ensure the integrity and confidentiality of data while leveraging digital technologies to advance their mission and serve their communities.

Chapter 15:

Utilizing Social Media for Awareness and Fundraising

Social media platforms have emerged as powerful tools for charity organizations to raise awareness, engage supporters, and drive fundraising efforts. With billions of users worldwide, social media provides charities with unprecedented reach and accessibility to connect with donors, volunteers, and advocates. This chapter explores effective strategies for utilizing social media to increase awareness and fundraising for charitable causes:

1. Establishing a Strong Social Media Presence:

    - Create and maintain active profiles on popular social media platforms, including Facebook, Twitter, Instagram, LinkedIn, and YouTube. Customize profiles with compelling visuals, mission statements, and links to donation pages or fundraising campaigns to make it easy for followers to support the cause.

2. Sharing Compelling Content:

    - Share engaging and visually appealing content, including stories, photos, videos, and infographics, that resonate with your audience and highlight the impact of your organization's work. Use storytelling to evoke emotion, inspire action, and connect followers with the mission and beneficiaries of the charity.

3. Leveraging Hashtags and Trends:

   - Utilize relevant hashtags and trending topics to increase the visibility and reach of your social media posts. Research popular hashtags related to charitable causes, holidays, or awareness campaigns and incorporate them into your posts to amplify your message and attract a broader audience.

4. Engaging with Followers:

   - Foster meaningful interactions with followers by responding to comments, messages, and mentions promptly. Encourage dialogue, ask questions, and solicit feedback from followers to cultivate a sense of community and engagement around the charity's mission and initiatives.

5. Hosting Live Events and Q&A Sessions:

   - Host live streaming events, such as Facebook Live sessions, Instagram Live broadcasts, or Twitter chats, to engage followers in real-time and provide insights into the organization's work. Conduct Q&A sessions, interviews with staff or beneficiaries, or behind-the-scenes tours to offer exclusive content and foster connection with supporters.

6. Encouraging User-Generated Content:

- Encourage followers to create and share user-generated content, such as personal stories, testimonials, or fundraising challenges, related to the charity's mission. Highlight user-generated content on social media channels to showcase the diverse voices and experiences of supporters and donors.

7. Promoting Fundraising Campaigns:

- Promote fundraising campaigns, donation drives, and special events through social media channels to mobilize support and encourage donations. Create compelling fundraising appeals, donation challenges, and matching gift opportunities to incentivize giving and motivate followers to take action.

8. Partnering with Influencers and Ambassadors:

- Partner with influencers, celebrities, or influential figures in your community who are passionate about your cause to amplify your message and reach new audiences. Collaborate with ambassadors or brand advocates who can help raise awareness, drive engagement, and mobilize support through their social networks.

9. Tracking Performance and Analytics:

- Monitor social media performance metrics, such as engagement rates, reach, and conversion rates, to assess the effectiveness of your social media efforts. Use analytics tools and platforms, such as Facebook Insights, Twitter Analytics, or Google Analytics, to track key performance indicators and optimize social media strategies based on data-driven insights.

10. Cultivating Long-Term Relationships:

- Focus on building and nurturing long-term relationships with followers, donors, and supporters on social media. Show appreciation for their contributions, recognize milestones, and celebrate achievements to foster a sense of belonging and loyalty to the charity's mission and community.

By leveraging the power of social media to raise awareness, engage supporters, and drive fundraising efforts, charity organizations can amplify their impact, expand their reach, and mobilize resources to address pressing social and humanitarian challenges. By adopting effective social media strategies and cultivating an active and engaged online community, charities can harness the collective power of social networks to effect positive change and make a meaningful difference in the world.

Strategies for Building a Strong Social Media Presence

Building a strong social media presence is essential for charity organizations to effectively reach and engage their target audience, raise awareness about their mission, and drive fundraising efforts. Here are key strategies to help charities build a strong social media presence:

1. Define Your Goals and Audience:

   - Clearly define your social media goals, whether it's increasing brand awareness, driving donations, or fostering community engagement. Identify your target audience, including donors, volunteers, beneficiaries, and advocates, and tailor your messaging and content to resonate with their interests and preferences.

2. Choose the Right Platforms:

   - Select the social media platforms that align with your audience demographics, organizational goals, and content strategy. Focus on platforms where your target audience is most active, whether it's Facebook, Instagram, Twitter, LinkedIn, YouTube, or others, and prioritize building a presence on those channels.

3. Create a Consistent Brand Identity:

   - Develop a consistent brand identity across all social media platforms, including a cohesive profile picture, cover photo, bio, and branding elements such as colours, fonts, and logos. Maintain consistency in tone, voice, and messaging to reinforce your organization's values and mission.

4. Share Compelling Content:

- Share high-quality, compelling content that educates, entertains, inspires, or informs your audience. Mix different types of content, including stories, photos, videos, infographics, testimonials, and behind-the-scenes glimpses, to keep your audience engaged and interested.

5. Engage and Interact with Your Audience:

- Actively engage with your audience by responding to comments, messages, and mentions promptly. Foster conversations, ask questions and encourage user-generated content to create a sense of community and belonging among your followers.

6. Utilize Hashtags and Trending Topics:

- Use relevant hashtags and trending topics to increase the visibility and reach of your social media posts. Research popular hashtags related to your cause, events, or campaigns, and incorporate them into your posts to expand your audience and join relevant conversations.

7. Post Regularly and Consistently:

- Maintain a regular posting schedule to stay top-of-mind with your audience and keep them engaged. Experiment with different posting times and frequencies to determine the optimal schedule for reaching your audience effectively.

8. Leverage Visual Storytelling:

    -   Use visual storytelling techniques to convey your organization's impact and mission effectively. Share compelling visuals, such as photos and videos, that showcase the people, projects, and stories behind your cause and evoke emotion and empathy from your audience.

9. Collaborate with Influencers and Partners:

    -   Collaborate with influencers, brand ambassadors, or partners who share your organization's values and can help amplify your message to a broader audience. Partner with influencers to co-create content, host takeover events, or participate in joint campaigns to reach new followers and supporters.

10. Track and Analyze Performance:

    -   Monitor your social media performance metrics, including engagement rates, reach, follower growth, and conversion rates, to evaluate the effectiveness of your social media efforts. Use analytics tools and platforms to track key performance indicators and refine your strategy based on data-driven insights.

By implementing these strategies, charity organizations can build a strong social media presence that effectively engages their audience, raises awareness about their cause, and drives meaningful action and support for their mission. Consistent effort, creativity, and strategic planning are key to successfully building and maintaining a robust social media presence that contributes to the overall success of the organization.

Engaging Supporters and Amplifying Messages through Social Platforms

Engaging supporters and amplifying messages through social platforms are essential strategies for charity organizations to expand their reach, mobilize support, and drive impact. By fostering meaningful interactions, cultivating a sense of community, and leveraging the power of social networks, charities can effectively engage supporters and amplify their messages to create positive change. Here are key strategies for engaging supporters and amplifying messages through social platforms:

1. Cultivate Authentic Connections:
    - Foster authentic connections with supporters by actively engaging with them on social platforms. Respond to comments, messages, and mentions promptly, and personalize interactions to make supporters feel valued and appreciated.

2. Encourage User Participation:
    - Encourage user participation and contributions by inviting supporters to share their stories, experiences, and perspectives

related to your cause. Create opportunities for user-generated content, such as sharing photos, testimonials, or personal fundraising campaigns, to amplify supporter voices and experiences.

3. Facilitate Two-Way Communication:

- Facilitate two-way communication by listening to feedback, soliciting input, and responding to inquiries from supporters. Use social platforms as a channel for dialogue, discussion, and collaboration, and actively involve supporters in decision-making processes related to your organization's initiatives and programs.

4. Empower Advocacy and Activism:

- Empower supporters to become advocates and activists for your cause by providing them with resources, tools, and opportunities to take action. Encourage supporters to share your content, sign petitions, participate in advocacy campaigns, and mobilize their networks to support your organization's mission.

5. Host Interactive Events and Campaigns:

- Host interactive events and campaigns on social platforms to engage supporters in meaningful ways. Organize virtual fundraisers, live streaming events, Twitter chats, or Instagram takeovers to create interactive experiences that encourage participation, collaboration, and community building.

6. Leverage Social Proof and Social Sharing:

- Leverage social proof and social sharing to amplify your organization's messages and reach new audiences. Highlight success stories, testimonials, and impact metrics to demonstrate the tangible outcomes of your work and inspire others to get involved. Encourage supporters to share your content with their networks to increase visibility and engagement.

7. Utilize Influencer Partnerships:

- Partner with influencers, brand ambassadors, or advocates who have a strong presence on social platforms and share an affinity with your cause. Collaborate with influencers to co-create content, host events, or endorse your organization's initiatives to reach new audiences and amplify your message.

8. Harness the Power of Visual Storytelling:

- Harness the power of visual storytelling to captivate and inspire supporters on social platforms. Use compelling visuals, such as photos, videos, and infographics, to convey your organization's impact, evoke emotion, and drive engagement. Share stories of beneficiaries, projects, and milestones to

humanize your cause and resonate with your
audience.

9. Create Shareable and Viral Content:

    •   Create shareable and viral content that
        resonates with your audience and
        encourages social sharing and engagement.
        Develop content that is informative,
        entertaining, inspiring, or emotionally
        compelling, and optimize it for virality by
        incorporating trending topics, humour, or
        interactive elements.

10. Measure and Optimize Performance:

    •   Measure the performance of your social
        media engagement efforts using analytics
        tools and platforms. Track key performance
        indicators, such as engagement rates, reach,
        shares, and conversions, to assess the
        effectiveness of your strategies and identify
        areas for optimization. Use insights from
        analytics to refine your approach and improve
        engagement over time.

By implementing these strategies, charity organizations can
effectively engage supporters and amplify their messages
through social platforms, ultimately driving greater
awareness, support, and impact for their mission.
Consistent effort, creativity, and strategic planning are key to
building and maintaining meaningful connections with
supporters and leveraging social platforms to advance the
organization's goals.

Measuring the Impact of Social Media Campaigns on Donation Efforts

Measuring the impact of social media campaigns on donation efforts is crucial for charity organizations to assess the effectiveness of their strategies, optimize their campaigns, and demonstrate the return on investment to stakeholders. By tracking key performance indicators (KPIs) and analyzing data from social media platforms, charities can gain insights into the impact of their campaigns on donation acquisition, engagement, and conversion. Here are key steps for measuring the impact of social media campaigns on donation efforts:

1. Define Clear Objectives and Goals:

    - Establish clear objectives and goals for your social media campaigns related to donation efforts. Determine specific metrics you want to measure, such as donation conversions, fundraising revenue, donor acquisition, or engagement rates, and align them with your organization's overall fundraising and marketing objectives.

2. Set Up Tracking Mechanisms:

    - Implement tracking mechanisms to monitor and measure the impact of your social media campaigns on donation efforts. Use tracking links, campaign tags, and conversion tracking tools provided by social media platforms, such as Facebook Pixel or Google Analytics, to attribute donations and conversions to specific campaign sources and activities.

3. Track Key Performance Indicators (KPIs):

- Track key performance indicators (KPIs) related to donation efforts to assess the effectiveness of your social media campaigns. Some relevant KPIs to track include:

  - Donation Conversion Rate: Measure the percentage of social media visitors who convert into donors by donating.

  - Donation Revenue: Track the total revenue generated from donations attributed to social media campaigns.

  - Donor Acquisition: Monitor the number of new donors acquired through social media channels.

  - Engagement Metrics: Analyze engagement metrics, such as likes, comments, shares, and click-through rates, to assess the level of audience engagement and interaction with your donation-related content.

4. Use Advanced Analytics and Attribution Models:

- Utilize advanced analytics tools and attribution models to analyze the impact of your social media campaigns on donation efforts more comprehensively. Implement multi-touch attribution models, such as first-click, last-click, or multi-touch attribution, to attribute conversions and donations accurately across multiple touchpoints and channels.

5. Conduct A/B Testing and Experimentation:

   - Conduct A/B testing and experimentation to optimize your social media campaigns for donation conversions. Test different campaign elements, such as ad creatives, messaging, targeting criteria, and call-to-action buttons, to identify the most effective strategies for driving donations and maximizing conversion rates.

6. Monitor Campaign Performance in Real-Time:

   - Monitor the performance of your social media campaigns in real time to identify trends, opportunities, and areas for improvement. Use social media analytics dashboards and reporting tools to track campaign metrics, assess performance against benchmarks, and make data-driven decisions to optimize campaign tactics and strategies.

7. Analyze Conversion Paths and User Behavior:

   - Analyze conversion paths and user behaviour to understand how social media engagement influences the donation journey. Track the steps users take from initial interaction with your social media content to completing a donation, and identify common paths, touchpoints, and barriers that impact conversion rates.

8. Integrate Data Across Channels:

- Integrate data across multiple channels and touchpoints to gain a holistic view of the donor journey and assess the overall impact of your organization's marketing and fundraising efforts. Combine data from social media platforms, email marketing campaigns, website analytics, and donor management systems to track donor behaviour across channels and optimize campaign strategies accordingly.

9. Evaluate Return on Investment (ROI):

- Evaluate the return on investment (ROI) of your social media campaigns by comparing the costs of campaign execution with the revenue generated from donations. Calculate the cost per donation acquired through social media channels and assess the cost-effectiveness and efficiency of your donation acquisition strategies.

10. Continuously Iterate and Improve:

- Continuously iterate and improve your social media campaigns based on insights gathered from data analysis and performance monitoring. Use learnings from past campaigns to refine targeting strategies, optimize messaging and creative assets, and experiment with new approaches to drive donation conversions effectively.

By following these steps and implementing a comprehensive measurement and analysis framework, charity organizations can effectively evaluate the impact of their social media campaigns on donation efforts, identify opportunities for improvement, and optimize their strategies to maximize fundraising success. By leveraging data-driven insights and adopting a continuous improvement mindset, charities can enhance their ability to engage supporters, drive donations, and achieve their fundraising goals through social media channels.

Chapter 16:

Donation Collection Management Plans

Effective donation collection management is essential for charity organizations to efficiently and securely collect, process, and manage donations from supporters. A well-structured donation collection management plan helps ensure transparency, accountability, and compliance with regulatory requirements while maximizing fundraising efforts. Here are the key components of a comprehensive donation collection management plan:

1. Donation Collection Channels:

    - Identify and establish multiple donation collection channels to provide supporters with convenient and diverse ways to contribute. Common donation collection channels include online platforms, fundraising events, direct mail campaigns, phone-in donations, corporate partnerships, and peer-to-peer fundraising campaigns.

2. Online Donation Platforms:

    - Select and utilize reputable online donation platforms that offer secure payment processing, customizable donation forms, and integration with your website and social media channels. Ensure that online donation platforms comply with data protection regulations and provide options for recurring donations, matching gifts, and donor acknowledgements.

3. Fundraising Events and Campaigns:

   - Plan and organize fundraising events, campaigns, and appeals to engage supporters and solicit donations. Develop compelling event concepts, set fundraising goals, and implement strategies for promoting events, selling tickets, and generating donations before, during, and after the event.

4. Direct Mail and Email Campaigns:

   - Implement direct mail and email fundraising campaigns to reach donors through traditional and digital channels. Develop targeted mailing lists, craft persuasive fundraising appeals, and personalize communications to inspire donor generosity and encourage contributions.

5. Mobile Giving and Text-to-Donate:

   - Leverage mobile giving and text-to-donate platforms to facilitate quick and easy donations via mobile devices. Promote text-to-donate campaigns through social media, email, and offline channels, and provide clear instructions for supporters to make donations using their smartphones.

6. Corporate Partnerships and Sponsorships:

- Cultivate relationships with corporate partners and sponsors to secure funding, in-kind donations, and sponsorship support for your organization's programs and initiatives. Collaborate with corporate partners on cause-related marketing campaigns, employee giving programs, and corporate social responsibility initiatives to maximize fundraising opportunities.

7. Peer-to-Peer Fundraising:

- Empower supporters to become fundraisers on behalf of your organization through peer-to-peer fundraising campaigns. Provide supporters with fundraising tools, resources, and support to create personalized fundraising pages, set fundraising goals, and solicit donations from their networks.

8. Donor Recognition and Stewardship:

- Implement donor recognition and stewardship strategies to acknowledge and appreciate donors for their contributions. Send personalized thank-you messages, recognition certificates, and impact reports to donors to demonstrate appreciation and showcase the impact of their donations.

9. Compliance and Data Security:

- Ensure compliance with regulatory requirements and data security standards when collecting and processing donations.

Implement procedures for handling sensitive donor information, maintaining donor privacy, and protecting against fraud, identity theft, and cybersecurity threats.

10. Reporting and Accountability:

- Establish reporting and accountability mechanisms to track donation collection activities, monitor fundraising performance, and report on financial outcomes. Maintain accurate records of donations received, track fundraising expenses, and prepare financial reports for stakeholders, donors, and regulatory agencies.

11. Continuous Improvement:

- Continuously evaluate and refine your donation collection management processes to improve efficiency, effectiveness, and donor satisfaction. Solicit feedback from donors, volunteers, and staff, and use insights from performance metrics and data analysis to identify areas for optimization and enhancement.

By developing and implementing a robust donation collection management plan, charity organizations can streamline donation processes, enhance donor engagement, and maximize fundraising success. By diversifying donation collection channels, leveraging technology, and prioritizing transparency and accountability, charities can effectively mobilize support, achieve their fundraising goals, and advance their mission to make a positive impact in the community.

Establishing Robust Systems for Donation Collection and Processing

Establishing robust systems for donation collection and processing is essential for charity organizations to efficiently manage incoming donations, maintain donor trust, and ensure compliance with regulatory requirements. By implementing standardized procedures, utilizing appropriate technology, and prioritizing transparency and accountability, charities can streamline donation processing workflows and optimize their fundraising efforts. Here are key steps for establishing robust systems for donation collection and processing:

1. Define Clear Processes and Procedures:

    - Develop clear, documented processes and procedures for donation collection and processing to ensure consistency and adherence to best practices. Outline step-by-step guidelines for receiving donations, recording donor information, issuing receipts, and depositing funds into designated accounts.

2. Utilize Technology Solutions:

    - Invest in technology solutions and fundraising platforms to streamline donation collection and processing tasks. Choose reputable donation management software or customer relationship management (CRM) systems that offer features such as online donation forms, donor databases, donation tracking, and reporting capabilities.

3. Implement Secure Payment Processing:

   - Implement secure payment processing solutions to protect donor information and prevent fraud. Choose payment gateways and processors that comply with Payment Card Industry Data Security Standard (PCI DSS) requirements and encrypt sensitive donor data during transmission and storage.

4. Provide Multiple Donation Channels:

   - Offer multiple donation channels to accommodate donor preferences and facilitate convenient giving. Establish online donation portals, accept donations via mail or phone, and provide options for recurring donations, direct debits, and electronic fund transfers (EFTs) to maximize accessibility and flexibility for donors.

5. Train Staff and Volunteers:

   - Provide comprehensive training to staff and volunteers involved in donation collection and processing to ensure they understand their roles, responsibilities, and the importance of following established procedures. Train staff on using donation management software, handling donor inquiries, and maintaining donor confidentiality.

6. Establish Internal Controls:

   • Implement internal controls and segregation of duties to prevent errors, fraud, and misuse of funds in donation processing. Assign roles and responsibilities for donation handling, verification, and reconciliation to different staff members to ensure accountability and oversight.

7. Maintain Donor Privacy and Confidentiality:

   • Maintain strict confidentiality and privacy protections for donor information collected during the donation process. Adhere to data protection regulations, such as the General Data Protection Regulation (GDPR) or the Health Insurance Portability and Accountability Act (HIPAA), and obtain donor consent for data processing and communication preferences.

8. Ensure Compliance with Regulatory Requirements:

   • Stay informed about relevant regulatory requirements and legal obligations governing donation collection and processing in your jurisdiction. Comply with tax laws, fundraising regulations, and reporting requirements imposed by government agencies and oversight bodies to avoid penalties and legal liabilities.

9. Monitor and Audit Donation Processes:

- Implement monitoring and auditing procedures to regularly review donation processes, identify potential issues or discrepancies, and ensure compliance with organizational policies and external regulations. Conduct internal audits, reconciliation checks, and spot audits to validate donation records and transactions.

10. Communicate Transparency and Accountability:

- Communicate transparency and accountability in donation collection and processing practices to donors, supporters, and stakeholders. Provide clear information about how donations are collected, processed, and utilized to support the organization's mission and demonstrate financial stewardship and integrity in fundraising activities.

By establishing robust systems for donation collection and processing, charity organizations can enhance operational efficiency, safeguard donor trust, and maximize the impact of their fundraising efforts. By implementing standardized procedures, leveraging technology solutions, and prioritizing transparency and accountability, charities can effectively manage donations and advance their mission to create positive change in the community.

Ensuring Transparency and Accountability in Donation Management

Transparency and accountability are fundamental principles in donation management that help charity organizations build trust with donors, maintain integrity in fundraising practices, and demonstrate responsible stewardship of donated funds. By implementing transparent processes, disclosing financial information, and providing regular updates to stakeholders, charities can foster confidence and credibility in their donation management practices. Here are key strategies for ensuring transparency and accountability in donation management:

1. Clear Communication of Financial Information:

   - Provide clear and accessible information about your organization's financial status, including income, expenses, and use of donated funds. Publish annual reports, financial statements, and audited accounts on your website or in donor communications to demonstrate fiscal transparency and accountability.

2. Donor Transparency and Disclosure:

   - Disclose information about how donated funds are utilized, including program expenses, overhead costs, and administrative fees. Provide donors with detailed breakdowns of how their contributions are allocated to specific programs, projects, or initiatives to ensure transparency in fund utilization.

3. Donor Privacy and Data Protection:

   - Safeguard donor privacy and protect sensitive donor information collected during the donation process. Implement data protection measures, such as encryption, secure storage, and access controls, to prevent unauthorized access, disclosure, or misuse of donor data.

4. Compliance with Regulatory Requirements:

   - Ensure compliance with regulatory requirements and legal obligations governing donation management, including tax laws, fundraising regulations, and reporting standards. Stay informed about changes in legislation and update your practices accordingly to avoid non-compliance and regulatory penalties.

5. Donor Acknowledgment and Recognition:

   - Acknowledge donors promptly and express gratitude for their contributions to your organization. Provide donors with acknowledgement receipts, thank-you letters, or personalized messages to recognize their generosity and reinforce the value of their support.

6. Transparent Fundraising Practices:

- Be transparent about your fundraising practices and methods used to solicit donations. Disclose any fees, commissions, or third-party costs associated with fundraising activities to donors and ensure that fundraising appeals accurately represent the organization's mission and activities.

7. Board Oversight and Governance:

   - Establish robust governance structures and oversight mechanisms to ensure accountability in donation management. Engage an independent board of directors or trustees responsible for overseeing fundraising activities, financial management, and compliance with ethical standards and organizational policies.

8. Independent Audits and Reviews:

   - Conduct regular independent audits and reviews of donation management processes to assess compliance with internal controls, financial regulations, and best practices. Engage external auditors or financial consultants to perform audits and provide recommendations for improving transparency and accountability.

9. Donor Feedback and Engagement:

   - Solicit feedback from donors and stakeholders about their donation experiences and preferences. Conduct donor surveys, focus groups, or feedback sessions to gather insights into donor expectations, concerns, and suggestions for improving donation management practices.

10. Public Disclosure and Reporting:

- Publicly disclose information about your organization's fundraising activities, financial performance, and impact achievements to stakeholders, regulators, and the general public. Publish annual reports, impact reports, and progress updates on your website or through other communication channels to enhance transparency and accountability.

By prioritizing transparency and accountability in donation management practices, charity organizations can build trust with donors, strengthen relationships with stakeholders, and demonstrate their commitment to ethical fundraising standards. By communicating openly, disclosing financial information, and engaging donors in meaningful ways, charities can uphold integrity and credibility in their fundraising efforts while advancing their mission to make a positive impact in the community.

Handling Donor Data and Privacy Safely and Ethically

Safeguarding donor data and privacy is paramount for charity organizations to maintain trust, comply with legal requirements, and protect sensitive information. By implementing robust data protection measures, adhering to ethical guidelines, and prioritizing donor confidentiality, charities can ensure the safe and ethical handling of donor data. Here are key principles for handling donor data and privacy safely and ethically:

1. Data Protection Compliance:

    - Ensure compliance with data protection regulations, such as the General Data Protection Regulation (GDPR), the California Consumer Privacy Act (CCPA), and other applicable laws governing the collection, processing, and storage of donor data. Familiarize yourself with legal requirements, including consent mechanisms, data access rights, and breach notification obligations.

2. Transparent Data Collection Practices:

    - Practice transparency in data collection by informing donors about the types of information collected, the purposes for which it will be used, and any third parties with whom it may be shared. Obtain explicit consent from donors before collecting their personal data and provide options for donors to control their privacy settings and communication preferences.

3. Minimization of Data Collection:

    - Minimize the collection of personal data to only what is necessary for legitimate fundraising purposes. Avoid collecting excessive or irrelevant information and limit access to donor data to authorized personnel who require it for specific tasks or functions.

4. Secure Data Storage and Transmission:

   - Implement robust security measures to protect donor data from unauthorized access, disclosure, or misuse. Encrypt sensitive data during transmission and storage, use secure servers and databases and implement access controls and authentication mechanisms to restrict access to authorized users only.

5. Confidentiality and Non-Disclosure:

   - Maintain strict confidentiality and non-disclosure of donor information to third parties without explicit consent from donors. Ensure that staff and volunteers handling donor data are trained on confidentiality obligations and understand the importance of protecting donor privacy.

6. Data Accuracy and Integrity:

   - Ensure the accuracy and integrity of donor data by regularly updating and verifying information to prevent errors, duplicates, or inconsistencies. Establish procedures for data validation, cleansing, and deduplication to maintain high-quality donor records and improve fundraising effectiveness.

7. Transparent Data Use and Sharing:

- Be transparent about how donor data will be used and shared within your organization and with external partners or service providers. Provide donors with clear information about data-sharing practices, including any data transfers to subcontractors, vendors, or affiliated organizations, and obtain consent for such activities where required.

8. Data Retention and Deletion:

   - Establish data retention policies and procedures to determine the appropriate length of time to retain donor data and the conditions for its deletion or disposal. Regularly review and purge outdated or unnecessary data following legal requirements and organizational policies.

9. Consent Management:

   - Implement robust consent management processes to obtain and record donor consent for the collection, processing, and use of their personal data. Allow donors to easily withdraw consent at any time and provide mechanisms for donors to update their preferences or opt out of communications.

10. Accountability and Oversight:

   - Assign responsibility for data protection and privacy compliance to designated individuals or teams within your organization. Establish oversight mechanisms, such as data protection officers or privacy committees, to monitor compliance, address data breaches, and handle inquiries or complaints related to donor data privacy.

By adhering to these principles and best practices for handling donor data and privacy, charity organizations can demonstrate their commitment to ethical fundraising practices, protect donor confidentiality, and maintain trust with supporters. By implementing robust data protection measures, ensuring transparency in data practices, and prioritizing donor consent and control, charities can uphold the highest standards of integrity and accountability in their fundraising efforts while safeguarding donor privacy and confidentiality.

Chapter 17:

Strategies to Increase Donations

Increasing donations is a critical goal for charity organizations seeking to expand their impact and sustain their programs and initiatives. By implementing effective fundraising strategies and engaging donors in meaningful ways, charities can inspire generosity, cultivate donor relationships, and drive greater support for their mission. Here are key strategies to increase donations:

1. Develop Compelling Fundraising Appeals:

    *   Craft compelling fundraising appeals that resonate with donors' values, emotions, and interests. Tell compelling stories, highlight the impact, and communicate the urgency of the cause to inspire donors to take action and make a difference.

2. Segment Donor Communications:

    *   Segment donor communications based on donors' preferences, behaviours, and giving history to tailor messages and appeals to their specific interests and motivations. Personalize communications to foster stronger connections and increase relevance and engagement.

3. Leverage Matching Gifts and Challenges:

    *   Encourage donors to increase their impact through matching gift programs and

fundraising challenges. Partner with corporate sponsors or donors willing to match donations or provide challenge grants to incentivize giving and motivate supporters to maximize their contributions.

4. Implement Recurring Giving Programs:

   - Launch recurring giving programs to encourage donors to make ongoing, monthly contributions to support your organization's mission. Promote the benefits of recurring donations, such as convenience, sustainability, and long-term impact, and provide incentives or recognition for recurring donors.

5. Offer Donation Incentives and Rewards:

   - Offer incentives or rewards to donors as a token of appreciation for their contributions. Provide exclusive perks, such as branded merchandise, VIP access to events, or recognition in donor honour rolls, to incentivize giving and enhance donor satisfaction and loyalty.

6. Host Fundraising Events and Campaigns:

   - Host fundraising events, campaigns, and appeals to engage donors and generate excitement and momentum for your cause. Organize virtual or in-person events, such as galas, auctions, peer-to-peer fundraisers, or crowdfunding campaigns, to mobilize support and raise funds for specific projects or initiatives.

7. Utilize Social Proof and Testimonials:

- Utilize social proof and testimonials to showcase the impact of donations and inspire confidence in your organization. Share success stories, testimonials from beneficiaries, and examples of tangible outcomes to demonstrate the value and effectiveness of donor support.

8. Cultivate Major Donors and Partnerships:

- Cultivate relationships with major donors, corporate sponsors, and philanthropic partners who can make significant contributions to your organization. Develop personalized cultivation strategies, stewardship plans, and recognition opportunities to engage major donors and secure transformative gifts.

9. Optimize Donation Processes and Channels:

- Streamline donation processes and optimize donation channels to make giving easy, convenient, and accessible for donors. Implement user-friendly donation forms, offer multiple payment options, and optimize mobile compatibility to reduce friction and barriers to giving.

10. Foster Donor Engagement and Stewardship:

- Foster ongoing engagement with donors through regular communication, updates, and stewardship activities. Show appreciation for donor support, recognize milestones and achievements, and involve donors in the impact of their contributions to cultivate deeper connections and loyalty.

11. Invest in Donor Acquisition and Retention:

- Invest in donor acquisition and retention strategies to attract new donors and retain existing supporters over time. Implement targeted marketing campaigns, donor acquisition initiatives, and donor retention programs to expand your donor base and increase donor lifetime value.

12. Measure and Evaluate Fundraising Performance:

- Measure and evaluate fundraising performance regularly to assess the effectiveness of your strategies and identify areas for improvement. Track key performance indicators (KPIs), such as donation revenue, donor acquisition rates, retention rates, and return on investment (ROI), to inform strategic decision-making and optimize fundraising efforts.

By implementing these strategies to increase donations, charity organizations can effectively mobilize support, drive fundraising success, and advance their mission to create positive change in the community. By leveraging storytelling, segmentation, incentives, and engagement tactics, charities can inspire generosity, deepen donor relationships, and achieve greater impact through increased donations.

Identifying and Targeting Potential Donors

Identifying and targeting potential donors is a fundamental aspect of fundraising for charity organizations. By understanding the characteristics, interests, and motivations of potential donors, charities can tailor their outreach efforts and engage individuals or groups who are most likely to support their mission. Here are key strategies for identifying and targeting potential donors:

1. Define Ideal Donor Profiles:

    - Define ideal donor profiles based on demographic, psychographic, and behavioural characteristics that align with your organization's mission and fundraising goals. Consider factors such as age, gender, income level, interests, values, and philanthropic motivations to create detailed donor personas.

2. Analyze Existing Donor Data:

    - Analyze existing donor data and historical giving patterns to identify common characteristics and trends among your current supporters. Use donor management software or CRM systems to segment donors based on giving history, donation frequency, gift size, and other relevant factors to inform targeted outreach strategies.

3. Conduct Prospect Research:

    - Conduct prospect research to identify individuals, corporations, foundations, or affinity groups with the capacity and inclination to support your organization. Utilize prospect research tools, wealth screening services, and public databases to gather information about potential donors' wealth, giving history, philanthropic interests, and connections.

4. Engage Board Members and Volunteers:

    - Engage board members, volunteers, and key stakeholders in the donor identification process by leveraging their networks, connections, and relationships. Encourage board members to make introductions, host cultivation events, or facilitate meetings with potential donors who may have a personal or professional affinity for your cause.

5. Cultivate Corporate Partnerships:

    - Cultivate relationships with corporate partners and businesses that share your organization's values and objectives. Research companies with corporate social responsibility (CSR) initiatives, grantmaking programs, or employee giving campaigns and explore opportunities for strategic partnerships, sponsorships, or cause-related marketing collaborations.

6. Target Affinity Groups and Communities:

   - Target affinity groups, communities, or networks that have a natural affinity for your cause or share common interests and values. Identify professional associations, clubs, alumni groups, religious congregations, or cultural organizations where potential donors may congregate and tailor your outreach efforts to resonate with their interests and affiliations.

7. Leverage Online and Social Media Channels:

   - Leverage online and social media channels to reach and engage potential donors in digital spaces. Utilize targeted advertising, social media platforms, and email marketing campaigns to raise awareness about your organization's mission, showcase impact stories, and solicit support from online audiences.

8. Participate in Networking Events and Conferences:

   - Participate in networking events, conferences, and community gatherings to connect with potential donors, influencers, and thought leaders in your field. Attend industry conferences, fundraising events, or networking meetups to expand your professional network, build relationships, and identify new funding opportunities.

9. Collaborate with Peer-to-Peer Fundraisers:

- Collaborate with peer-to-peer fundraisers, advocates, and supporters who are passionate about your cause and willing to fundraise on your behalf. Empower volunteers, donors, and community champions to create personal fundraising pages, share their stories, and mobilize support from their networks to amplify your fundraising efforts.

10. Build Strategic Partnerships and Alliances:

- Build strategic partnerships and alliances with other nonprofit organizations, foundations, or community groups that share similar missions or serve complementary populations. Explore opportunities for collaborative fundraising campaigns, joint events, or shared resources to expand your reach and attract new donors collectively.

By implementing these strategies to identify and target potential donors, charity organizations can effectively expand their donor base, diversify funding sources, and increase financial support for their mission-driven initiatives. By leveraging data analysis, prospect research, stakeholder engagement, and strategic partnerships, charities can identify and cultivate meaningful relationships with individuals, businesses, and organizations who are aligned with their cause and eager to make a positive impact in the community.

Cultivating Relationships with Major Donors and Corporate Partners

Cultivating relationships with major donors and corporate partners is essential for charity organizations seeking significant financial support and strategic alliances. By building meaningful connections, demonstrating impact, and fostering trust and mutual benefit, charities can engage major donors and corporate partners as long-term supporters and advocates for their mission. Here are key strategies for cultivating relationships with major donors and corporate partners:

1. Conduct Prospect Research:

   - Conduct comprehensive prospect research to identify potential major donors and corporate partners who have the capacity and inclination to support your organization's mission and initiatives. Utilize wealth screening services, prospect research tools, and public databases to gather information about prospects' philanthropic interests, giving capacity, and connections.

2. Customize Engagement Strategies:

   - Tailor engagement strategies and cultivation approaches to align with the interests, preferences, and motivations of major donors and corporate partners. Customize communication channels, messaging, and engagement opportunities to resonate with their values, priorities, and philanthropic objectives.

3. Establish Personal Connections:

- Invest time in building personal connections and rapport with major donors and corporate partners through face-to-face meetings, phone calls, or personalized correspondence. Take the time to listen, understand their philanthropic goals and aspirations, and demonstrate genuine appreciation for their support and partnership.

4. Share Impact Stories and Successes:

- Share compelling impact stories, success stories, and testimonials that illustrate the tangible outcomes and transformative effects of their contributions. Provide regular updates and progress reports to demonstrate the impact of their support and showcase the value of their investment in your organization's mission.

5. Offer Recognition and Stewardship:

- Offer meaningful recognition and stewardship opportunities to major donors and corporate partners to express gratitude for their generosity and commitment.

Recognize donors publicly through donor honour rolls, naming opportunities, or special events, and provide exclusive perks or privileges as a token of appreciation for their support.

6. Provide Opportunities for Engagement:

   - Provide opportunities for major donors and corporate partners to engage directly with your organization, programs, and beneficiaries. Invite them to participate in site visits, program demonstrations, or volunteer opportunities to experience firsthand the impact of their contributions and deepen their connection to your cause.

7. Foster Two-Way Communication:

   - Foster open, transparent, and two-way communication with major donors and corporate partners to solicit feedback, address concerns, and maintain alignment with their philanthropic objectives. Listen actively, respond promptly to inquiries or requests, and seek input on strategic decisions or funding priorities.

8. Collaborate on Strategic Initiatives:

   - Collaborate with major donors and corporate partners on strategic initiatives, projects, or campaigns that align with their interests and expertise. Explore opportunities for joint funding, co-branding, or shared resources to maximize impact, leverage strengths, and address common goals collaboratively.

9. Engage Leadership and Decision-Makers:

    - Engage senior leadership and decision-makers within major donor organizations and corporate partners to build trust and credibility at the highest levels. Cultivate relationships with executives, board members, and key stakeholders to secure buy-in, alignment, and long-term commitment to your partnership.

10. Demonstrate Accountability and Impact:

    - Demonstrate accountability and transparency in your organization's operations, financial management, and program outcomes to instil confidence and trust in major donors and corporate partners. Provide regular updates on fundraising progress, financial stewardship, and programmatic achievements to reinforce the value and impact of their support.

By implementing these strategies for cultivating relationships with major donors and corporate partners, charity organizations can strengthen partnerships, secure significant funding, and advance their mission-driven initiatives collaboratively. By prioritizing personalized engagement, meaningful recognition, and strategic collaboration, charities can foster long-term relationships with major donors and corporate partners who are committed to making a lasting difference in the community.

Implementing Creative Fundraising Initiatives to Drive Donor Giving

Implementing creative fundraising initiatives is essential for charity organizations seeking to engage donors, inspire generosity, and drive financial support for their mission-driven initiatives. By innovating new fundraising approaches, leveraging technology, and tapping into donors' passions and interests, charities can cultivate excitement and enthusiasm for giving. Here are key strategies for implementing creative fundraising initiatives to drive donor giving:

1. Host Signature Fundraising Events:

   - Host signature fundraising events, galas, or charity auctions that offer unique experiences, entertainment, or opportunities for engagement. Create memorable event themes, interactive activities, or celebrity appearances to attract donors and drive participation while raising funds for your cause.

2. Launch Peer-to-Peer Fundraising Campaigns:

   - Launch peer-to-peer fundraising campaigns that empower supporters, volunteers, and advocates to fundraise on behalf of your organization. Provide fundraising toolkits, personalized fundraising pages, and incentives for participants to mobilize their networks, amplify your message, and drive donations.

3. Organize Virtual Fundraising Challenges:

    - Organize virtual fundraising challenges, competitions, or campaigns that encourage donors to set and achieve fundraising milestones or goals. Create friendly competitions, leaderboard rankings, or incentives for donors to participate, donate, or recruit others to join the challenge.

4. Create Crowdfunding Campaigns:

    - Create crowdfunding campaigns on online platforms or social media channels to raise funds for specific projects, campaigns, or urgent needs. Develop compelling campaign narratives, set achievable fundraising targets, and leverage storytelling, visuals, and multimedia content to attract donors and solicit support.

5. Offer Creative Fundraising Incentives:

    - Offer creative fundraising incentives, rewards, or perks to incentivize donors to give. Provide exclusive rewards, experiences, or recognition for donors who reach specific giving levels, milestones, or achievements to enhance donor motivation and engagement.

6. Launch Cause-Related Marketing Campaigns:

- Launch cause-related marketing campaigns or corporate partnerships that align with your organization's mission and values. Collaborate with businesses, brands, or influencers to create co-branded products, promotions, or events that generate proceeds or donations in support of your cause.

7. Develop Creative Fundraising Products:

    - Develop creative fundraising products or merchandise that supporters can purchase to support your organization. Create branded merchandise, apparel, or accessories that showcase your cause, raise awareness, and generate revenue through sales or proceeds.

8. Organize DIY Fundraising Events:

    - Organize do-it-yourself (DIY) fundraising events or initiatives that empower supporters to create their own fundraising campaigns or events in support of your cause. Provide fundraising toolkits, resources, and guidance for individuals or groups to organize DIY events, such as bake sales, garage sales, or virtual challenges.

9. Engage Donors Through Gamification:

    - Engage donors through gamification techniques that turn fundraising into a fun and interactive experience. Implement gamified fundraising challenges, leaderboards, or incentives that reward donors for their participation, engagement, and contribution to fundraising goals.

10. Leverage Matching Gifts and Challenges:

- Leverage matching gifts and fundraising challenges to incentivize donor giving and maximize the impact of donations. Secure matching gift pledges from corporate sponsors or major donors to match donations up to a certain amount or timeframe, or create fundraising challenges with specific targets or milestones to motivate donors to give.

By implementing these creative fundraising initiatives, charity organizations can engage donors, inspire giving, and drive financial support for their mission-driven initiatives. By leveraging events, campaigns, challenges, and incentives, charities can cultivate excitement, generate momentum, and mobilize donors to make a meaningful difference in the community.

Chapter 18:

Challenges of Charity Organizations

Charity organizations face a myriad of challenges in their efforts to fulfil their missions, address social issues, and make a positive impact in communities. These challenges can range from financial constraints and operational hurdles to regulatory compliance and external factors affecting fundraising efforts. Understanding and effectively navigating these challenges are essential for charities to sustain their operations, adapt to changing circumstances, and maximize their effectiveness. Here are some of the key challenges faced by charity organizations:

1. Financial Constraints:

    - Limited funding sources, fluctuating donations, and budgetary constraints can pose significant challenges for charity organizations, impacting their ability to deliver programs and services, cover operational costs, and sustain long-term initiatives.

2. Fundraising Fatigue:

    - Donor fatigue, market saturation, and competition for charitable dollars can make fundraising efforts increasingly challenging for charity organizations, requiring innovative strategies to attract and retain donor support amidst a crowded philanthropic landscape.

3. Regulatory Compliance:

- Compliance with complex and evolving regulatory requirements, tax laws, and reporting standards presents challenges for charity organizations, requiring careful oversight, transparency, and adherence to legal obligations to maintain nonprofit status and uphold public trust.

4. Volunteer Recruitment and Retention:

- Recruiting and retaining volunteers with the necessary skills, time availability, and commitment to support charity operations and programs can be challenging, particularly in competitive volunteer markets or for specialized roles requiring specific expertise.

5. Capacity Building:

- Building organizational capacity, leadership development, and staff training to effectively manage growth, scale programs, and adapt to changing needs requires investment in infrastructure, systems, and human resources, which may be limited for smaller or grassroots organizations.

6. Impact Measurement and Evaluation:

- Measuring and evaluating the impact of programs, assessing outcomes, and demonstrating effectiveness to donors, stakeholders, and funders can be challenging for charity organizations, requiring robust monitoring and evaluation frameworks, data

collection methods, and reporting
mechanisms.

7. Technological Adoption:

    - Adopting and integrating technology
      solutions, fundraising platforms, and digital
      tools to streamline operations, enhance
      donor engagement, and optimize fundraising
      efforts can be challenging for charity
      organizations with limited resources,
      technical expertise, or resistance to change.

8. Public Perception and Trust:

    - Maintaining public trust, credibility, and
      reputation in the face of scandals,
      controversies, or negative perceptions within
      the nonprofit sector or broader community
      can pose challenges for charity organizations,
      requiring proactive communication,
      transparency, and ethical conduct.

9. Diversity, Equity, and Inclusion:

    - Promoting diversity, equity, and inclusion
      within charity organizations, addressing
      systemic barriers, and ensuring
      representation and participation of
      marginalized or underserved communities in
      decision-making processes and program
      delivery can be challenging but essential for
      achieving equitable outcomes.

10. External Factors:

- External factors such as economic downturns, political instability, natural disasters, or global crises can impact charity organizations' operations, fundraising revenues, and program delivery, requiring agility, resilience, and adaptability to navigate unforeseen challenges and maintain organizational sustainability.

By acknowledging and addressing these challenges proactively, charity organizations can strengthen their resilience, enhance their effectiveness, and advance their mission to create positive change and improve lives in communities. By leveraging strategic planning, collaboration, innovation, and stakeholder engagement, charities can overcome obstacles, seize opportunities, and drive meaningful impact in the pursuit of social good.

Addressing Funding Instability and Resource Constraints

Funding instability and resource constraints pose significant challenges for charity organizations, impacting their ability to sustain operations, deliver programs, and achieve their mission objectives. Addressing these challenges requires proactive strategies, innovative approaches, and diversified funding sources to mitigate risks and build organizational resilience. Here are key strategies for addressing funding instability and resource constraints:

1. Diversify Revenue Streams:

    - Diversify revenue streams beyond traditional sources of funding, such as individual donations and grants, to reduce reliance on a single funding source and mitigate the impact of fluctuations in donor giving or grant funding. Explore earned income opportunities, fee-for-service models, corporate sponsorships, and social enterprise ventures to generate additional revenue streams.

2. Develop Sustainable Fundraising Strategies:

   - Develop sustainable fundraising strategies that prioritize long-term donor relationships, donor retention, and donor stewardship to cultivate a reliable base of support. Focus on building a pipeline of recurring donors, major donors, and corporate partners through targeted cultivation, engagement, and personalized stewardship efforts.

3. Pursue Grant Opportunities Strategically:

   - Pursue grant opportunities strategically by identifying funders aligned with your organization's mission, programs, and impact objectives. Conduct thorough research, cultivate relationships with grantmakers, and tailor grant proposals to meet funders' priorities and requirements to increase the likelihood of securing funding.

4. Invest in Fundraising Capacity:

   - Invest in fundraising capacity building, staff training, and professional development to strengthen fundraising skills, techniques, and strategies within your organization. Provide ongoing training, mentorship, and resources to empower staff, volunteers, and board members to effectively execute fundraising initiatives and maximize fundraising success.

5. Explore Collaborative Funding Models:

- Explore collaborative funding models, partnerships, and consortia with other nonprofit organizations, government agencies, or philanthropic entities to pool resources, share costs, and leverage collective expertise to address common challenges and achieve shared objectives collaboratively.

6. Engage in Donor Cultivation and Stewardship:

- Engage in proactive donor cultivation and stewardship activities to nurture relationships with donors, demonstrate impact, and communicate the value of their support to inspire continued giving. Provide personalized acknowledgement, recognition, and gratitude to donors, and keep them informed about the progress and outcomes of their contributions.

7. Build Financial Reserves:

- Build financial reserves and contingency funds to buffer against unexpected revenue fluctuations, economic downturns, or emergencies that may impact fundraising revenues or operational stability. Establish reserve policies, set aside designated funds, and prioritize financial planning to ensure organizational sustainability and resilience.

8. Leverage Technology and Data Analytics:

- Leverage technology and data analytics tools to optimize fundraising efforts, identify donor trends, and target fundraising appeals more effectively. Utilize donor management systems, fundraising software, and data analytics platforms to track donor behaviour, segment donor audiences, and personalize communication and outreach strategies.

9. Advocate for Policy and Funding Support:

- Advocate for policy reforms, government funding, and sector-wide support to address systemic challenges, resource constraints, and regulatory barriers affecting charity organizations. Engage in advocacy campaigns, coalition building, and public awareness efforts to raise awareness about the importance of nonprofit funding and advocate for policies that support a thriving nonprofit sector.

10. Foster a Culture of Philanthropy:

- Foster a culture of philanthropy within your organization by engaging staff, board members, volunteers, and stakeholders as ambassadors and advocates for your mission and fundraising initiatives. Cultivate a shared commitment to fundraising, transparency, and donor-centric values to instil a culture of philanthropy that permeates throughout your organization.

By implementing these strategies for addressing funding instability and resource constraints, charity organizations can strengthen their financial sustainability, enhance fundraising effectiveness, and navigate challenges with resilience and adaptability. By diversifying revenue streams, building donor relationships, and investing in organizational capacity, charities can overcome funding challenges and continue to advance their mission to create positive change in communities.

Navigating Regulatory Compliance and Reporting Requirements

Charity organizations are subject to a complex array of regulatory compliance and reporting requirements, which can vary depending on factors such as organizational structure, activities, and geographic location. Navigating these requirements effectively is essential for ensuring legal compliance, maintaining nonprofit status, and upholding public trust and accountability. Here are key strategies for navigating regulatory compliance and reporting requirements:

1. Understand Legal Obligations:
   - Develop a thorough understanding of the legal obligations, regulations, and reporting requirements applicable to charity

organizations in your jurisdiction. Stay informed about changes in relevant laws, tax codes, and regulatory frameworks that may impact your organization's operations or compliance obligations.

2. Establish Governance Policies:

   - Establish governance policies, procedures, and internal controls to ensure compliance with legal and regulatory requirements, promote transparency, and mitigate the risk of noncompliance. Adopt written policies for governance, financial management, conflict of interest, whistleblower protection, and other areas of organizational governance.

3. Maintain Nonprofit Status:

   - Take steps to maintain nonprofit status and tax-exempt status by adhering to IRS guidelines, state regulations, and filing requirements for nonprofit organizations. File annual tax returns, such as Form 990, with the IRS and state regulatory agencies to report financial activities, governance practices, and programmatic accomplishments.

4. Implement Financial Controls:

   - Implement robust financial controls, accounting practices, and record-keeping systems to ensure accurate financial reporting, compliance with accounting standards, and transparency in financial management. Maintain detailed financial records, audit trails, and documentation to support financial transactions and reporting.

5. Comply with Donor Restrictions:

    - Comply with donor restrictions, grant agreements, and funding requirements governing the use of restricted funds, designated gifts, and grant funds. Ensure that funds are used for their intended purpose, following donor preferences, restrictions, and legal guidelines.

6. Monitor Compliance Risks:

    - Monitor compliance risks, identify potential areas of vulnerability, and conduct regular compliance assessments or audits to evaluate adherence to legal requirements, internal policies, and industry standards. Implement corrective actions, remediation plans, or policy updates to address compliance deficiencies or mitigate risks proactively.

7. Seek Legal and Financial Guidance:

    - Seek legal counsel, financial advice, or professional assistance from qualified experts, attorneys, or consultants with expertise in nonprofit law, governance, and compliance matters. Consult with legal advisors, accountants, or compliance specialists to interpret complex regulations, resolve compliance issues, and ensure adherence to best practices.

8. Train Staff and Board Members:

   - Provide training, education, and ongoing professional development for staff, board members, and volunteers on compliance responsibilities, ethical standards, and legal obligations. Ensure that personnel are aware of regulatory requirements, reporting deadlines, and their roles in maintaining compliance with organizational policies and procedures.

9. Engage in Transparent Reporting:

   - Engage in transparent reporting and disclosure practices to provide stakeholders, donors, and the public with accurate, timely, and accessible information about your organization's activities, finances, and impact. Publish annual reports, financial statements, and impact assessments to demonstrate accountability and transparency in operations.

10. Stay Informed and Adaptive:

   - Stay informed about emerging regulatory trends, legislative developments, and industry best practices affecting charity organizations. Adapt your compliance practices, policies, and procedures in response to changes in regulations, shifts in the nonprofit landscape, and evolving stakeholder expectations.

By implementing these strategies for navigating regulatory compliance and reporting requirements, charity organizations can mitigate compliance risks, uphold legal obligations, and maintain the trust and confidence of stakeholders. By prioritizing transparency, accountability, and proactive compliance efforts, charities can demonstrate their commitment to ethical conduct, good governance, and mission-driven impact.

Managing Stakeholder Expectations and Public Perception

Effective management of stakeholder expectations and public perception is crucial for charity organizations to build trust, foster credibility, and cultivate support for their mission-driven initiatives. By understanding stakeholders' needs, communicating transparently, and proactively addressing concerns, charities can enhance their reputation, engage stakeholders effectively, and achieve their organizational objectives. Here are key strategies for managing stakeholder expectations and public perception:

1. Identify Key Stakeholders:

   - Identify and prioritize key stakeholders, including donors, volunteers, beneficiaries, board members, staff, government agencies, community partners, and the general public, who have a vested interest in your organization's mission, activities, and outcomes.

2. Conduct Stakeholder Analysis:

   - Conduct stakeholder analysis to assess stakeholders' interests, expectations, concerns, and influence on your organization. Identify stakeholders' needs, preferences, and communication preferences to tailor engagement strategies and communication approaches accordingly.

3. Establish Open Communication Channels:

   - Establish open, transparent communication channels to facilitate dialogue, feedback, and engagement with stakeholders. Create opportunities for two-way communication, such as town hall meetings, feedback sessions, surveys, and online forums, to solicit input, address concerns, and foster collaboration.

4. Set Realistic Expectations:

   - Set realistic expectations with stakeholders regarding your organization's goals, capabilities, and limitations. Provide clear, transparent information about your organization's mission, programs, impact metrics, and financial stewardship to manage stakeholders' expectations effectively.

5. Demonstrate Accountability and Transparency:

- Demonstrate accountability and transparency in your organization's operations, decision-making processes, and financial management practices. Publish annual reports, financial statements, impact assessments, and governance documents to provide stakeholders with insight into your organization's activities and outcomes.

6. Deliver on Promises:

   - Deliver on promises and commitments made to stakeholders, including donors, volunteers, and beneficiaries, to build trust and credibility. Fulfil obligations, honour donor restrictions, and communicate progress, achievements, and challenges transparently to maintain stakeholder confidence and support.

7. Address Stakeholder Concerns Promptly:

   - Address stakeholder concerns, feedback, and complaints promptly and constructively. Establish protocols and procedures for handling stakeholder inquiries, grievances, or feedback, and ensure timely responses, resolution, and follow-up to demonstrate responsiveness and commitment to stakeholder satisfaction.

8. Engage in Community Outreach and Engagement:

   - Engage in community outreach and engagement activities to build relationships, foster goodwill, and demonstrate your organization's commitment to the communities you serve. Participate in community events, collaborate with local partners, and support grassroots initiatives to strengthen ties with stakeholders and enhance public perception.

9. Leverage Digital and Social Media Platforms:

- Leverage digital and social media platforms to amplify your organization's message, reach new audiences, and engage stakeholders online. Use social media channels, blogs, and email newsletters to share stories, impact updates, and calls to action, and encourage dialogue and interaction with your organization's supporters.

10. Monitor and Respond to Public Feedback:

- Monitor public feedback, sentiment, and media coverage about your organization through media monitoring, social media listening, and online reputation management tools. Monitor online conversations, news articles, and social media mentions to identify emerging issues, respond to criticism, and address misinformation promptly and effectively.

By implementing these strategies for managing stakeholder expectations and public perception, charity organizations can enhance their reputation, build trust, and strengthen relationships with stakeholders. By prioritizing transparency, accountability, and proactive communication, charities can foster positive perceptions, mobilize support, and advance their mission to create positive change in communities.

Chapter 19:

Understanding Why Charity Organizations Fail

Despite their noble intentions and efforts to make a positive impact, charity organizations sometimes face challenges that lead to failure. Understanding the underlying reasons for failure is essential for identifying potential pitfalls, implementing corrective measures, and improving organizational resilience. Here are key factors contributing to why charity organizations fail:

1. Financial Mismanagement:

    - Poor financial management practices, including budget deficits, cash flow problems, and misallocation of funds, can undermine a charity's financial stability and sustainability. Lack of financial oversight, inadequate budgeting, and overreliance on restricted funds or unreliable revenue sources can contribute to financial distress and organizational failure.

2. Ineffective Fundraising Strategies:

    - Ineffective fundraising strategies, such as limited donor outreach, stagnant fundraising efforts, or overemphasis on short-term revenue generation, can hinder a charity's ability to generate sufficient funding to support its programs and operations. Failure to diversify funding sources, adapt to changing donor preferences, or engage donors effectively can lead to fundraising shortfalls and organizational stagnation.

3. Lack of Strategic Planning:

    - Lack of strategic planning, vision, and organizational direction can result in a charity's inability to define clear goals, prioritize initiatives, and allocate resources effectively. Failure to develop a strategic plan, monitor progress, or adapt to changing external conditions can leave a charity vulnerable to strategic drift, mission creep, or operational inefficiency.

4. Governance and Leadership Issues:

    - Governance and leadership challenges, such as ineffective board governance, leadership turnover, or conflicts of interest, can undermine a charity's governance structure and decision-making processes. Lack of board oversight, strategic leadership, or succession planning can lead to governance failures, organizational instability, and reputational damage.

5. Mission Drift or Lack of Impact:

    - Mission drift, where a charity deviates from its core mission or loses sight of its intended impact, can erode donor trust, confuse stakeholders, and diminish organizational effectiveness. Failure to articulate a clear mission, measure impact, or adapt programs to address evolving community needs can result in mission drift and loss of relevance.

6. Legal and Compliance Issues:

   - Legal and compliance issues, such as failure to comply with regulatory requirements, tax laws, or reporting obligations, can expose a charity to legal liabilities, fines, or loss of nonprofit status. Inadequate governance practices, financial mismanagement, or ethical lapses can lead to legal challenges, reputational harm, and organizational downfall.

7. Insufficient Capacity and Resources:

   - Insufficient organizational capacity, including limited staff expertise, volunteer shortages, or inadequate infrastructure, can hamper a charity's ability to deliver programs effectively and sustain operations. Failure to invest in capacity building, talent development, or resource mobilization can constrain organizational growth and resilience.

8. Lack of Stakeholder Engagement:

   - Lack of meaningful stakeholder engagement, including limited community involvement, donor communication, or beneficiary feedback, can hinder a charity's ability to build trust, mobilize support, and achieve meaningful impact. Failure to engage stakeholders as partners, advocates, or collaborators can lead to disconnects between the organization and its stakeholders.

9. External Factors and Environmental Challenges:

- External factors, such as economic downturns, political instability, or natural disasters, can pose significant challenges for charity organizations, impacting fundraising revenues, program delivery, and organizational sustainability. Failure to adapt to external changes, anticipate emerging trends, or mitigate environmental risks can leave a charity vulnerable to external shocks and organizational failure.

10. Lack of Adaptability and Innovation:

- Lack of adaptability and innovation, including resistance to change, organizational inertia, or complacency, can hinder a charity's ability to respond to evolving needs, seize opportunities, and stay relevant in a dynamic operating environment. Failure to embrace innovation, experimentation, or strategic adaptation can lead to organizational stagnation and eventual failure.

By recognizing these factors contributing to why charity organizations fail, nonprofit leaders, board members, and stakeholders can take proactive steps to mitigate risks, strengthen organizational resilience, and foster long-term sustainability. By prioritizing financial stewardship, strategic planning, governance excellence, and stakeholder engagement, charities can overcome challenges, learn from failures, and continue to advance their mission to create positive change in communities.

Common Reasons for Organizational Failure in the Charity Sector

Organizational failure within the charity sector can stem from various factors, many of which are unique to the nonprofit landscape. Understanding these common reasons for failure is essential for charity leaders to preemptively address challenges and mitigate risks. Here are some prevalent reasons for organizational failure in the charity sector:

1. **Financial Mismanagement:** Poor financial management, including overspending, budget deficits, and lack of financial transparency, can lead to financial instability and eventual organizational collapse.

2. **Ineffective Fundraising Strategies:** Reliance on limited fundraising channels, donor fatigue, and failure to adapt to changing donor preferences can result in insufficient funding to sustain operations and programs.

3. **Governance Issues:** Weak governance structures, lack of board oversight, and conflicts of interest can impede decision-making processes, erode donor trust, and undermine organizational effectiveness.

4. **Mission Drift:** Losing sight of the organization's core mission, pursuing unrelated programs or initiatives, or failing to align activities with the organization's stated objectives can lead to loss of focus and donor disillusionment.

5. **Legal and Compliance Challenges:** Noncompliance with regulatory requirements, tax laws, and reporting obligations can result in legal liabilities, fines, and damage to the organization's reputation.

6. **Insufficient Capacity:** Inadequate staffing, volunteer shortages, and lack of organizational infrastructure can hinder program delivery, operational efficiency, and long-term sustainability.

7. **Lack of Stakeholder Engagement:** Failure to engage stakeholders effectively, including donors, beneficiaries, and community members, can lead to loss of support, diminished impact, and organizational isolation.

8. **External Environmental Factors:** Economic downturns, changes in government policies, and unforeseen external events such as natural disasters or pandemics can pose significant challenges to organizational viability and resilience.

9. **Leadership Issues:** Poor leadership, including ineffective management practices, lack of strategic vision, and failure to inspire and motivate staff and volunteers, can contribute to organizational dysfunction and decline.

10. **Resistance to Change:** Inability or unwillingness to adapt to changing circumstances, embrace innovation, or address organizational weaknesses can lead to stagnation and eventual irrelevance in a dynamic operating environment.

By proactively addressing these common reasons for organizational failure, charity leaders can enhance their organization's resilience, sustainability, and ability to achieve its mission. Through strategic planning, effective governance, transparent communication, and a commitment to continuous improvement, charities can navigate challenges and thrive in the face of adversity.

Learning from Past Failures to Inform Future Strategies

In the charity sector, learning from past failures is crucial for organizations to evolve, adapt, and improve their strategies for long-term success. By analyzing the root causes of failure, identifying key lessons learned, and implementing corrective measures, charities can build resilience, enhance organizational effectiveness, and advance their mission. Here's how charity organizations can leverage past failures to inform future strategies:

1. **Conduct Comprehensive Post-Mortems:** After experiencing failure, conduct thorough post-mortem analyses to identify the underlying causes, contributing factors, and lessons learned from the experience. Engage stakeholders, including board members, staff, volunteers, and beneficiaries, in reflective discussions to gain diverse perspectives and insights.

2. **Identify Patterns and Trends:** Look for patterns and trends across past failures within the organization and the broader charity sector. Identify common themes, recurring challenges, and systemic issues that may indicate underlying weaknesses or areas for improvement.

3. **Evaluate Organizational Culture:** Assess the organization's culture, values, and norms to determine how they may have contributed to past failures. Foster a culture of transparency, accountability, and continuous learning that encourages open dialogue, constructive feedback, and innovation.

4. **Acknowledge and Accept Failure:** Cultivate a culture that acknowledges and accepts failure as an inevitable part of the learning process. Encourage staff and stakeholders to embrace failure as an opportunity for growth, experimentation, and improvement rather than a cause for blame or punishment.

5. **Implement Corrective Actions:** Based on lessons learned from past failures, develop and implement corrective actions, process improvements, and policy changes to address identified weaknesses and mitigate future risks. Prioritize action items, assign responsibilities, and establish timelines for implementation to ensure accountability and follow-through.

6. **Strengthen Governance and Oversight:** Enhance governance structures, board oversight, and

leadership accountability to prevent the recurrence of past failures. Improve transparency, communication, and decision-making processes within the organization to foster greater trust and confidence among stakeholders.

7. **Invest in Capacity Building:** Invest in capacity-building initiatives, staff training, and professional development programs to strengthen organizational capabilities and resilience. Equip staff and volunteers with the skills, knowledge, and resources they need to navigate challenges and succeed in their roles.

8. **Embrace Innovation and Adaptation:** Foster a culture of innovation, experimentation, and adaptive learning that encourages creativity, flexibility, and agility in response to changing circumstances. Encourage staff to explore new ideas, test innovative approaches, and learn from both successes and failures.

9. **Establish Metrics for Success:** Define clear metrics, benchmarks, and performance indicators to measure the effectiveness of strategies implemented in response to past failures. Monitor progress, track outcomes, and adjust strategies as needed to ensure continuous improvement and alignment with organizational goals.

10. **Share Insights and Best Practices:** Share insights, best practices, and lessons learned from past failures with other organizations in the charity sector. Contribute to knowledge sharing, peer learning, and

collaborative initiatives that promote collective learning and drive sector-wide improvement.

By learning from past failures and applying these lessons to inform future strategies, charity organizations can become more resilient, adaptive, and impactful in their mission to create positive change in communities. Through a commitment to continuous improvement, reflection, and learning, charities can navigate challenges with greater confidence and effectiveness, ultimately achieving greater success in advancing their mission and serving their beneficiaries.

Building Resilience and Adaptability to Overcome Challenges

Resilience and adaptability are essential qualities for charity organizations to thrive in the face of adversity, uncertainty, and change. By cultivating these attributes within their organizations, charity leaders can better equip their teams to navigate challenges, seize opportunities, and sustain long-term impact. Here's how charity organizations can build resilience and adaptability to overcome challenges:

1. **Foster a Culture of Resilience:** Cultivate a culture that values resilience, perseverance, and optimism in the face of adversity. Encourage staff, volunteers, and stakeholders to embrace challenges as opportunities for growth, learning, and innovation.

2. **Prioritize Strategic Planning:** Invest in strategic planning processes that anticipate potential challenges, identify risks, and develop contingency

plans to mitigate adverse effects. Set clear goals, objectives, and performance indicators to guide organizational decision-making and resource allocation.

3. **Embrace Change as an Opportunity:** Encourage a mindset of embracing change as an opportunity for growth and improvement rather than a threat to stability. Foster a spirit of innovation, experimentation, and adaptation to respond effectively to evolving needs and circumstances.

4. **Build Organizational Agility:** Develop organizational structures, processes, and systems that promote agility, flexibility, and responsiveness to changing conditions. Streamline decision-making, empower frontline staff, and decentralize authority to enable quick and effective responses to emerging challenges.

5. **Diversify Funding Streams:** Reduce reliance on a single source of funding by diversifying revenue streams and cultivating relationships with a diverse range of donors, funders, and partners. Explore alternative funding models, earned income opportunities, and social enterprise ventures to supplement traditional fundraising efforts.

6. **Invest in Capacity Building:** Invest in capacity-building initiatives, staff training, and professional development programs to strengthen organizational capabilities and resilience. Equip staff and volunteers with the skills, knowledge, and resources

they need to adapt to changing circumstances and overcome challenges.

7. **Strengthen Stakeholder Relationships:** Build strong relationships with stakeholders, including donors, beneficiaries, volunteers, and community partners, based on trust, transparency, and mutual respect. Engage stakeholders as partners in problem-solving, decision-making, and program development to foster collaboration and collective action.

8. **Promote Well-being and Self-care:** Prioritize the well-being and self-care of staff, volunteers, and stakeholders to prevent burnout, fatigue, and disengagement. Provide resources, support, and opportunities for self-care activities, mental health awareness, and work-life balance to foster resilience and sustainability.

9. **Learn from Failure and Adapt:** Embrace failure as a natural part of the learning process and an opportunity for growth and improvement. Encourage a culture of learning, reflection, and adaptation where lessons learned from past failures inform future strategies and decision-making.

10. **Stay Connected and Informed:** Stay connected to external networks, industry peers, and stakeholders to stay informed about emerging trends, best practices, and opportunities for collaboration. Participate in sector-wide initiatives, knowledge-sharing platforms, and networking events to leverage collective wisdom and expertise.

By building resilience and adaptability into their organizational DNA, charity organizations can better withstand challenges, navigate uncertainty, and seize opportunities for positive change. Through a commitment to continuous learning, innovation, and collaboration, charities can build a more sustainable and impactful future for themselves and the communities they serve.

Chapter 20:

Obstacles, Needs, and Demands of Charity Organizations

Charity organizations face a myriad of obstacles, needs, and demands as they strive to fulfil their missions and make a positive impact in their communities. Understanding and addressing these challenges is essential for building resilient, effective, and sustainable charitable organizations. Here are some of the key obstacles, needs, and demands faced by charity organizations:

1. **Limited Resources:** One of the most significant challenges for charity organizations is the scarcity of resources, including financial, human, and material resources. Limited funding, volunteer shortages, and lack of access to essential resources can hinder organizations' ability to deliver programs and services effectively.

2. **Fundraising Pressure:** Charity organizations often face immense pressure to raise funds to support their operations and programs. Meeting fundraising targets, securing grants, and competing for donor dollars can be time-consuming and stressful, particularly for smaller organizations with limited fundraising capacity.

3. **Capacity Constraints:** Many charity organizations struggle with capacity constraints, including limited staff expertise, organizational infrastructure, and technical capabilities. Insufficient capacity can impede organizations' ability to scale their impact,

respond to emerging needs, and adapt to changing circumstances.

4. **Competition for Funding:** The competitive funding landscape presents a significant challenge for charity organizations, particularly in sectors with high demand for resources. Competition for grants, corporate sponsorships, and individual donations can intensify, making it difficult for organizations to secure funding for their programs and initiatives.

5. **Regulatory Compliance:** Charity organizations must navigate a complex web of regulatory requirements, reporting obligations, and compliance standards. Ensuring compliance with legal and regulatory frameworks, tax laws, and reporting requirements can be time-consuming and resource-intensive for organizations of all sizes.

6. **Public Trust and Accountability:** Maintaining public trust and accountability is essential for charity organizations to retain donor support, attract volunteers, and engage stakeholders effectively. Any perceived lapse in transparency, ethical conduct, or financial stewardship can damage an organization's reputation and credibility.

7. **Community Needs and Expectations:** Charity organizations must continually assess and respond to evolving community needs, priorities, and expectations. Failure to address pressing social issues, engage with marginalized communities, or adapt to changing demographics can undermine organizations' relevance and effectiveness.

8. **Staff and Volunteer Burnout:** The demanding nature of charity work can take a toll on staff and volunteers, leading to burnout, fatigue, and turnover. High levels of stress, emotional exhaustion, and compassion fatigue can impact organizational morale, productivity, and sustainability.

9. **Technology and Digital Divide:** Access to technology and digital tools is increasingly important for charity organizations to communicate with stakeholders, deliver services, and operate efficiently. However, many organizations struggle with limited access to technology, digital literacy barriers, and the digital divide among their beneficiaries.

10. **Political and Economic Instability:** Charity organizations are often vulnerable to political and economic instability, including changes in government policies, funding cuts, and economic downturns. Uncertainty in the political and economic landscape can disrupt funding streams, impact program delivery, and create challenges for long-term planning.

Addressing these obstacles, needs, and demands requires a multifaceted approach that includes strategic planning, capacity building, stakeholder engagement, and collaboration. By building resilience, fostering innovation, and leveraging collective resources, charity organizations can overcome these challenges and continue to make a meaningful difference in the lives of those they serve.

Identifying Key Challenges Faced by Charity Organizations

Charity organizations, despite their noble intentions and dedication to making a positive impact, encounter numerous challenges that can impede their effectiveness and sustainability. Identifying these key challenges is essential for developing targeted strategies to address them effectively. Here are some of the primary challenges faced by charity organizations:

1. **Resource Constraints:** Limited financial resources, insufficient funding streams, and a scarcity of skilled personnel pose significant challenges for charity organizations. Without adequate resources, organizations may struggle to implement programs, cover operational costs, and expand their reach.

2. **Fundraising Pressure:** Charity organizations face constant pressure to raise funds to support their activities and fulfil their mission. Competition for donor dollars, donor fatigue, and economic uncertainties can make fundraising efforts challenging and unpredictable.

3. **Capacity Limitations:** Many charity organizations operate with limited capacity in terms of staff expertise, organizational infrastructure, and technological capabilities. Lack of capacity can hinder organizations' ability to scale their impact, deliver programs efficiently, and adapt to changing needs.

4. **Regulatory Compliance:** Navigating complex regulatory environments, compliance requirements,

and reporting obligations can be daunting for charity organizations. Ensuring compliance with legal and regulatory frameworks while maintaining transparency and accountability is a significant challenge for many organizations.

5. **Public Trust and Perception:** Maintaining public trust, credibility, and transparency is crucial for charity organizations to attract donors, volunteers, and supporters. Negative publicity, scandals, or perceived misuse of funds can damage an organization's reputation and erode public trust.

6. **Mission Drift:** Charity organizations may face challenges in staying true to their mission and core values amid external pressures, donor expectations, and changing social needs. Mission drift, where organizations deviate from their original purpose or priorities, can dilute impact and undermine organizational effectiveness.

7. **Community Engagement:** Engaging with diverse communities, building partnerships, and addressing community need effectively require skillful communication, cultural sensitivity, and active collaboration. Charity organizations may encounter challenges in understanding community needs, gaining trust, and fostering meaningful participation.

8. **Technology and Digital Divide:** Access to technology, digital literacy, and infrastructure pose challenges for charity organizations, particularly in reaching and serving marginalized communities. The digital divide can exacerbate inequalities and limit

organizations' ability to leverage technology for outreach, fundraising, and service delivery.

9. **Volunteer Management:** Recruiting, training, and retaining volunteers is a critical aspect of charity operations, but it can also present challenges. Managing volunteer schedules, expectations, and motivations while ensuring their meaningful contribution to organizational goals requires effective volunteer management practices.

10. **Adapting to External Factors:** Charity organizations must be resilient and adaptable to external factors such as economic fluctuations, changes in government policies, and unforeseen crises or disasters. Adapting to external shocks and uncertainties while maintaining organizational stability and continuity is a significant challenge for charities.

Addressing these key challenges requires strategic planning, capacity building, stakeholder engagement, and a commitment to continuous improvement. By identifying and understanding these challenges, charity organizations can develop targeted strategies to overcome them, enhance their resilience, and achieve greater impact in serving their communities.

Addressing the Diverse Needs and Demands of Beneficiaries

Charity organizations play a vital role in addressing the diverse needs and demands of their beneficiaries, who often come from various backgrounds and face unique challenges. Meeting these diverse needs requires a nuanced understanding of beneficiaries' circumstances, preferences, and aspirations. Here are key strategies for charity organizations to effectively address the diverse needs and demands of their beneficiaries:

1. **Conduct Comprehensive Needs Assessments:** Conduct thorough needs assessments to identify the specific needs, priorities, and aspirations of different beneficiary groups. Engage directly with beneficiaries through surveys, focus groups, and community consultations to gather insights and feedback.

2. **Tailor Programs and Services:** Design programs and services that are tailored to the unique needs, preferences, and cultural contexts of different beneficiary groups. Offer a range of services that address various aspects of beneficiaries' lives, such as education, healthcare, livelihoods, and social support.

3. **Promote Inclusivity and Accessibility:** Ensure that programs and services are accessible and inclusive to all beneficiaries, regardless of their background, abilities, or circumstances. Remove barriers to participation, provide accommodations as needed,

and promote diversity and inclusion in all aspects of organizational operations.

4. **Empower Beneficiaries:** Empower beneficiaries to actively participate in decision-making processes, program design, and implementation. Provide opportunities for beneficiaries to voice their opinions, express their needs, and contribute their expertise to shape programs that meet their needs effectively.

5. **Offer Holistic Support:** Take a holistic approach to addressing beneficiaries' needs by providing comprehensive support that addresses their physical, emotional, social, and economic well-being. Offer integrated services that address multiple dimensions of beneficiaries' lives and promote long-term resilience and self-sufficiency.

6. **Build Community Partnerships:** Collaborate with community organizations, local authorities, and other stakeholders to leverage resources, expertise, and networks in meeting beneficiaries' needs. Build strong partnerships that enable coordinated and sustainable interventions that maximize impact.

7. **Provide Culturally Sensitive Services:** Respect and honour the cultural traditions, values, and beliefs of beneficiaries in delivering services. Ensure that programs are culturally sensitive, relevant, and responsive to the cultural diversity within beneficiary communities.

8. **Offer Flexibility and Choice:** Recognize that beneficiaries have different preferences, priorities,

and circumstances, and offer flexibility and choice in accessing services. Provide options and alternatives that allow beneficiaries to choose the services that best meet their needs and preferences.

9. **Ensure Accountability and Transparency:** Maintain transparency and accountability in the delivery of services by providing clear information about program objectives, eligibility criteria, and available resources. Solicit feedback from beneficiaries, monitor program outcomes, and communicate openly about successes, challenges, and areas for improvement.

10. **Continuously Evaluate and Adapt:** Regularly evaluate program effectiveness, solicit feedback from beneficiaries, and adapt interventions based on changing needs and circumstances. Use monitoring and evaluation data to identify areas for improvement and refine program strategies to better meet beneficiaries' needs over time.

By adopting these strategies, charity organizations can effectively address the diverse needs and demands of their beneficiaries, empower individuals and communities, and create lasting positive change in society. Through a commitment to inclusivity, responsiveness, and continuous improvement, charities can maximize their impact and ensure that all beneficiaries have the opportunity to thrive and achieve their full potential.

Collaborating with Stakeholders to Overcome Obstacles and Drive Impact

In the dynamic landscape of charity work, collaboration with stakeholders is instrumental in overcoming obstacles and achieving meaningful impact. By fostering partnerships and engaging with diverse stakeholders, charity organizations can leverage collective resources, expertise, and networks to address complex challenges more effectively. Here are key strategies for collaborating with stakeholders to overcome obstacles and drive impact:

1. **Identify Key Stakeholders:** Identify and map out the key stakeholders who play a role in addressing the issues your charity aims to tackle. These stakeholders may include government agencies, community organizations, businesses, donors, volunteers, and beneficiaries.

2. **Build Trust and Relationships:** Invest time and effort in building trust-based relationships with stakeholders based on mutual respect, transparency, and shared values. Foster open communication, active listening, and collaborative problem-solving to strengthen relationships over time.

3. **Define Shared Goals and Objectives:** Work collaboratively with stakeholders to define shared goals, objectives, and outcomes that align with the collective mission and vision. Ensure that all stakeholders have a clear understanding of the roles, responsibilities, and contributions expected from each party.

4. **Encourage Inclusive Participation:** Ensure that stakeholders from diverse backgrounds, perspectives, and expertise are included in decision-making processes and collaborative initiatives. Empower stakeholders to contribute their unique insights, knowledge, and resources to co-create solutions that reflect the needs and aspirations of all stakeholders.

5. **Facilitate Communication and Coordination:** Establish channels for regular communication, information sharing, and coordination among stakeholders to facilitate collaboration and ensure alignment of efforts. Utilize technology, online platforms, and networking events to foster ongoing dialogue and engagement.

6. **Promote Shared Learning and Capacity Building:** Create opportunities for stakeholders to learn from each other, share best practices, and build their capacity to address common challenges more effectively. Offer training, workshops, and peer-learning opportunities that enable stakeholders to acquire new skills, knowledge, and perspectives.

7. **Leverage Resources and Expertise:** Pool together resources, expertise, and networks from different stakeholders to maximize impact and efficiency. Tap into the unique strengths and capabilities of each stakeholder to address specific aspects of the problem and achieve collective goals.

8. **Adapt and Flexibility:** Be flexible and adaptable in response to changing needs, circumstances, and

priorities. Embrace a spirit of experimentation, innovation, and continuous improvement in collaborative initiatives, allowing room for iteration and adjustment based on feedback and evolving conditions.

9. **Celebrate Successes and Milestones:** Recognize and celebrate successes, achievements, and milestones reached through collaborative efforts. Acknowledge the contributions of all stakeholders and highlight the positive impact generated through collective action, fostering a sense of pride and motivation to sustain collaborative efforts.

10. **Evaluate and Reflect:** Regularly evaluate the effectiveness of collaborative initiatives, measure outcomes, and reflect on lessons learned to inform future collaboration efforts. Solicit feedback from stakeholders, identify areas for improvement, and iterate on strategies to enhance collaboration and drive greater impact over time.

By collaborating with stakeholders effectively, charity organizations can overcome obstacles, amplify their impact, and create sustainable change that addresses the needs of communities and beneficiaries. Through shared vision, shared responsibility, and shared action, stakeholders can collectively contribute to building a more equitable, resilient, and thriving society.

Chapter 21:

How to Start Your Own Charity Organization

Starting your own charity organization can be a fulfilling and impactful way to make a difference in your community or address a pressing social issue. However, launching a charity requires careful planning, dedication, and adherence to legal and regulatory requirements. Here are key steps to help you start your own charity organization:

1. **Define Your Mission and Vision:** Clarify the purpose and objectives of your charity by defining a clear mission and vision statement. Identify the social issue or cause you want to address and articulate the impact you aim to achieve.

2. **Conduct Research:** Conduct thorough research to understand the need for your charity's services or interventions, as well as the existing landscape of similar organizations and potential gaps or opportunities. Identify your target beneficiaries and assess their needs, preferences, and priorities.

3. **Develop a Strategic Plan:** Create a strategic plan that outlines your charity's goals, objectives, strategies, and activities. Define your target outcomes, target population, geographic scope, and timelines for implementation. Consider how you will measure success and evaluate the impact of your programs.

4. **Choose a Legal Structure:** Decide on the legal structure for your charity, such as a nonprofit

corporation, charitable trust, or unincorporated association. Consult with legal experts or professionals to understand the legal requirements and implications of each structure, including tax-exempt status and liability considerations.

5. **Register Your Charity:** Register your charity with the relevant government authorities or regulatory bodies to obtain legal recognition and tax-exempt status. Familiarize yourself with the registration process, required documents, and compliance requirements in your jurisdiction.

6. **Develop Governing Documents:** Prepare governing documents, such as articles of incorporation, bylaws, and a constitution, to establish the governance structure, operating procedures, and decision-making processes of your charity. Ensure that your governing documents comply with legal requirements and reflect your organization's mission and values.

7. **Establish a Board of Directors:** Recruit a diverse and qualified board of directors to provide strategic leadership, oversight, and governance for your charity. Select individuals with relevant expertise, experience, and connections who are committed to advancing your organization's mission.

8. **Secure Funding:** Develop a fundraising plan to secure the financial resources needed to launch and sustain your charity's operations and programs. Explore diverse funding sources, such as grants, donations, sponsorships, crowdfunding, and earned

income streams. Develop relationships with potential donors, funders, and partners to support your cause.

9. **Build Partnerships:** Forge strategic partnerships with other organizations, community groups, government agencies, businesses, and stakeholders who share your goals and can support your efforts. Collaborate with partners to leverage resources, expertise, and networks to maximize your impact and reach.

10. **Launch and Promote Your Charity:** Officially launch your charity and promote your mission, programs, and initiatives to raise awareness and attract supporters. Develop a marketing and communications strategy to engage stakeholders, cultivate donors, and mobilize volunteers. Utilize various channels, such as websites, social media, press releases, and events, to amplify your message and expand your reach.

11. **Monitor and Evaluate:** Establish systems for monitoring and evaluating your charity's performance, tracking progress toward goals, and measuring the impact of your programs. Collect data, analyze outcomes, and solicit feedback from stakeholders to inform decision-making, improve effectiveness, and demonstrate accountability to donors and supporters.

Starting your own charity organization requires careful planning, perseverance, and collaboration with stakeholders. By following these steps and staying committed to your mission, you can build a successful charity that makes a meaningful difference in the lives of others and contributes to positive social change.

Steps to Establishing a New Charity Organization

Establishing a new charity organization requires careful planning, legal compliance, and strategic decision-making. Here are the key steps to guide you through the process:

1. **Define Your Mission and Vision:** Clearly define the purpose and goals of your charity organization by developing a mission statement that outlines the issues you aim to address and the impact you seek to achieve. Establish a vision statement that articulates your long-term aspirations and the positive change you hope to create.

2. **Conduct Market Research:** Conduct comprehensive research to understand the social or community needs your charity will address. Identify gaps in existing services, assess the demand for your proposed programs or initiatives, and gather insights into the demographics and characteristics of your target beneficiaries.

3. **Develop a Strategic Plan:** Create a strategic plan that outlines the objectives, strategies, and activities of your charity organization. Define your target outcomes, key performance indicators, and timelines for implementation. Consider how you will measure success and adapt your strategies over time.

4. **Choose a Legal Structure:** Select a suitable legal structure for your charity organization, such as a nonprofit corporation, charitable trust, or

unincorporated association. Consult legal experts or professionals to understand the legal requirements and implications of each structure, including tax-exempt status and liability considerations.

5. **Register Your Charity:** Register your charity with the appropriate government authorities or regulatory bodies to obtain legal recognition and tax-exempt status. Familiarize yourself with the registration process, required documents, and compliance requirements in your jurisdiction.

6. **Draft Governing Documents:** Prepare governing documents, including articles of incorporation, bylaws, and a constitution, to establish the governance structure, operating procedures, and decision-making processes of your charity organization. Ensure that your governing documents comply with legal requirements and reflect your organization's mission and values.

7. **Recruit Board Members:** Recruit a diverse and qualified board of directors to provide strategic leadership, oversight, and governance for your charity organization. Select individuals with relevant expertise, experience, and connections who are committed to advancing your organization's mission.

8. **Develop a Fundraising Plan:** Develop a fundraising plan to secure the financial resources needed to launch and sustain your charity's operations and programs. Explore diverse funding sources, such as grants, donations, sponsorships, crowdfunding, and earned income streams. Cultivate relationships with

potential donors, funders, and partners to support your cause.

9. **Establish Operational Infrastructure:** Set up the operational infrastructure of your charity organization, including administrative systems, financial controls, and human resources policies. Develop policies and procedures for governance, finance, fundraising, volunteer management, and program delivery.

10. **Launch Your Charity:** Officially launch your charity organization and promote your mission, programs, and initiatives to raise awareness and attract supporters. Develop a marketing and communications strategy to engage stakeholders, cultivate donors, and mobilize volunteers. Utilize various channels, such as websites, social media, press releases, and events, to amplify your message and expand your reach.

11. **Monitor and Evaluate:** Establish systems for monitoring and evaluating your charity's performance, tracking progress toward goals, and measuring the impact of your programs. Collect data, analyze outcomes, and solicit feedback from stakeholders to inform decision-making, improve effectiveness, and demonstrate accountability to donors and supporters.

By following these steps and staying committed to your mission, you can establish a new charity organization that makes a meaningful difference in the lives of others and contributes to positive social change.

Legal and Regulatory Requirements for Charity Registration

Registering a charity involves complying with specific legal and regulatory requirements to obtain legal recognition and tax-exempt status. Here are the key legal and regulatory requirements for charity registration:

1. **Choose a Legal Structure:** Select a suitable legal structure for your charity, such as a nonprofit corporation, charitable trust, or unincorporated association. Each structure has different legal implications, including governance, liability, and tax-exempt status. Consult legal experts or professionals to determine the most appropriate structure for your organization.

2. **Articles of Incorporation or Trust Deed:** Prepare and file articles of incorporation or a trust deed with the appropriate government authorities to formally establish your charity as a legal entity. These documents outline the purpose, governance structure, and operational details of your charity organization.

3. **Bylaws or Constitution:** Develop and adopt bylaws or a constitution that governs the internal operations, decision-making processes, and procedures of your charity. These documents outline the roles and responsibilities of the board of directors, officers, members, and committees within your organization.

4. **Registration with Government Authorities:** Register your charity with the relevant government authorities or regulatory bodies responsible for overseeing

charitable organizations. This may include federal, state, or provincial agencies, depending on your jurisdiction. Submit required forms, documents, and fees to complete the registration process.

5. **Tax-Exempt Status:** Apply for tax-exempt status with the appropriate tax authorities to receive favourable tax treatment for your charity organization. This typically involves applying for recognition as a tax-exempt entity under the applicable tax laws or regulations. Provide documentation of your charitable activities, governance structure, and financial accountability to support your application.

6. **Compliance with Charitable Purposes:** Ensure that your charity's activities and programs align with its charitable purposes as defined by law. Charitable purposes typically include advancing education, relieving poverty, promoting health, supporting religious or cultural activities, or benefiting the community in other ways. Avoid engaging in activities that are prohibited or restricted under charity laws.

7. **Financial Accountability:** Establish financial controls, reporting procedures, and accountability mechanisms to ensure transparent and responsible stewardship of charitable funds. Maintain accurate financial records, prepare annual financial statements, and comply with reporting requirements specified by regulatory authorities.

8. **Governance and Accountability:** Maintain effective governance structures, practices, and procedures to ensure accountability, transparency, and ethical

conduct within your charity organization. Adopt best practices for board governance, conflicts of interest, whistleblower protection, and ethical fundraising.

9. **Compliance with Regulatory Requirements:** Stay informed about legal and regulatory requirements that apply to charitable organizations in your jurisdiction. This may include registration renewal, annual reporting, fundraising regulations, disclosure obligations, and other compliance requirements.

10. **Legal Advice and Assistance:** Seek legal advice and assistance from qualified professionals or legal experts specializing in nonprofit and charity law. They can guide navigating the registration process, complying with legal requirements, and addressing any legal issues or challenges that may arise.

By fulfilling these legal and regulatory requirements, your charity can obtain official recognition, maintain tax-exempt status, and operate in compliance with applicable laws and regulations. This ensures the credibility, legitimacy, and sustainability of your charity organization as it works to achieve its charitable mission and serve the community.

Building a Solid Foundation: Mission, Vision, and Values

Establishing a strong foundation for your charity organization begins with defining its mission, vision, and values. These foundational elements provide clarity, purpose, and direction for your organization's activities and guide its decision-making processes. Here's how to develop a solid foundation for your charity:

1. **Mission Statement:** Your mission statement succinctly describes the core purpose and reason for the existence of your charity. It articulates what your organization does, who it serves, and the impact it seeks to achieve. When crafting your mission statement, consider the specific needs or issues your charity aims to address, the target beneficiaries, and the outcomes you aspire to accomplish. Keep it clear, concise, and inspiring to resonate with stakeholders and motivate action.

2. **Vision Statement:** Your vision statement outlines the desired future state or long-term aspirations of your charity. It paints a compelling picture of the positive change your organization seeks to create in the world. Think about the ultimate goals or outcomes you hope to achieve, the broader impact you aspire to make, and the legacy you aim to leave behind. Your vision statement should inspire and rally stakeholders around a shared vision of a better future.

3. **Core Values:** Your organization's core values represent its fundamental beliefs, principles, and guiding principles that inform its culture, behaviours, and decisions. Identify the values that are central to your charity's identity and ethos, such as integrity, compassion, inclusivity, accountability, and transparency. These values serve as the moral compass that guides your organization's actions and relationships with stakeholders.

4. **Align Mission, Vision, and Values:** Ensure that your mission, vision, and values are aligned and mutually reinforcing. Your mission statement should reflect your organization's purpose and activities, while your vision statement should capture its aspirations and long-term impact. Your core values should underpin both your mission and vision, shaping how your organization operates and interacts with stakeholders.

5. **Communicate Effectively:** Once you've defined your mission, vision, and values, communicate them clearly and consistently to stakeholders. Incorporate them into your organization's communications, branding, and messaging to convey your organization's identity, purpose, and values to the wider community. Engage stakeholders in conversations about your mission, vision, and values to build understanding, trust, and support.

6. **Live Your Values:** Demonstrate your organization's commitment to its values through its actions, decisions, and behaviours. Integrate your values into all aspects of your organization's operations, from governance and leadership to program delivery and stakeholder engagement. Lead by example and cultivate a culture that embodies your organization's values in everything it does.

7. **Review and Revise:** Periodically review and revisit your mission, vision, and values to ensure they remain relevant, aspirational, and aligned with your organization's evolving needs and priorities. Revisit

them during strategic planning processes, organizational assessments, and times of change or transition. Be open to revising or refining your mission, vision, and values as needed to reflect your organization's growth, learning, and adaptation over time.

By establishing a solid foundation built on a clear mission, inspiring vision, and values-driven culture, your charity organization can effectively navigate challenges, inspire stakeholders, and achieve meaningful impact in pursuit of its charitable mission.

Chapter 22:

Aims and Objectives of Charity Organizations

The aims and objectives of charity organizations serve as guiding principles that define their purpose, goals, and desired outcomes. These aims and objectives provide a clear direction for the organization's activities and initiatives, helping to focus efforts and resources on achieving meaningful impact. Here are the key aims and objectives of charity organizations:

1. **Addressing Social Needs:** Charity organizations aim to address pressing social needs and challenges within communities, such as poverty, hunger, homelessness, education inequality, healthcare disparities, environmental degradation, and social exclusion. They work to improve the well-being and quality of life of individuals and communities facing adversity or disadvantage.

2. **Promoting Social Justice and Equity:** Charity organizations strive to promote social justice, equity, and human rights by advocating for the rights and dignity of marginalized and vulnerable populations. They work to challenge systemic inequalities, discrimination, and oppression, and to empower individuals and communities to advocate for their rights and access to opportunities.

3. **Providing Humanitarian Assistance:** Charity organizations provide humanitarian assistance and relief to communities affected by emergencies, disasters, conflicts, and crises. They offer immediate

assistance, such as food, shelter, water, healthcare, and psychosocial support, to alleviate suffering and meet the urgent needs of affected populations.

4. **Advancing Education and Empowerment:** Charity organizations aim to advance education, skills development, and empowerment opportunities for individuals and communities, particularly those facing barriers to accessing quality education and opportunities for personal and professional growth. They promote lifelong learning, literacy, vocational training, and capacity-building initiatives to empower individuals to reach their full potential.

5. **Supporting Health and Well-being:** Charity organizations work to improve health outcomes and promote well-being by providing access to healthcare services, preventive care, mental health support, nutrition programs, and public health initiatives. They address health disparities, promote healthy behaviours, and advocate for universal access to healthcare services.

6. **Protecting the Environment:** Charity organizations play a vital role in protecting and preserving the environment by promoting environmental conservation, sustainability, and climate resilience. They undertake initiatives to address environmental degradation, pollution, deforestation, biodiversity loss, and climate change, and to promote sustainable practices and stewardship of natural resources.

7. **Fostering Community Development:** Charity organizations contribute to community development by fostering social cohesion, civic engagement, and community resilience. They facilitate community-led initiatives, participatory decision-making processes, and collective action to address local priorities, build social capital, and strengthen community networks.

8. **Promoting Cultural Preservation and Heritage:** Charity organizations support cultural preservation and heritage conservation efforts to safeguard cultural diversity, traditions, languages, and intangible cultural heritage. They promote cultural exchange, intercultural dialogue, and cultural enrichment initiatives that celebrate and preserve cultural identities and heritage assets.

9. **Building Sustainable Livelihoods:** Charity organizations work to promote economic empowerment and sustainable livelihoods for individuals and communities, particularly those living in poverty or facing economic marginalization. They support income-generating activities, entrepreneurship development, vocational training, microfinance programs, and job creation initiatives to enhance economic opportunities and resilience.

10. **Fostering Global Solidarity and Cooperation:** Charity organizations promote global solidarity, cooperation, and mutual support to address global challenges, promote peace, and build a more just and sustainable world. They advocate for international cooperation, humanitarian principles,

and human rights frameworks to address global inequities, conflicts, and humanitarian crises.

By pursuing these aims and objectives, charity organizations contribute to building a more equitable, inclusive, and sustainable society where all individuals have the opportunity to thrive and fulfil their potential. Through their commitment to serving others and advancing social change, charity organizations play a crucial role in creating a positive impact and building a better world for future generations.

Defining the Purpose and Goals of Charity Organizations

Charity organizations play a crucial role in addressing societal needs, promoting social justice, and fostering positive change. Defining their purpose and goals is essential for guiding their actions, mobilizing resources, and measuring impact. Here's how charity organizations define their purpose and goals:

1. **Addressing Social Needs:** The primary purpose of charity organizations is to address pressing social needs and challenges within communities. These needs may include poverty alleviation, hunger relief, access to education and healthcare, housing assistance, disaster relief, and support for vulnerable populations such as children, the elderly, and individuals with disabilities.

2. **Promoting Social Justice and Equity:** Charity organizations aim to promote social justice, equity, and human rights by advocating for the rights and dignity of marginalized and vulnerable populations. They work to challenge systemic inequalities,

discrimination, and oppression, and to empower individuals and communities to advocate for their rights and access to opportunities.

3. **Providing Humanitarian Assistance:** Charity organizations provide humanitarian assistance and relief to communities affected by emergencies, disasters, conflicts, and crises. Their goals include providing immediate assistance such as food, shelter, water, healthcare, and psychosocial support to alleviate suffering and meet the urgent needs of affected populations.

4. **Advancing Education and Empowerment:** Charity organizations aim to advance education, skills development, and empowerment opportunities for individuals and communities. Their goals include promoting access to quality education, vocational training, and capacity-building initiatives to empower individuals to reach their full potential and participate fully in society.

5. **Supporting Health and Well-being:** Charity organizations work to improve health outcomes and promote well-being by providing access to healthcare services, preventive care, mental health support, nutrition programs, and public health initiatives. Their goals include addressing health disparities, promoting healthy behaviours, and advocating for universal access to healthcare services.

6. **Protecting the Environment:** Charity organizations contribute to protecting and preserving the environment by promoting environmental

conservation, sustainability, and climate resilience. Their goals include addressing environmental degradation, pollution, deforestation, biodiversity loss, and climate change, and promoting sustainable practices and stewardship of natural resources.

7. **Fostering Community Development:** Charity organizations contribute to community development by fostering social cohesion, civic engagement, and community resilience. Their goals include facilitating community-led initiatives, participatory decision-making processes, and collective action to address local priorities, build social capital, and strengthen community networks.

8. **Promoting Cultural Preservation and Heritage:** Charity organizations support cultural preservation and heritage conservation efforts to safeguard cultural diversity, traditions, languages, and intangible cultural heritage. Their goals include promoting cultural exchange, intercultural dialogue, and cultural enrichment initiatives that celebrate and preserve cultural identities and heritage assets.

9. **Building Sustainable Livelihoods:** Charity organizations work to promote economic empowerment and sustainable livelihoods for individuals and communities. Their goals include supporting income-generating activities, entrepreneurship development, vocational training, microfinance programs, and job creation initiatives to enhance economic opportunities and resilience.

10. **Fostering Global Solidarity and Cooperation:** Charity organizations promote global solidarity, cooperation, and mutual support to address global challenges and build a more just and sustainable world. Their goals include advocating for international cooperation, humanitarian principles, and human rights frameworks to address global inequities, conflicts, and humanitarian crises.

By defining their purpose and goals in alignment with these overarching objectives, charity organizations can effectively channel their efforts, resources, and energy toward making a positive impact and advancing social change in communities locally and globally.

Aligning Objectives with Mission to Drive Impact

For charity organizations to maximize their impact and effectively address societal needs, it's crucial to align their objectives with their mission. This alignment ensures that organizational efforts are focused, strategic, and directed towards achieving meaningful outcomes. Here's how charity organizations can align their objectives with their mission to drive impact:

1. **Mission Clarity:** Start by clearly defining the mission of the charity organization. The mission statement should succinctly articulate the organization's purpose, values, and the specific societal issue it aims to address. Ensure that all stakeholders understand and are aligned with the mission.

2. **Identify Key Objectives:** Based on the mission, identify key objectives that outline the specific goals

and desired outcomes the organization seeks to achieve. Objectives should be SMART (Specific, Measurable, Achievable, Relevant, Time-bound) and directly linked to addressing the societal need identified in the mission statement.

3. **Prioritize Impact Areas:** Prioritize impact areas that are most closely aligned with the mission and where the organization can make the greatest difference. Focus on addressing root causes rather than symptoms to drive sustainable change and long-term impact.

4. **Set Clear Goals:** Set clear, quantifiable goals for each objective to measure progress and success. Goals should be aligned with the mission and reflect the organization's commitment to addressing societal needs effectively.

5. **Develop Strategic Initiatives:** Develop strategic initiatives and programs that directly contribute to achieving the organization's objectives. Ensure that initiatives are designed to address the identified societal need in a targeted and impactful manner.

6. **Allocate Resources Wisely:** Allocate resources, including financial, human, and material resources, strategically to support the implementation of initiatives aligned with the organization's objectives. Prioritize investments that have the potential to generate the greatest impact and outcomes.

7. **Monitor and Evaluate Progress:** Establish systems for monitoring and evaluating progress towards

achieving objectives and desired outcomes. Regularly assess the effectiveness and impact of initiatives, adjust strategies as needed, and celebrate successes along the way.

8. **Collaborate with Stakeholders:** Collaborate with stakeholders, including beneficiaries, partners, donors, and community members, to align objectives with their needs and priorities. Engage stakeholders in the planning, implementation, and evaluation of initiatives to ensure relevance and effectiveness.

9. **Communicate Impact:** Communicate the organization's impact and progress towards achieving its mission and objectives transparently and effectively. Share success stories, data, and testimonials to demonstrate the tangible difference the organization is making in addressing societal needs.

10. **Iterate and Adapt:** Continuously iterate and adapt strategies based on lessons learned, changing needs, and external factors. Stay flexible and responsive to emerging challenges and opportunities, while remaining steadfast in the organization's commitment to its mission.

By aligning objectives with the mission, charity organizations can focus their efforts, resources, and energies on driving meaningful impact in addressing societal needs and advancing positive change in communities. This alignment ensures that organizational actions are purposeful, and strategic, and ultimately contribute to fulfilling the organization's mission and vision.

Balancing Short-term and Long-term Goals for Sustainability

Sustainability is crucial for charity organizations to continue making a positive impact over the long term. Balancing short-term and long-term goals is essential to ensure that organizations can address immediate needs while also building capacity, resilience, and lasting impact. Here are strategies for balancing short-term and long-term goals for sustainability:

1. **Strategic Planning:** Develop a strategic plan that integrates both short-term and long-term goals. Identify immediate priorities that address pressing needs in the community while also setting strategic objectives that contribute to the organization's long-term vision and sustainability.

2. **Priority Setting:** Prioritize short-term goals that are aligned with the organization's mission and have the potential to generate immediate impact. Simultaneously, prioritize long-term goals that build organizational capacity, enhance sustainability, and address systemic issues for lasting change.

3. **Resource Allocation:** Allocate resources effectively to support both short-term and long-term goals. Ensure that resources are distributed in a balanced manner, considering the urgency of short-term needs and the importance of investing in long-term initiatives that contribute to sustainability.

4. **Flexible Funding:** Secure funding that allows flexibility to address both short-term emergencies and long-term strategic priorities. Diversify funding sources to reduce dependence on unstable or restricted funding streams, enabling the organization to adapt to changing needs and priorities.

5. **Capacity Building:** Invest in organizational capacity-building initiatives that strengthen infrastructure, governance, leadership, and staff capabilities. Building internal capacity enables the organization to effectively deliver programs, manage resources, and adapt to changing circumstances over the long term.

6. **Collaboration and Partnerships:** Collaborate with other organizations, community groups, government agencies, and stakeholders to leverage resources, expertise, and networks. Forming strategic partnerships can enhance the organization's ability to address both short-term crises and long-term challenges more effectively.

7. **Monitoring and Evaluation:** Establish robust monitoring and evaluation mechanisms to track progress towards both short-term and long-term goals. Regularly assess the impact of interventions, collect feedback from stakeholders, and use data to inform decision-making and program improvements.

8. **Adaptability and Innovation:** Foster a culture of adaptability and innovation within the organization. Encourage staff and volunteers to explore creative solutions to address immediate needs while also experimenting with new approaches and

technologies to achieve long-term sustainability and impact.

9. **Community Engagement:** Engage with the community to understand their needs, priorities, and aspirations. Involve beneficiaries and stakeholders in the planning, implementation, and evaluation of programs to ensure relevance, ownership, and sustainability over time.

10. **Continuous Learning:** Embrace a culture of continuous learning and improvement. Reflect on successes and challenges, learn from experiences, and apply insights to refine strategies and approaches for achieving both short-term results and long-term sustainability.

By balancing short-term and long-term goals effectively, charity organizations can respond to immediate needs while also building resilience, capacity, and lasting impact. This balanced approach enables organizations to thrive in the face of uncertainty, adapt to changing circumstances, and continue making a positive difference in the lives of those they serve over the long term.

Chapter 23:

Successful Charity Organization Strategies

Successful charity organizations employ strategic approaches that enable them to achieve their mission, maximize impact, and ensure sustainability. These organizations leverage innovative practices, effective management techniques, and collaborative partnerships to address societal needs effectively. Here are key strategies employed by successful charity organizations:

1. **Clear Mission and Vision:** Successful charity organizations have a clear and compelling mission that guides their activities and inspires stakeholders. They articulate a vision for the future that reflects their aspirations and the positive change they seek to create in the world.

2. **Strategic Planning:** They develop strategic plans that outline specific goals, objectives, and initiatives aligned with their mission and vision. These plans provide a roadmap for action, prioritize areas of focus, and allocate resources effectively to achieve desired outcomes.

3. **Impact-driven Programs:** Successful charity organizations design and implement programs that are evidence-based, outcome-focused, and responsive to community needs. They prioritize interventions with measurable impact and continually evaluate their effectiveness to ensure accountability and learning.

4. **Diversified Funding:** They diversify their funding sources to reduce dependence on any single revenue stream and mitigate financial risks. Successful organizations leverage a mix of government grants, private donations, corporate partnerships, earned income ventures, and fundraising events to sustain their operations.

5. **Transparent Financial Management:** They maintain transparent financial management practices, with robust systems for budgeting, accounting, and reporting. Successful organizations demonstrate fiscal responsibility, integrity, and accountability to donors, funders, and stakeholders.

6. **Effective Governance:** They have strong governance structures in place, with engaged and knowledgeable board members providing strategic oversight and guidance. Successful organizations adhere to best practices in governance, with clear roles, responsibilities, and accountability mechanisms.

7. **Collaborative Partnerships:** They collaborate with other nonprofits, government agencies, businesses, and community groups to leverage resources, expertise, and networks. Successful organizations forge strategic partnerships that amplify their impact, enhance their reach, and foster collective action to address complex challenges.

8. **Innovative Approaches:** Successful charity organizations embrace innovation and creativity in their approaches to addressing societal needs. They explore new technologies, methodologies, and

solutions to improve the efficiency, effectiveness, and scalability of their programs and services.

9. **Community Engagement:** They actively engage with beneficiaries, community members, and stakeholders to understand their needs, priorities, and aspirations. Successful organizations involve the community in decision-making, program design, and implementation to ensure relevance, ownership, and sustainability.

10. **Continuous Learning and Improvement:** They foster a culture of learning, reflection, and adaptation within the organization. Successful organizations regularly evaluate their performance, gather feedback from stakeholders, and apply insights to refine strategies, innovate solutions, and enhance impact.

By implementing these strategies, charity organizations can strengthen their capacity, increase their effectiveness, and make a lasting difference in the lives of individuals and communities they serve. Successful organizations demonstrate resilience, adaptability, and commitment to their mission, driving positive change and creating a better world for all.

Developing Effective Strategic Plans for Charity Organizations

Effective strategic planning is essential for charity organizations to clarify their mission, set clear objectives, allocate resources efficiently, and achieve meaningful impact. Here's a step-by-step guide to developing strategic plans for charity organizations:

1. **Mission Review:** Begin by reviewing and reaffirming the organization's mission statement. Ensure that the mission statement accurately reflects the organization's purpose, values, and the societal needs it seeks to address.

2. **Stakeholder Engagement:** Engage key stakeholders, including board members, staff, volunteers, beneficiaries, donors, and community members, in the strategic planning process. Seek input, feedback, and perspectives to ensure that the strategic plan reflects diverse viewpoints and priorities.

3. **Environmental Scan:** Conduct a thorough analysis of the internal and external environment in which the organization operates. Assess internal strengths and weaknesses, as well as external opportunities and threats, to inform strategic decision-making.

4. **SWOT Analysis:** Based on the environmental scan, conduct a SWOT analysis (Strengths, Weaknesses, Opportunities, Threats) to identify key strategic issues and priorities. Identify areas of competitive advantage, areas for improvement, emerging opportunities, and potential challenges or risks.

5. **Goal Setting:** Set clear, specific, and measurable goals that align with the organization's mission and address strategic priorities. Goals should be SMART (Specific, Measurable, Achievable, Relevant, Time-

bound) and reflect both short-term and long-term objectives.

6. **Strategic Objectives:** Develop strategic objectives that outline the specific actions and initiatives needed to achieve each goal. Each objective should be linked to one or more goals and include clear targets, timelines, and responsible parties for implementation.

7. **Resource Allocation:** Determine the resources required to support the implementation of strategic objectives, including financial, human, and material resources. Develop a budget that aligns with the strategic plan and ensures adequate funding for priority initiatives.

8. **Action Planning:** Develop detailed action plans for each strategic objective, outlining specific activities, milestones, deadlines, and resource requirements. Assign responsibilities to individuals or teams accountable for implementation, and establish mechanisms for monitoring progress.

9. **Performance Metrics:** Define key performance indicators (KPIs) and metrics to track progress towards achieving strategic goals and objectives. Establish benchmarks, targets, and timelines for measuring success, and regularly review and report on performance against targets.

10. **Evaluation and Review:** Establish a process for ongoing evaluation and review of the strategic plan to assess its effectiveness, relevance, and impact.

Schedule regular check-ins, progress reviews, and strategic retreats to monitor implementation, identify lessons learned, and make adjustments as needed.

11. **Communication and Alignment:** Communicate the strategic plan to all stakeholders to ensure understanding, buy-in, and alignment with organizational goals and priorities. Engage staff, volunteers, donors, and partners in the strategic planning process to foster ownership and commitment to implementation.

12. **Flexibility and Adaptation:** Remain flexible and adaptive in responding to changing circumstances, emerging opportunities, and unforeseen challenges. Continuously monitor the external environment, evaluate the effectiveness of strategies, and adjust the strategic plan as needed to stay responsive and relevant.

By following these steps, charity organizations can develop effective strategic plans that provide a roadmap for achieving their mission, driving impact, and ensuring sustainability over the long term. A well-crafted strategic plan serves as a guiding framework for organizational decision-making, resource allocation, and performance management, enabling charity organizations to fulfil their purpose and make a meaningful difference in the communities they serve.

Leveraging Partnerships and Collaborations for Greater Impact

Partnerships and collaborations are powerful tools for charity organizations to amplify their impact, leverage resources, and address complex social challenges more effectively. By partnering with other nonprofits, government agencies, businesses, and community groups, charity organizations can combine their strengths, expertise, and networks to achieve shared goals and create positive change. Here's how charity organizations can leverage partnerships and collaborations for greater impact:

1. **Identify Strategic Partners:** Identify potential partners that share similar values, missions, and objectives. Look for organizations with complementary strengths, resources, and expertise that can enhance your own capabilities and expand your reach.

2. **Build Relationships:** Invest time and effort in building strong relationships with potential partners. Engage in open, transparent communication, and seek opportunities for collaboration based on mutual trust, respect, and shared goals.

3. **Define Shared Goals:** Work collaboratively with partners to define shared goals and objectives that align with the mission and priorities of all parties involved. Ensure that each partner has a clear understanding of their roles, responsibilities, and contributions to the collaboration.

4. **Collaborative Planning:** Engage in collaborative planning processes to develop joint initiatives, programs, or projects that leverage the strengths and resources of all partners. Foster creativity and innovation by exploring new approaches and solutions to address shared challenges.

5. **Resource Sharing:** Pool resources, expertise, and networks to maximize impact and efficiency. Share financial resources, staff time, technical expertise, and in-kind support to support joint initiatives and programs.

6. **Capacity Building:** Support capacity-building initiatives that strengthen the capabilities and sustainability of partner organizations. Provide training, technical assistance, and mentorship to build skills, enhance organizational effectiveness, and promote long-term resilience.

7. **Advocacy and Policy Change:** Collaborate on advocacy and policy change initiatives to address systemic issues and create lasting impact. Mobilize collective voices, resources, and networks to advocate for policy reforms, legislative changes, and social justice issues.

8. **Community Engagement:** Involve beneficiaries, community members, and stakeholders in collaborative efforts to ensure relevance, ownership, and sustainability. Engage communities in decision-making, program design, and implementation to promote inclusivity and empowerment.

9. **Measure and Evaluate Impact:** Establish shared metrics, indicators, and evaluation frameworks to measure the impact and effectiveness of collaborative efforts. Regularly assess progress towards shared goals, gather feedback from stakeholders, and use data to inform decision-making and program improvements.

10. **Adaptability and Learning:** Remain flexible and adaptive in responding to changing circumstances, emerging opportunities, and lessons learned from collaborative efforts. Foster a culture of continuous learning, reflection, and improvement to enhance the effectiveness and sustainability of partnerships over time.

By leveraging partnerships and collaborations effectively, charity organizations can multiply their impact, expand their reach, and create lasting change in the communities they serve. Through shared vision, shared goals, and shared action, collaborative efforts have the potential to address complex social challenges and build a more just, equitable, and sustainable world for all.

Innovating and Adapting to Changing Needs and Circumstances

In today's dynamic and ever-changing landscape, charity organizations must continuously innovate and adapt to meet evolving needs and circumstances effectively. By embracing creativity, flexibility, and resilience, charity organizations can remain responsive and relevant in addressing societal challenges and driving positive change. Here are strategies for innovating and adapting to changing needs and circumstances:

1. **Continuous Needs Assessment:** Conduct regular needs assessments to understand emerging challenges, trends, and priorities within communities. Stay connected with beneficiaries,

stakeholders, and partners to gather feedback, identify gaps, and assess evolving needs effectively.

2. **Flexibility in Programming:** Maintain flexibility in programming to respond promptly to changing circumstances and emerging needs. Design programs and services that can be adapted, scaled, or modified based on feedback, data, and evolving community needs.

3. **Innovative Solutions:** Foster a culture of innovation within the organization by encouraging staff, volunteers, and stakeholders to generate creative ideas and solutions. Explore new approaches, technologies, and methodologies that have the potential to address complex challenges more effectively.

4. **Pilot Projects:** Implement pilot projects or experimental initiatives to test innovative ideas and solutions in a controlled environment. Evaluate the feasibility, effectiveness, and scalability of pilot projects before scaling them up or integrating them into core programming.

5. **Partnerships and Collaboration:** Collaborate with other organizations, businesses, academia, and government agencies to access expertise, resources, and networks that can support innovation and adaptation efforts. Leverage partnerships to co-create solutions, share best practices, and amplify impact.

6. **Data-driven Decision Making:** Utilize data and evidence to inform decision-making and resource allocation. Collect, analyze, and utilize data effectively to identify trends, measure impact, and assess the effectiveness of interventions in addressing community needs.

7. **Technology Integration:** Embrace technology and digital solutions to enhance efficiency, reach, and impact. Leverage technology for data management, communication, fundraising, program delivery, and community engagement to streamline operations and improve outcomes.

8. **Capacity Building:** Invest in staff training, skill development, and capacity-building initiatives to equip teams with the knowledge and tools needed to innovate and adapt effectively. Foster a learning culture that encourages experimentation, reflection, and continuous improvement.

9. **Risk Management:** Anticipate and mitigate risks associated with innovation and adaptation efforts. Develop contingency plans, risk management strategies, and crisis response protocols to address unforeseen challenges and ensure organizational resilience.

10. **Feedback Mechanisms:** Establish feedback mechanisms to gather input, insights, and perspectives from beneficiaries, stakeholders, and partners. Actively solicit feedback through surveys, focus groups, community meetings, and digital

platforms to inform decision-making and program improvements.

11. **Learning from Failures:** Embrace failures as learning opportunities and catalysts for innovation. Encourage a culture of experimentation and risk-taking, where failures are analyzed, lessons are learned, and insights are applied to improve future efforts.

By embracing innovation and adaptation, charity organizations can effectively navigate uncertainty, address evolving needs, and remain agile in achieving their mission and driving positive change in communities. Through a commitment to continuous learning, collaboration, and creativity, charity organizations can innovate solutions that have the potential to transform lives and create a more equitable and sustainable future for all.

Chapter 24:

Charity Organization Organizational Chart

Creating a clear and effective organizational chart is essential for charity organizations to establish accountability, define roles and responsibilities, and promote efficient communication and decision-making. The organizational chart provides a visual representation of the organization's structure, hierarchy, and reporting relationships. Here's an example of a typical organizational chart for a charity organization:

1. **Board of Directors:** The Board of Directors is the governing body responsible for providing strategic direction, oversight, and governance for the charity organization. Board members are elected or appointed and represent the interests of stakeholders, donors, and the community.

2. **Executive Director/CEO:** The Executive Director or Chief Executive Officer (CEO) is responsible for leading the organization, implementing the strategic plan, and managing day-to-day operations. The Executive Director reports to the Board of Directors and oversees all staff and programs.

3. **Senior Leadership Team:** The Senior Leadership Team consists of key executives and department heads who work closely with the Executive Director to develop and execute organizational strategies, policies, and initiatives. This team typically includes positions such as Chief Operating Officer (COO),

Chief Financial Officer (CFO), Chief Programs Officer (CPO), and Chief Development Officer (CDO).

4. **Departments/Programs:** The organization's departments or programs are responsible for delivering specific services, programs, or functions aligned with the organization's mission and objectives. Common departments include Programs/Services, Finance/Administration, Fundraising/Development, Marketing/Communications, Human Resources, and IT/Technology.

5. **Staff Teams:** Within each department or program, there are staff members responsible for executing tasks, implementing projects, and achieving goals. Staff members report to department heads or program managers and collaborate with colleagues across the organization.

6. **Volunteers:** Volunteers play a crucial role in supporting the organization's mission and activities. They may assist with program delivery, fundraising events, administrative tasks, and advocacy efforts. Volunteer coordinators or managers oversee volunteer recruitment, training, and engagement.

7. **Advisory Committees/Task Forces:** The organization may establish advisory committees or task forces composed of experts, stakeholders, or community members to provide input, guidance, and support on specific issues, initiatives, or projects.

8. **External Partners/Partnerships:** Charity organizations often collaborate with external partners, including other nonprofits, government agencies, businesses, foundations, and community organizations. These partnerships enable the organization to leverage resources, expertise, and networks to achieve shared goals and maximize impact.

9. **Beneficiaries/Community Members:** The ultimate beneficiaries of the charity organization's programs and services are the individuals, families, or communities it serves. Their needs, interests, and feedback inform the organization's decision-making and programmatic priorities.

By establishing a clear organizational chart, charity organizations can promote transparency, accountability, and efficiency in their operations, ensuring that resources are effectively utilized to advance their mission and serve their constituents. Regular review and adaptation of the organizational structure can help charity organizations remain responsive to changing needs and evolving priorities over time.

Roles and Responsibilities within a Charity Organization

In a charity organization, each member of the team plays a vital role in fulfilling the organization's mission, delivering programs and services, and ensuring effective operations. Here are common roles and their associated responsibilities within a charity organization:

1. **Board of Directors:**
   - Provide strategic direction and governance oversight.
   - Set organizational policies, goals, and priorities.
   - Ensure legal and ethical compliance.
   - Hire, evaluate, and support the Executive Director.
   - Monitor financial performance and accountability.
2. **Executive Director/CEO:**
   - Provide visionary leadership and strategic direction.
   - Oversee day-to-day operations and program implementation.
   - Develop and execute organizational strategies and plans.
   - Manage organizational finances, budgets, and resources.
   - Build and maintain relationships with stakeholders, donors, and partners.
   - Represent the organization in the community and advocate for its mission.
3. **Senior Leadership Team:**
   - Collaborate with the Executive Director to develop organizational strategies and plans.
   - Lead and manage departments or functional areas within the organization.
   - Implement policies, procedures, and initiatives to achieve organizational goals.
   - Provide guidance, support, and mentorship to staff members.

- Monitor and evaluate program performance and impact.
- Communicate effectively with the Board of Directors, staff, and external stakeholders.

4. **Departments/Programs:**
   - Plan, implement, and evaluate programs and services aligned with the organization's mission.
   - Manage budgets, resources, and timelines for program delivery.
   - Recruit, train, and supervise staff and volunteers.
   - Collect and analyze data to measure program effectiveness and outcomes.
   - Collaborate with other departments and stakeholders to achieve shared objectives.

5. **Staff Members:**
   - Execute tasks, projects, and responsibilities within their respective roles and departments.
   - Adhere to organizational policies, procedures, and standards of conduct.
   - Communicate effectively with colleagues, supervisors, and stakeholders.
   - Participate in training, professional development, and performance evaluation processes.
   - Contribute ideas, feedback, and solutions to improve organizational effectiveness and impact.

6. **Volunteers:**

- Support program delivery, events, and initiatives as assigned by staff members.
- Follow instructions, guidelines, and protocols provided by staff and supervisors.
- Demonstrate commitment, reliability, and professionalism in volunteer roles.
- Attend training sessions, orientations, and meetings as required.
- Provide feedback and suggestions for improving the volunteer experience and program effectiveness.

7. **External Partners/Partnerships:**
- Collaborate with the organization to achieve shared goals and objectives.
- Provide financial support, resources, expertise, or in-kind contributions.
- Participate in joint initiatives, projects, or events.
- Communicate openly, transparently, and respectfully with organizational representatives.
- Foster positive relationships and maintain mutual trust and accountability.

By clearly defining roles and responsibilities within the charity organization, individuals can work together effectively to advance the organization's mission, serve its constituents, and make a positive impact in the community. Regular communication, collaboration, and alignment of efforts ensure that everyone is working towards shared goals and objectives, fostering a culture of teamwork, accountability, and success.

Hierarchical Structure and Reporting Lines

A hierarchical structure and clearly defined reporting lines are essential components of organizational effectiveness within a charity organization. This structure helps streamline communication, facilitate decision-making, and promote accountability at all levels. Here's an example of a hierarchical structure and reporting lines within a charity organization:

1. **Board of Directors:**
   - The highest governing body is responsible for providing strategic oversight and direction to the organization.
   - Reports to: Shareholders (if applicable) and stakeholders, including donors, community members, and beneficiaries.

2. **Executive Director/CEO:**
   - The senior executive is responsible for overseeing the day-to-day operations and implementing the strategic direction set by the Board of Directors.
   - Reports to: Board of Directors.

3. **Senior Leadership Team:**
   - Consists of key executives and department heads responsible for leading various functional areas within the organization.
   - Typically includes positions such as Chief Operating Officer (COO), Chief Financial Officer (CFO), Chief Programs Officer (CPO), and Chief Development Officer (CDO).
   - Reports to: Executive Director/CEO.

4. **Departments/Programs:**
   - Organizational units are responsible for delivering specific programs, services, or functions aligned with the organization's mission and objectives.
   - Departments may include Programs/Services, Finance/Administration, Fundraising/Development, Marketing/Communications, Human Resources, and IT/Technology.
   - Reports to: Senior Leadership Team or directly to the Executive Director/CEO, depending on the organizational structure.

5. **Managers/Supervisors:**
   - Oversee the day-to-day operations of their respective departments or teams.
   - Responsible for assigning tasks, supervising staff, and ensuring the efficient delivery of programs and services.
   - Reports to: Department Heads or Senior Leadership Team.

6. **Staff Members:**
   - Execute tasks, projects, and responsibilities within their respective roles and departments.
   - Follow instructions, guidelines, and protocols provided by managers and supervisors.
   - Collaborate with colleagues and contribute to achieving departmental and organizational goals.
   - Reports to: Managers or Supervisors within their respective departments.

7. **Volunteers:**
   - Support program delivery, events, and initiatives as assigned by staff members.
   - Follow instructions and guidelines provided by volunteer coordinators or managers.
   - Work alongside staff members to achieve program objectives and goals.
   - Reports to: Volunteer Coordinators or Managers.
8. **External Partners/Partnerships:**
   - Collaborate with the organization to achieve shared goals and objectives.
   - Provide support, resources, expertise, or in-kind contributions as needed.
   - Participate in joint initiatives, projects, or events.
   - Reports to: Designated staff members or project leads within the organization.

By establishing a hierarchical structure and clear reporting lines, charity organizations can promote accountability, efficiency, and alignment across all levels of the organization. Effective communication and collaboration between different levels and departments ensure that everyone is working towards common goals, fostering a culture of teamwork and success within the organization.

Ensuring Clarity and Efficiency in Organizational Operations

Clarity and efficiency in organizational operations are critical for charity organizations to fulfil their mission effectively, maximize impact, and steward resources responsibly. Here are key strategies to ensure clarity and efficiency in organizational operations:

1. **Clear Mission and Objectives:** Ensure that the organization's mission and objectives are clearly defined, understood, and communicated to all stakeholders. Align operational activities with the organization's mission to maintain focus and clarity in decision-making.
2. **Transparent Communication:** Foster open, transparent communication channels within the organization. Ensure that information flows freely between departments, teams, and hierarchical levels to facilitate collaboration, problem-solving, and decision-making.
3. **Defined Roles and Responsibilities:** Clearly define roles, responsibilities, and reporting lines for all staff members, volunteers, and stakeholders. Ensure that each individual understands their contribution to the organization's mission and how their work aligns with broader objectives.
4. **Streamlined Processes and Procedures:** Identify and eliminate unnecessary bureaucracy, red tape, and inefficiencies in organizational processes and procedures. Streamline workflows, standardize practices, and automate routine tasks to increase productivity and reduce administrative burden.
5. **Regular Performance Reviews:** Implement regular performance reviews and feedback mechanisms to evaluate individual and team performance against established goals and objectives. Provide constructive feedback, recognition, and support to motivate and empower staff members.
6. **Data-Driven Decision-Making:** Utilize data and evidence to inform decision-making and resource

allocation. Collect, analyze, and utilize data effectively to measure performance, track progress, and identify areas for improvement in organizational operations.

7. **Training and Development:** Invest in staff training and professional development initiatives to enhance skills, knowledge, and competencies relevant to organizational roles and responsibilities. Provide opportunities for continuous learning and growth to support career advancement and organizational effectiveness.

8. **Collaborative Problem-Solving:** Encourage collaborative problem-solving and decision-making processes that involve input from diverse perspectives and stakeholders. Foster a culture of innovation, creativity, and adaptability to address challenges and seize opportunities effectively.

9. **Effective Meetings and Communication:** Conduct efficient and productive meetings that have clear agendas, objectives, and outcomes. Ensure that meetings are well-prepared, focused, and action-oriented, with follow-up actions assigned and tracked for accountability.

10. **Resource Optimization:** Optimize the allocation and utilization of resources, including financial, human, and material resources, to maximize impact and efficiency. Prioritize investments in high-impact programs, initiatives, and activities aligned with organizational priorities.

11. **Continuous Improvement:** Foster a culture of continuous improvement and learning within the organization. Encourage staff members to identify

areas for improvement, experiment with new approaches, and share best practices to enhance organizational effectiveness over time.

By implementing these strategies, charity organizations can create a culture of clarity, efficiency, and effectiveness in their operations. Clarity in mission, roles, and communication, coupled with streamlined processes, data-driven decision-making, and a commitment to continuous improvement, enables organizations to achieve their goals, maximize impact, and make a positive difference in the communities they serve.

Chapter 25:

A-Z Charity Terminology

A comprehensive understanding of charity terminology is essential for effective communication and decision-making within the nonprofit sector. Here's an A-Z guide to common charity terminology:

A. **501(c)(3):** A section of the Internal Revenue Code that designates an organization as tax-exempt and eligible to receive tax-deductible charitable contributions.

B. **Beneficiary:** The individual, group, or community that receives assistance, services, or support from a charity organization.

C. **Community Outreach:** Activities and initiatives aimed at engaging and serving communities, raising awareness, and addressing local needs.

D. **Donor:** An individual, corporation, foundation, or organization that provides financial or in-kind contributions to support the mission and activities of a charity organization.

E. **Endowment:** Funds set aside and invested to provide income for ongoing support of a charity organization's programs and operations.

F. **Fundraising:** The process of soliciting donations, grants, sponsorships, and other sources of funding to support a charity organization's activities and programs.

G. **Grant:** Financial assistance provided by a foundation, government agency, or other funding entity to support specific projects or initiatives.

H. **Humanitarian Aid:** Assistance provided to alleviate human suffering and address basic needs, often in response to emergencies, disasters, or crises.

I. **Impact Assessment:** Evaluation of a charity organization's programs and activities to measure their effectiveness, outcomes, and social impact.

J. **Joint Venture:** Collaboration between two or more organizations to undertake a specific project, initiative, or program.

K. **Key Performance Indicators (KPIs):** Quantifiable metrics used to measure the success and performance of a charity organization's programs, operations, and impact.

L. **Legacy Giving:** Donations made through wills, bequests, or estate planning to support a charity organization's work beyond the donor's lifetime.

M. **Mission Statement:** A concise statement that defines the purpose, values, and goals of a charity organization, guiding its activities and decision-making.

N. **Nonprofit Organization:** An organization that operates for purposes other than profit-making, typically focused on advancing a charitable, educational, religious, or social cause.

O. **Outreach Programs:** Initiatives and activities aimed at reaching out to underserved communities, populations, or individuals to provide support, resources, and services.

P. **Philanthropy:** The practice of promoting the welfare of others through charitable giving, volunteerism, and advocacy to address social issues and improve quality of life.

Q. **Quality Standards:** Guidelines, benchmarks, or criteria used to assess and ensure the quality, effectiveness, and ethical conduct of charity organization's programs and operations.

R. **Resilience:** The ability of a charity organization to adapt, recover, and thrive in the face of challenges, setbacks, and changing circumstances.

S. **Social Impact:** The measurable, positive change or outcomes resulting from a charity organization's activities, programs, and interventions.

T. **Transparency:** Openness, honesty, and accountability in charity organization's operations, governance, and financial management, including clear reporting to stakeholders.

U. **Unrestricted Funds:** Funds received by a charity organization that can be used for any purpose or program, providing flexibility in addressing emerging needs and priorities.

V. **Volunteerism:** The act of offering one's time, skills, and resources to support a charity organization's mission and activities without financial compensation.

W. **Workforce Development:** Programs and initiatives aimed at enhancing the skills, knowledge, and employability of individuals to improve their economic prospects and well-being.

X. **eXcellence:** Commitment to achieving high standards of performance, impact, and service delivery in charity organization's operations and programs.

Y. **Youth Engagement:** Involvement of young people in charity organization's activities, decision-making, and advocacy efforts to address issues affecting their communities and futures.

Z. **Zero-Based Budgeting:** Budgeting approach where a charity organization starts from scratch each budget cycle, re-evaluating all expenses and justifying each expenditure based on needs and priorities.

By familiarizing themselves with these terms, charity organizations can enhance their capacity for effective communication, collaboration, and decision-making, ultimately contributing to their ability to achieve their mission and make a positive impact in the communities they serve.

Glossary of Key Terms and Concepts in the Charity Sector

1. **501(c)(3):** A section of the Internal Revenue Code (USA)that designates an organization as tax-exempt and eligible to receive tax-deductible charitable contributions. Check your local/national Authority and Tax department.

2. **Advocacy:** Efforts to promote or support a particular cause, policy, or issue through public awareness campaigns, lobbying, and community mobilization.

3. **Board of Directors:** The governing body of a charity organization responsible for providing strategic direction, oversight, and governance.
4. **Capacity Building:** Initiatives and activities aimed at strengthening the skills, resources, and effectiveness of charity organizations to achieve their mission and goals.
5. **Charitable Giving:** Donations, gifts, or contributions made by individuals, corporations, or foundations to support charity organizations and their activities.
6. **Community Engagement:** Collaboration and involvement of community members, stakeholders, and beneficiaries in charity organization's programs, decision-making, and activities.
7. **Donor Stewardship:** Practices and strategies aimed at cultivating, recognizing, and retaining donors through effective communication, relationship-building, and acknowledgement of their contributions.
8. **Endowment Fund:** Funds set aside and invested to provide income for ongoing support of charity organization's programs and operations.
9. **Ethical Fundraising:** Practices and principles that promote honesty, integrity, and accountability in soliciting and managing donations and funds for charity organizations.
10. **Grantmaking:** The process of awarding grants or financial assistance to nonprofit organizations, individuals, or projects to support specific initiatives or objectives.
11. **Impact Assessment:** Evaluation of charity organization's programs and activities to measure their effectiveness, outcomes, and social impact.
12. **Nonprofit Organization:** An organization that operates for purposes other than profit-making, typically focused on advancing a charitable, educational, religious, or social cause.

13. **Philanthropy:** The practice of promoting the welfare of others through charitable giving, volunteerism, and advocacy to address social issues and improve quality of life.
14. **Program Evaluation:** Systematic assessment of charity organization's programs and activities to determine their efficiency, effectiveness, and impact on intended beneficiaries.
15. **Social Entrepreneurship:** Innovative approaches to addressing social problems and creating sustainable solutions through entrepreneurial ventures and business models.
16. **Stakeholder Engagement:** Involvement and collaboration of individuals, groups, and organizations with an interest or stake in the charity organization's mission, activities, or outcomes.
17. **Sustainability:** The ability of a charity organization to maintain and continue its programs, operations, and impact over the long term, often through diversified funding sources and strategic planning.
18. **Transparency:** Openness, honesty, and accountability in charity organization's operations, governance, and financial management, including clear reporting to stakeholders.
19. **Volunteerism:** The act of offering one's time, skills, and resources to support a charity organization's mission and activities without financial compensation.
20. **Workforce Development:** Programs and initiatives aimed at enhancing the skills, knowledge, and employability of individuals to improve their economic prospects and well-being.

This glossary provides a foundation for understanding key terms and concepts in the charity sector, supporting effective communication, collaboration, and decision-making among stakeholders within the nonprofit community.

Definitions of Commonly Used Jargon and Acronyms

1. **NGO:** Non-Governmental Organization - A nonprofit organization that operates independently of government control, often focused on addressing social, environmental, or humanitarian issues.

2. **CSR:** Corporate Social Responsibility - A business model that encourages companies to be socially accountable by considering the impact of their activities on society and the environment.

3. **NPO:** Nonprofit Organization - An organization that uses surplus revenues to achieve its goals rather than distributing them as profit or dividends.

4. **IRS:** Internal Revenue Service - The federal agency responsible for collecting taxes and enforcing tax laws in the United States. Check Your local/National Authorities.

5. **ROI:** Return on Investment - A measure of the profitability of an investment relative to its cost, often used to evaluate the effectiveness of fundraising efforts.

6. **EIN:** Employer Identification Number - A unique nine-digit number assigned by the IRS to identify a business entity for tax purposes.

7. **FTE:** Full-Time Equivalent - A unit of measurement used to represent the workload of an employee or group of employees on a full-time basis.

8. **KPI:** Key Performance Indicator - Quantifiable metrics used to evaluate the success or effectiveness of an organization's activities, often

used in strategic planning and performance management.

9. **RFP:** Request for Proposal - A document soliciting bids from vendors or service providers to complete a project or provide goods or services.

10. **ROI:** Return on Investment - A measure of the profitability of an investment relative to its cost, often used to evaluate the effectiveness of fundraising efforts.

11. **CBO:** Community-Based Organization - An organization that operates at the local level and is focused on addressing the needs and interests of a specific community or population.

12. **GDP:** Gross Domestic Product - The total value of goods and services produced within a country's borders during a specific period, often used as a measure of economic performance.

13. **UNICEF:** United Nations International Children's Emergency Fund - An international organization that provides humanitarian aid and development assistance to children and mothers in developing countries.

14. **USAID:** United States Agency for International Development - The federal agency responsible for administering civilian foreign aid and development assistance programs on behalf of the United States government.

15. **IRS:** Internal Revenue Service - The federal agency responsible for collecting taxes and enforcing tax laws in the United States.

16. **CEO:** Chief Executive Officer - The highest-ranking executive in a company or organization, responsible

for making major corporate decisions, managing operations, and implementing policies.

17. **SME:** Subject Matter Expert - An individual with specialized knowledge, skills, or expertise in a particular field or subject area.

18. **DOS:** Department of State - The federal agency responsible for conducting U.S. foreign policy and representing the United States abroad.

19. **HR:** Human Resources - The department within an organization responsible for managing personnel-related matters, including recruitment, hiring, training, and employee relations.

20. **SOP:** Standard Operating Procedure - A set of step-by-step instructions or protocols outlining how to complete a specific task or activity within an organization.

Understanding this jargon and acronyms commonly used in the nonprofit sector can help facilitate effective communication and collaboration among stakeholders, ensuring clarity and efficiency in organizational operations and decision-making processes.

Enhancing Understanding and Communication within the Charity Community

Effective communication is crucial for fostering collaboration, sharing best practices, and advancing common goals within the charity community. Here are strategies to enhance understanding and communication within the charity community:

1. **Clear Communication Channels:** Establish clear and accessible communication channels, including email lists, newsletters, social media groups, and

online forums, to facilitate information sharing and networking among charity professionals.

2. **Regular Networking Events:** Organize regular networking events, workshops, and conferences where charity professionals can meet, exchange ideas, and build relationships. These events provide opportunities for learning, collaboration, and mutual support.

3. **Knowledge Sharing Platforms:** Create online platforms or databases where charity organizations can share resources, case studies, and best practices. Encourage members to contribute articles, reports, and success stories to enrich the collective knowledge base.

4. **Training and Capacity Building:** Offer training sessions, webinars, and workshops on topics relevant to charity management, fundraising, program development, and governance. Provide opportunities for skill-building and professional development tailored to the needs of charity professionals.

5. **Collaborative Projects:** Encourage collaboration on joint projects, initiatives, or campaigns that address common challenges or objectives within the charity community. Collaborative projects foster teamwork, innovation, and collective impact.

6. **Mentorship Programs:** Establish mentorship programs where experienced charity professionals can mentor emerging leaders and newcomers in the sector. Mentorship programs facilitate knowledge transfer, skill development, and career advancement.

7. **Peer Learning Groups:** Form peer learning groups or communities of practice focused on specific areas of

interest or expertise, such as fundraising, program evaluation, or advocacy. Peer learning groups provide opportunities for peer-to-peer support, feedback, and learning.

8. **Feedback Mechanisms:** Solicit feedback from charity professionals through surveys, focus groups, or feedback forms to identify areas for improvement and address community needs. Actively listen to feedback and incorporate suggestions to enhance communication and engagement.

9. **Diversity and Inclusion:** Foster diversity and inclusion within the charity community by promoting representation and participation from individuals of diverse backgrounds, perspectives, and experiences. Embrace diversity as a source of strength and innovation.

10. **Recognition and Appreciation:** Recognize and appreciate the contributions of charity professionals through awards, honours, or appreciation events. Celebrate achievements and milestones to boost morale and reinforce a sense of community.

11. **Transparency and Accountability:** Practice transparency and accountability in communication, decision-making, and resource allocation within the charity community. Build trust and credibility by being open, honest, and accountable to stakeholders.

12. **Cross-Sector Collaboration:** Foster collaboration and partnerships with other sectors, including government, academia, business, and civil society, to leverage resources, expertise, and networks for collective impact.

By implementing these strategies, the charity community can strengthen understanding, collaboration, and communication, ultimately enhancing its ability to address social challenges, advance its mission, and make a positive impact on society.

Chapter 26:

Effective management of a charity organization requires adherence to certain principles and practices. Here are some key do's and don'ts for charity organization management:

Do's:

1. **Do Establish Clear Goals and Objectives:** Clearly define the mission, vision, and objectives of the charity organization to guide decision-making and resource allocation.

2. **Do Prioritize Transparency and Accountability:** Maintain transparency in financial management, operations, and governance practices to build trust with donors, beneficiaries, and stakeholders.

3. **Do Foster a Culture of Ethical Conduct:** Promote ethical behaviour and integrity among staff, volunteers, and board members, ensuring adherence to ethical standards in all organizational activities.

4. **Do Cultivate Relationships with Donors:** Build strong relationships with donors through personalized communication, regular updates on impact, and acknowledgement of their contributions.

5. **Do Invest in Capacity Building:** Invest in staff training, professional development, and organizational capacity building to enhance skills, knowledge, and effectiveness.

6. **Do Measure and Evaluate Impact:** Implement systems for monitoring, evaluation, and impact assessment to track progress towards goals and improve program effectiveness.

7. **Do Embrace Innovation:** Embrace innovation and creativity in program design, fundraising strategies, and organizational practices to adapt to changing needs and trends.

8. **Do Collaborate with Partners:** Collaborate with other organizations, government agencies, and stakeholders to leverage resources, expertise, and networks for greater impact.

Don'ts:
1. **Don't Misuse Funds:** Avoid misusing funds or diverting resources intended for charitable purposes for personal gain or unauthorized expenses.
2. **Don't Neglect Legal Compliance:** Ensure compliance with relevant laws, regulations, and reporting requirements governing charity organizations to avoid legal issues and penalties.
3. **Don't Overlook Risk Management:** Identify and mitigate risks associated with financial management, program delivery, and organizational operations to safeguard the organization's reputation and sustainability.
4. **Don't Operate in Isolation:** Avoid operating in isolation from the communities and beneficiaries served, and actively seek input and participation from stakeholders in decision-making processes.
5. **Don't Ignore Donor Relations:** Avoid neglecting donor relations or taking donors for granted, as maintaining strong donor relationships is crucial for long-term sustainability.
6. **Don't Engage in Discriminatory Practices:** Refrain from engaging in discriminatory practices or policies based on race, gender, ethnicity, religion, or other factors, and promote diversity and inclusion within the organization.
7. **Don't Lose Sight of Mission:** Avoid mission drift or losing sight of the organization's core mission and values, and ensure that all activities and decisions align with the organization's purpose.
8. **Don't Rely Solely on Fundraising:** While fundraising is essential, don't rely solely on fundraising efforts for

financial sustainability. Diversify revenue streams and explore innovative funding models.

By adhering to these do's and don'ts, charity organizations can uphold ethical standards, promote transparency and accountability, and maximize their impact in serving their beneficiaries and communities.

Best Practices for Ethical and Effective Leadership

Ethical and effective leadership is essential for guiding charity organizations toward their mission and achieving a positive impact. Here are some best practices for ethical and effective leadership in the charity sector:

1. **Lead by Example:** Demonstrate integrity, honesty, and ethical behaviour in all aspects of leadership, serving as a role model for staff, volunteers, and stakeholders.
2. **Communicate Vision and Values:** Clearly communicate the organization's mission, vision, and values to inspire and align stakeholders toward common goals.
3. **Foster Trust and Transparency:** Build trust and transparency through open communication, active listening, and accountability in decision-making and operations.
4. **Empower and Delegate:** Empower staff and volunteers by delegating authority, providing autonomy, and encouraging innovation and initiative.
5. **Promote Diversity and Inclusion:** Foster a culture of diversity and inclusion by valuing and respecting the perspectives, backgrounds, and contributions of all individuals.
6. **Develop Talent:** Invest in staff development, training, and mentorship programs to cultivate talent, build leadership capacity, and retain top performers.
7. **Collaborate and Build Partnerships:** Collaborate with other organizations, government agencies, and stakeholders to leverage resources, expertise, and networks for greater impact.

8. **Strategic Decision-Making:** Make strategic decisions based on evidence, data, and informed analysis, considering the long-term implications and potential risks and opportunities.
9. **Embrace Change and Adaptability:** Embrace change, innovation, and adaptability to respond effectively to evolving needs, challenges, and opportunities in the charity sector.
10. **Practice Self-Care:** Prioritize self-care, work-life balance, and personal well-being to sustain energy, resilience, and effectiveness as a leader.
11. **Promote Ethical Fundraising:** Ensure ethical fundraising practices by adhering to donor stewardship principles, respecting donor privacy, and maintaining transparency in financial management.
12. **Manage Conflict Constructively:** Address conflicts and disagreements constructively through open dialogue, mediation, and conflict resolution techniques, fostering a positive and respectful work environment.
13. **Accountability and Evaluation:** Establish systems for accountability and evaluation to monitor progress, measure impact, and learn from successes and challenges.
14. **Engage Stakeholders:** Engage stakeholders, including donors, beneficiaries, volunteers, and community members, in decision-making processes and program design to ensure relevance and ownership.
15. **Lead with Empathy and Compassion:** Demonstrate empathy, compassion, and humility in leadership, recognizing and valuing the dignity and worth of every individual.

By embracing these best practices, charity leaders can foster ethical conduct, inspire trust and confidence, and lead their organizations toward greater impact and sustainability.

Pitfalls to Avoid in Charity Operations and Fundraising

While charity operations and fundraising are crucial for supporting the organization's mission, several pitfalls can hinder effectiveness and ethical conduct. Here are some common pitfalls to avoid:

1. **Lack of Transparency:** Failing to maintain transparency in financial management, program delivery, and governance practices can erode trust with donors, beneficiaries, and stakeholders.
2. **Overhead Obsession:** Overemphasizing low overhead costs at the expense of investing in organizational capacity, program quality, and impact can undermine long-term sustainability and effectiveness.
3. **Mission Drift:** Losing focus on the organization's core mission and values, or pursuing activities outside its scope, can dilute impact and confuse stakeholders.
4. **Donor Dependency:** Relying too heavily on a small group of donors or a single source of funding can create financial instability and vulnerability to shifts in donor priorities or economic conditions.
5. **Ethical Concerns:** Engaging in unethical fundraising practices, such as pressuring donors, misrepresenting impact, or misusing funds, can damage the organization's reputation and credibility.
6. **Inadequate Risk Management:** Ignoring or underestimating risks associated with financial management, program delivery, or external factors can leave the organization vulnerable to crises or disruptions.
7. **Failure to Adapt:** Failing to adapt to changing needs, trends, or circumstances in the operating environment can result in irrelevance, inefficiency, or missed opportunities for impact.

8. **Burnout and Staff Turnover:** Neglecting staff well-being, work-life balance, and professional development can lead to burnout, high staff turnover, and diminished organizational capacity.
9. **Ineffective Communication:** Poor communication with donors, beneficiaries, and stakeholders can result in misunderstandings, missed opportunities for engagement, and loss of support.
10. **Lack of Evaluation:** Neglecting to monitor and evaluate program effectiveness, outcomes, and impact can limit learning, improvement, and accountability.
11. **Ignoring Legal Compliance:** Disregarding legal and regulatory requirements, such as tax laws, fundraising regulations, and reporting obligations, can result in legal liabilities and reputational damage.
12. **Ignoring Donor Stewardship:** Failing to steward donors through timely acknowledgement, appreciation, and recognition can lead to donor attrition and loss of support.
13. **Ineffective Fundraising Strategies:** Relying on outdated or ineffective fundraising strategies, without adapting to donor preferences or market trends, can result in stagnant revenue growth.
14. **Underinvesting in Capacity Building:** Neglecting to invest in organizational capacity building, staff training, and infrastructure improvements can limit the organization's ability to scale and deliver quality programs.
15. **Ignoring Diversity and Inclusion:** Neglecting to promote diversity, equity, and inclusion in organizational practices and decision-making can result in exclusion, discrimination, and missed opportunities for innovation and impact.

Here are additional some pitfalls to avoid:
1. **Lack of Transparency:** Failing to provide transparent and accurate information about the organization's

activities, finances, and impact can erode trust with donors, beneficiaries, and stakeholders.

2. **Mismanagement of Funds:** Poor financial management, including misappropriation of funds, inadequate budgeting, or failure to adhere to accounting standards, can lead to financial instability and damage the organization's reputation.

3. **Overreliance on a Single Source of Funding:** Depending heavily on a single source of funding, such as government grants or corporate donations, leaves the organization vulnerable to funding fluctuations and increases the risk of financial instability.

4. **Ineffective Governance:** Weak governance structures, including lack of oversight, conflicts of interest, or inadequate board engagement, can hinder decision-making, accountability, and organizational effectiveness.

5. **Mission Drift:** Losing sight of the organization's mission and core values, or pursuing activities outside of the organization's mandate, can dilute impact and undermine the organization's credibility and relevance.

6. **Ignoring Compliance Requirements:** Neglecting legal and regulatory requirements, such as tax filings, reporting obligations, or compliance with fundraising regulations, can result in legal sanctions, fines, or loss of tax-exempt status.

7. **Donor Mismanagement:** Failing to properly steward and cultivate donor relationships, including inadequate acknowledgement, recognition, or communication with donors, can lead to donor dissatisfaction and loss of support.

8. **Ignoring Risks and Contingencies:** Failing to identify and mitigate risks, such as cybersecurity threats, reputational risks, or programmatic risks, can leave the organization vulnerable to disruptions and crises.

9. **Ineffective Program Design:** Implementing programs without adequate needs assessment, planning, or evaluation can result in inefficiencies, ineffective use of resources, and limited impact on beneficiaries.
10. **Poor Volunteer Management:** Inadequate recruitment, training, or supervision of volunteers can lead to disengagement, turnover, and negative experiences for both volunteers and beneficiaries.
11. **Overhead Stigma:** Succumbing to pressure to minimize administrative costs and overhead expenses at the expense of organizational capacity and effectiveness can hinder long-term sustainability and impact.
12. **Failure to Adapt to Change:** Resisting change or failing to adapt to evolving needs, trends, and technologies can result in organizational stagnation, loss of relevance, and missed opportunities for innovation and growth.
13. **Donor-Driven Programs:** Designing programs solely based on donor preferences or funding restrictions, rather than the needs and priorities of beneficiaries, can compromise program quality and effectiveness.
14. **Lack of Diversity and Inclusion:** Failing to embrace diversity, equity, and inclusion in organizational policies, practices, and decision-making processes can result in exclusionary practices and limited representation of marginalized communities.
15. **Poor Communication and Engagement:** Inadequate communication with stakeholders, including donors, beneficiaries, and volunteers, can lead to misunderstandings, disengagement, and loss of support.

By proactively addressing these pitfalls and implementing sound management practices, charity organizations can enhance their effectiveness, sustainability, and ability to achieve their mission and make a positive impact in the communities they serve. By being mindful of these pitfalls and implementing proactive measures to address them, charity organizations can enhance their effectiveness, sustainability, and ethical conduct in operations and fundraising efforts.

While charity operations and fundraising are essential for achieving the mission of nonprofit organizations, there are common pitfalls that leaders should be aware of to ensure effectiveness and sustainability.

Upholding Integrity and Trustworthiness in all Activities

Maintaining integrity and trustworthiness is paramount for charity organizations to fulfil their missions effectively and earn the confidence of stakeholders. Here's how charity organizations can uphold integrity and trustworthiness in all activities:

1. **Adherence to Ethical Standards:** Ensure that all activities, decisions, and interactions are guided by ethical principles, honesty, and integrity.
2. **Transparency:** Practice openness and transparency in all organizational operations, including financial management, governance practices, and program outcomes.
3. **Accountability:** Hold yourself and your organization accountable for actions, commitments, and outcomes, and take responsibility for mistakes or shortcomings.
4. **Compliance with Regulations:** Abide by all relevant laws, regulations, and reporting requirements governing charity organizations to maintain legal compliance and credibility.
5. **Fair and Equitable Treatment:** Treat all stakeholders, including donors, beneficiaries, staff, volunteers, and partners, with fairness, respect, and dignity, regardless of their background or status.

6. **Confidentiality and Privacy:** Safeguard sensitive information and respect the confidentiality and privacy rights of individuals and organizations, particularly donors and beneficiaries.
7. **Conflict of Interest Management:** Implement policies and procedures to identify, disclose, and manage conflicts of interest among board members, staff, and volunteers to avoid real or perceived impropriety.
8. **Stewardship of Resources:** Use resources, including financial, human, and material resources, prudently, efficiently, and for their intended charitable purposes.
9. **Donor Relations:** Foster strong relationships with donors through clear communication, donor stewardship, and transparency in how their contributions are used to support the organization's mission.
10. **Program Integrity:** Ensure that all programs and activities are aligned with the organization's mission, goals, and values and that they deliver meaningful, measurable impact to beneficiaries.
11. **Whistleblower Protection:** Establish mechanisms for staff, volunteers, and stakeholders to report concerns or misconduct confidentially and without fear of retaliation, and take appropriate action to address reported issues.
12. **Continuous Improvement:** Commit to continuous learning, reflection, and improvement to strengthen organizational effectiveness, impact, and integrity over time.
13. **Code of Conduct:** Develop and enforce a code of conduct or ethics policy that outlines expected standards of behaviour and provides guidance on ethical decision-making for all members of the organization.

14. **Independent Oversight:** Maintain independent oversight mechanisms, such as an audit committee or external advisory board, to ensure accountability and integrity in organizational practices.
15. **Crisis Preparedness:** Develop and implement a crisis management plan to address potential reputational risks, emergencies, or unforeseen challenges, maintaining transparency and trust even in challenging circumstances.

By prioritizing integrity and trustworthiness in all activities, charity organizations can strengthen their credibility, build lasting relationships with stakeholders, and fulfil their missions with integrity and impact.

Chapter 27:

Best Practices in Charity Organization Management
Effective management is essential for charity organizations
to achieve their missions, maximize impact, and ensure
sustainability. Here are some best practices in charity
organization management:

1. **Strategic Planning:** Develop and implement a
   strategic plan that articulates the organization's
   mission, vision, goals, and strategies for achieving
   them. Regularly review and update the plan to adapt
   to changing circumstances and priorities.
2. **Governance:** Establish a strong governance
   structure with a board of directors that provides
   oversight, guidance, and support to the organization's
   leadership. Ensure that board members are diverse,
   knowledgeable, and committed to the organization's
   mission.
3. **Financial Management:** Maintain sound financial
   management practices, including budgeting,
   accounting, and internal controls, to ensure
   transparency, accountability, and compliance with
   regulatory requirements.
4. **Fundraising:** Implement a diversified fundraising
   strategy that includes individual giving, grants,
   corporate partnerships, events, and other revenue
   streams. Cultivate relationships with donors and
   supporters, communicate impact, and steward funds
   effectively.
5. **Program Development and Evaluation:** Design and
   implement programs that address identified needs
   and achieve measurable outcomes. Regularly
   evaluate program effectiveness, collect data, and
   use evidence-based practices to inform decision-
   making and improve results.

6. **Human Resources Management:** Recruit, retain, and develop a talented and committed staff team. Provide opportunities for professional growth, support staff well-being, and foster a culture of collaboration, inclusivity, and accountability.
7. **Volunteer Engagement:** Engage volunteers effectively by providing meaningful opportunities for involvement, training and support, recognition, and feedback. Leverage the skills and expertise of volunteers to augment the organization's capacity and impact.
8. **Partnerships and Collaboration:** Collaborate with other organizations, government agencies, businesses, and community groups to leverage resources, share expertise, and maximize impact. Build strategic partnerships that complement the organization's strengths and extend its reach.
9. **Risk Management:** Identify potential risks and develop strategies to mitigate them, including financial risks, operational risks, reputational risks, and risks related to external factors such as regulatory changes or economic downturns.
10. **Technology and Innovation:** Embrace technology and innovation to enhance organizational efficiency, effectiveness, and reach. Invest in technology infrastructure, digital platforms, and data analytics to streamline operations, improve communication, and amplify impact.
11. **Communication and Advocacy:** Develop a comprehensive communication strategy to raise awareness about the organization's mission, engage stakeholders, and advocate for social change. Use storytelling, media outreach, and digital channels to amplify the organization's voice and impact.
12. **Continuous Learning and Improvement:** Foster a culture of learning, reflection, and continuous improvement within the organization. Encourage staff

and board members to seek feedback, evaluate performance, and adapt strategies based on lessons learned.

13. **Ethical Leadership and Integrity:** Lead with integrity, honesty, and ethical behaviour, setting a positive example for staff, volunteers, and stakeholders. Uphold high ethical standards in all organizational activities, including fundraising, financial management, and program delivery.

14. **Adaptability and Resilience:** Be flexible and adaptive in response to changing circumstances, emerging needs, and unexpected challenges. Build organizational resilience by anticipating risks, diversifying revenue streams, and maintaining strong relationships with stakeholders.

15. **Measuring and Communicating Impact:** Develop systems for monitoring and evaluating impact, collecting data, and reporting outcomes to stakeholders. Communicate impact effectively through reports, dashboards, and storytelling to demonstrate the organization's effectiveness and accountability.

By implementing these best practices, charity organizations can strengthen their capacity, effectiveness, and impact, ultimately advancing their missions and making a meaningful difference in the lives of those they serve.

Implementing Governance and Accountability Measures

Governance and accountability are crucial aspects of effective charity organization management. Here's how charity organizations can implement governance and accountability measures:

1. **Establish a Board of Directors:** Form a board of directors composed of diverse individuals with relevant skills, experience, and a commitment to the organization's mission. The board should provide oversight, guidance, and strategic direction to the organization.

2. **Define Roles and Responsibilities:** Clearly define the roles and responsibilities of board members, officers, staff, and volunteers. Develop job descriptions, governance policies, and organizational bylaws outlining expectations and accountability mechanisms.
3. **Hold Regular Board Meetings:** Schedule regular board meetings to discuss organizational matters, review financial reports, evaluate programs, and make strategic decisions. Ensure that meeting agendas are structured, and minutes are documented to track decisions and actions taken.
4. **Promote Transparency:** Maintain transparency in organizational operations, decision-making processes, and financial management. Share relevant information with stakeholders, including donors, beneficiaries, staff, and the public, through annual reports, newsletters, and website updates.
5. **Financial Oversight:** Implement robust financial oversight mechanisms to ensure the responsible stewardship of resources. Develop annual budgets, conduct audits, and establish financial controls and policies to prevent fraud, mismanagement, or misuse of funds.
6. **Compliance with Legal and Regulatory Requirements:** Stay informed about applicable laws, regulations, and reporting requirements governing charity organizations. Ensure compliance with tax laws, charitable solicitation regulations, and other legal obligations to maintain the organization's nonprofit status and credibility.
7. **Conflict of Interest Policy:** Adopt a conflict of interest policy requiring board members, officers, staff, and volunteers to disclose potential conflicts of interest and abstain from participating in decisions where they have a personal or financial interest.

8. **Code of Ethics:** Develop and enforce a code of ethics or conduct that outlines expected standards of behaviour for all members of the organization. Emphasize integrity, honesty, fairness, and respect in all interactions and activities.
9. **Whistleblower Protection:** Establish procedures for reporting suspected misconduct, fraud, or ethical violations confidentially and without fear of retaliation. Protect whistleblowers from adverse consequences and investigate reported concerns promptly and impartially.
10. **Evaluation and Performance Monitoring:** Implement systems for evaluating organizational performance, assessing program effectiveness, and measuring outcomes. Use key performance indicators (KPIs) and benchmarks to track progress and inform strategic decision-making.
11. **Board Training and Development:** Provide orientation, training, and ongoing professional development opportunities for board members to enhance their understanding of governance principles, legal responsibilities, and best practices in nonprofit management.
12. **Annual Review and Assessment:** Conduct an annual review and assessment of board performance, governance practices, and organizational effectiveness. Solicit feedback from board members, staff, and stakeholders to identify areas for improvement and implement corrective actions.
13. **Collaborative Leadership:** Foster a culture of collaborative leadership, mutual respect, and shared accountability among board members, staff, and volunteers. Encourage open communication, active participation, and collective problem-solving to advance the organization's mission.

14. **Continuous Improvement:** Commit to continuous learning, adaptation, and improvement in governance and accountability practices. Stay informed about emerging trends, best practices, and evolving expectations in the nonprofit sector to maintain relevance and effectiveness.

By implementing robust governance and accountability measures, charity organizations can strengthen their capacity, credibility, and impact, ensuring that they fulfil their missions and serve their communities effectively.

Fostering a Culture of Transparency and Open Communication

Transparency and open communication are essential components of a healthy organizational culture within charity organizations. Here's how charity organizations can foster transparency and open communication:

1. **Lead by Example:** Leadership sets the tone for organizational culture. Leaders should demonstrate transparency and open communication in their actions, decisions, and interactions with staff, volunteers, donors, and beneficiaries.

2. **Establish Clear Communication Channels:** Create multiple channels for communication, including regular staff meetings, newsletters, email updates, and intranet platforms. Ensure that information flows freely and is accessible to all stakeholders.

3. **Share Organizational Information:** Share information about the organization's mission, vision, goals, strategies, and financial performance with staff, volunteers, donors, and beneficiaries. Provide updates on program activities, achievements, challenges, and impact.

4. **Encourage Dialogue and Feedback:** Encourage open dialogue, feedback, and constructive criticism from staff, volunteers, and stakeholders. Create forums for discussion, such as town hall meetings,

suggestion boxes, and feedback surveys, to gather input and address concerns.

5. **Transparency in Decision-Making:** Involve staff, volunteers, and stakeholders in the decision-making process whenever possible. Communicate the rationale behind decisions, solicit input from diverse perspectives, and be transparent about how decisions are made.

6. **Share Successes and Failures:** Celebrate successes and milestones, and acknowledge failures and challenges openly. Cultivate a culture where learning from mistakes is encouraged, and failures are viewed as opportunities for growth and improvement.

7. **Financial Transparency:** Be transparent about the organization's financial health, including budget allocations, income sources, and expenditure priorities. Provide regular updates on financial performance, audits, and fundraising efforts to donors and stakeholders.

8. **Honor Donor Intent:** Respect donor intent by communicating how their contributions are used to support the organization's mission and programs. Provide donors with reports and updates on the impact of their contributions.

9. **Accessibility of Leadership:** Ensure that organizational leaders are accessible and approachable to staff, volunteers, and stakeholders. Maintain an open-door policy and encourage communication at all levels of the organization.

10. **Training and Support:** Provide training and support to staff and volunteers on effective communication skills, conflict resolution, and cultural competency. Equip them with the tools and resources they need to communicate effectively in diverse contexts.

11. **Accountability Mechanisms:** Establish accountability mechanisms to ensure that

commitments are met, promises are kept, and actions align with organizational values. Hold individuals and teams accountable for their responsibilities and performance.

12. **Celebrate Transparency Champions:** Recognize and celebrate individuals and teams that demonstrate a commitment to transparency, open communication, and ethical conduct. Highlight their contributions as role models for the organization.

13. **Continuous Improvement:** Continuously assess and refine communication practices based on feedback, changing needs, and emerging trends. Solicit input from stakeholders on how communication can be improved and adapt accordingly.

By fostering a culture of transparency and open communication, charity organizations can build trust, foster collaboration, and strengthen relationships with staff, volunteers, donors, and beneficiaries. This, in turn, can enhance organizational effectiveness, resilience, and impact in serving their communities.

Continuous Learning and Improvement for Organizational Excellence

Continuous learning and improvement are essential for charity organizations to adapt to changing environments, address emerging challenges, and maximize their impact. Here's how charity organizations can foster a culture of continuous learning and improvement:

1. **Commitment to Learning:** Emphasize the importance of learning and professional development at all levels of the organization. Encourage staff, volunteers, and board members to embrace a growth mindset and pursue opportunities for learning and skill development.

2. **Training and Development:** Provide regular training and development opportunities to build the knowledge, skills, and competencies of staff and volunteers. Offer workshops, seminars, webinars,

and online courses on topics relevant to their roles and the organization's mission.

3. **Peer Learning and Knowledge Sharing:** Facilitate peer learning and knowledge sharing among staff, volunteers, and partners. Create opportunities for individuals to share best practices, lessons learned, and innovative approaches to program delivery, fundraising, and organizational management.

4. **Evaluation and Feedback:** Establish systems for monitoring and evaluating organizational performance, program effectiveness, and stakeholder satisfaction. Collect feedback from staff, volunteers, donors, and beneficiaries to identify areas for improvement and inform decision-making.

5. **Data-Informed Decision-Making:** Use data and evidence to inform decision-making and program planning. Collect and analyze data on program outcomes, financial performance, and stakeholder feedback to identify trends, measure impact, and make informed decisions.

6. **Quality Improvement Processes:** Implement quality improvement processes to continuously assess and enhance program quality, efficiency, and effectiveness. Use tools such as Plan-Do-Study-Act (PDSA) cycles or Lean Six Sigma methodologies to identify and address areas for improvement.

7. **Innovation and Experimentation:** Encourage innovation and experimentation within the organization. Create a culture where staff and volunteers feel empowered to propose new ideas, test innovative solutions, and take calculated risks to achieve better outcomes.

8. **Adaptive Management:** Embrace adaptive management principles to navigate uncertainty and complexity in the operating environment. Be flexible and responsive to changing needs, emerging trends,

and unexpected challenges, adjusting strategies and tactics as necessary.

9. **Learning from Failure:** View failure as an opportunity for learning and growth rather than a setback. Encourage staff and volunteers to reflect on failures, identify root causes, and apply lessons learned to improve future performance and decision-making.

10. **External Partnerships and Networks:** Collaborate with external partners, peer organizations, and professional networks to access expertise, share resources, and learn from collective experiences. Participate in conferences, workshops, and communities of practice to stay informed about emerging trends and best practices in the sector.

11. **Leadership Support:** Provide leadership support and commitment to learning and improvement initiatives. Allocate resources, time, and organizational support for training, evaluation, and innovation activities, and lead by example in embracing a culture of continuous learning.

12. **Celebrating Successes:** Celebrate successes, achievements, and milestones as a way to recognize and reinforce a culture of learning and improvement. Highlight examples of successful initiatives, innovations, and improvements to inspire and motivate staff, volunteers, and stakeholders.

By prioritizing continuous learning and improvement, charity organizations can enhance their organizational capacity, effectiveness, and resilience, ultimately advancing their mission and making a positive difference in the lives of those they serve.

Chapter 28:

Types of Charities and Charity Functions

Charities vary in their missions, focus areas, and approaches to addressing social needs. Understanding the different types of charities and their functions can help stakeholders identify opportunities for collaboration, funding, and support. Here are some common types of charities and their functions:

1. **Human Services Charities:** Human services charities focus on meeting the basic needs and improving the well-being of individuals and families. They provide services such as food assistance, housing support, healthcare, counselling, and disaster relief.

2. **Health Charities:** Health charities promote health and well-being by supporting medical research, disease prevention and treatment, access to healthcare services, and public health initiatives. They may focus on specific diseases or health issues, such as cancer research charities or mental health organizations.

3. **Education Charities:** Education charities support access to quality education and lifelong learning opportunities. They may provide scholarships, school supplies, literacy programs, vocational training, or support for schools and educational institutions.

4. **Environmental Charities:** Environmental charities work to protect and preserve the natural

environment, wildlife habitats, and ecosystems. They may engage in conservation efforts, environmental advocacy, climate action, pollution control, and sustainable development initiatives.

5. **Animal Welfare Charities:** Animal welfare charities advocate for the humane treatment and well-being of animals. They may provide shelter and care for abandoned or mistreated animals, promote animal adoption, and support spaying and neutering programs.

6. **Arts and Culture Charities:** Arts and culture charities promote creativity, cultural expression, and access to the arts. They support museums, galleries, theatres, music and dance programs, cultural festivals, and arts education initiatives.

7. **International Development Charities:** International development charities work to alleviate poverty, promote economic development, and improve living conditions in developing countries. They may provide humanitarian aid, support community development projects, and advocate for global justice and human rights.

8. **Religious Charities:** Religious charities provide spiritual support, social services, and community outreach based on religious principles and beliefs. They may operate churches, mosques, temples, or faith-based organizations that provide charitable services such as food pantries, shelters, and counselling.

9. **Disability and Special Needs Charities:** Disability and special needs charities support individuals with disabilities and their families by providing advocacy, resources, and specialized services. They may focus on accessibility, inclusion, and empowerment for people with disabilities.

10. **Community Development Charities:** Community development charities work to strengthen communities, promote social cohesion, and empower marginalized populations. They may support community centres, grassroots organizations, and initiatives that address local needs and priorities.

11. **Philanthropic Foundations:** Philanthropic foundations support charitable activities by providing grants, funding research, and investing in social change initiatives. They may focus on specific issue areas, geographic regions, or populations, and often play a key role in shaping philanthropic priorities and strategies.

12. **Advocacy and Policy Charities:** Advocacy and policy charities work to advance social justice, human rights, and systemic change through advocacy, lobbying, and policy reform efforts. They may engage in legislative advocacy, public education campaigns, and coalition building to address the root causes of social problems.

Understanding the diversity of charity types and functions is essential for donors, volunteers, policymakers, and other stakeholders to effectively support and engage with charitable organizations. By recognizing the unique contributions and challenges of different types of charities, stakeholders can work together to address complex social issues and create positive change in their communities and beyond.

Understanding the Diversity of Charitable Organizations

Charitable organizations are diverse in their missions, structures, and approaches to addressing social needs. Recognizing this diversity is essential for stakeholders to effectively engage, support, and collaborate with charitable organizations. Here are some key aspects to consider when understanding the diversity of charitable organizations:

1. **Mission and Focus Areas:** Charitable organizations vary in their mission statements and focus areas. Some may focus on providing basic needs such as food, shelter, and healthcare, while others may prioritize environmental conservation, education, animal welfare, or cultural preservation. Understanding each organization's mission and focus areas is crucial for aligning support and resources with their goals and priorities.

2. **Size and Scale:** Charitable organizations range in size and scale, from small grassroots initiatives to large international nonprofits. Small organizations may have limited resources and capacity but can be highly responsive to local needs and flexible in their approaches. Larger organizations may have greater resources and reach but may face challenges related

to bureaucracy and coordination across multiple locations or programs.

3. **Legal Structure:** Charitable organizations can have different legal structures, including nonprofit corporations, charitable trusts, foundations, and social enterprises. Each legal structure has its own requirements, governance mechanisms, and tax implications. Understanding the legal structure of an organization can provide insight into its accountability, transparency, and regulatory obligations.

4. **Funding Sources:** Charitable organizations rely on various sources of funding to support their operations and programs. These may include individual donations, corporate sponsorships, government grants, philanthropic foundations, earned income, and in-kind contributions. Understanding an organization's funding sources can shed light on its financial sustainability, independence, and potential funding gaps or vulnerabilities.

5. **Geographic Scope:** Charitable organizations operate at different geographic levels, ranging from local community-based organizations to national or international entities. Some organizations focus exclusively on serving a specific geographic area, while others may have a broader regional, national, or global mandate. Understanding an organization's geographic scope is important for assessing its relevance and impact within a given context.

6. **Target Populations:** Charitable organizations serve diverse populations, including children, youth, seniors, individuals with disabilities, refugees, immigrants, Indigenous communities, and marginalized or underserved groups. Some organizations may target specific demographic groups or populations facing particular challenges or vulnerabilities. Understanding the target population(s) served by an organization is critical for tailoring programs and services to meet their unique needs.

7. **Collaborative Partnerships:** Charitable organizations often collaborate with other nonprofits, government agencies, businesses, academic institutions, and community groups to leverage resources, share expertise, and maximize impact. Collaborative partnerships can enhance the effectiveness, efficiency, and sustainability of charitable efforts by pooling resources, coordinating activities, and addressing complex social problems collaboratively.

8. **Organizational Culture and Values:** Each charitable organization has its own organizational culture, values, and ethos that shape its identity, decision-making processes, and relationships with stakeholders. Understanding an organization's culture and values can provide insights into its priorities, priorities, and approaches to achieving its mission.

By recognizing and appreciating the diversity of charitable organizations, stakeholders can better understand the complexities of the nonprofit sector and effectively support initiatives that align with their values, interests, and objectives. Embracing this diversity can foster collaboration, innovation, and collective action towards addressing pressing social challenges and creating positive change in communities around the world.

Categorizing Charities by Focus Areas and Activities

Charities encompass a wide range of focus areas and activities, each dedicated to addressing specific social needs and challenges. Categorizing charities based on their focus areas and activities can help stakeholders understand the diverse landscape of charitable organizations and identify opportunities for collaboration, funding, and support. Here are some common categories of charities based on their focus areas and activities:

1. **Human Services:** Charities in this category focus on meeting the basic needs and improving the well-being of individuals and families. Activities may include providing food assistance, shelter, healthcare, counselling, emergency relief, and social services for vulnerable populations such as the homeless, low-income families, and survivors of domestic violence.

2. **Health and Medical Research:** Health charities support medical research, disease prevention, treatment, and access to healthcare services. They may fund research initiatives, advocacy campaigns, and community health programs targeting specific

diseases or health issues such as cancer, HIV/AIDS, mental health, maternal and child health, and infectious diseases.

3. **Education and Youth Development:** Charities in this category promote access to quality education, literacy, and youth development opportunities. They may support schools, afterschool programs, tutoring services, scholarships, vocational training, and initiatives to improve educational outcomes for children, youth, and underserved communities.

4. **Environmental Conservation:** Environmental charities work to protect and preserve natural habitats, wildlife, and ecosystems. They engage in conservation efforts, habitat restoration, environmental advocacy, climate action, pollution control, and sustainable development initiatives aimed at addressing environmental challenges such as deforestation, pollution, habitat loss, and climate change.

5. **Animal Welfare:** Charities focusing on animal welfare advocate for the humane treatment and well-being of animals. They may provide shelter and care for abandoned or mistreated animals, promote adoption, spaying and neutering programs, and advocate for policies and laws that protect animals from cruelty and exploitation.

6. **Arts and Culture:** Arts and culture charities promote creativity, cultural expression, and access to the arts. They support museums, galleries, theatres, music and dance programs, cultural festivals, arts

education initiatives, and efforts to preserve and celebrate cultural heritage and diversity.

7. **International Development:** International development charities work to alleviate poverty, promote economic development, and improve living conditions in developing countries. They may provide humanitarian aid, support community development projects, empower women and marginalized populations, and advocate for global justice and human rights.

8. **Community Development:** Charities focusing on community development work to strengthen communities, promote social cohesion, and empower residents. They support community centres, grassroots organizations, and initiatives that address local needs and priorities such as affordable housing, economic empowerment, civic engagement, and neighbourhood revitalization.

9. **Philanthropic Foundations:** Philanthropic foundations support charitable activities by providing grants, funding research, and investing in social change initiatives. They may focus on specific issue areas, geographic regions, or populations, and play a key role in shaping philanthropic priorities and strategies.

10. **Advocacy and Policy Reform:** Charities engaged in advocacy and policy reform work to advance social justice, human rights, and systemic change. They engage in legislative advocacy, public education campaigns, and coalition building to address the root

causes of social problems, promote equity and inclusion, and influence public policy and decision-making.

Categorizing charities based on their focus areas and activities can provide a framework for understanding their missions, priorities, and impact. However, it's important to recognize that many charities operate across multiple focus areas and engage in diverse activities to address complex social challenges comprehensively. Embracing this diversity and complexity can help stakeholders collaborate effectively and maximize collective efforts towards creating positive change in communities worldwide.

Exploring Different Models for Delivering Charitable Services

Charitable organizations employ various models for delivering services and programs to address social needs and improve the well-being of individuals and communities. Understanding these models can provide insights into how charities operate, allocate resources, and engage with stakeholders. Here are some different models for delivering charitable services:

1. **Direct Service Provision:** In this model, charitable organizations directly deliver services and programs to beneficiaries. This may involve operating shelters, food banks, healthcare clinics, counselling services, educational programs, and other direct service initiatives. These organizations often have staff, volunteers, and facilities dedicated to providing hands-on assistance and support to individuals in need.

2. **Grantmaking and Funding:** Some charitable organizations focus on grantmaking and funding initiatives to support other nonprofits, community groups, and grassroots organizations. They provide financial support through grants, scholarships, fellowships, and capacity-building initiatives to enable other organizations to implement programs and services that align with the funder's mission and priorities.

3. **Partnership and Collaboration:** Charitable organizations may engage in partnerships and collaborations with other nonprofits, government agencies, businesses, academic institutions, and community groups to leverage resources, share expertise, and maximize impact. These partnerships may involve joint programming, shared services, coalition building, and collaborative initiatives aimed at addressing complex social problems collaboratively.

4. **Advocacy and Policy Change:** Some charitable organizations focus on advocacy and policy change as a means of addressing the root causes of social issues and promoting systemic change. They engage in legislative advocacy, public education campaigns, community organizing, and policy reform efforts to influence laws, regulations, and public policies that impact the well-being of individuals and communities.

5. **Capacity Building and Technical Assistance:** Charitable organizations may provide capacity

building and technical assistance to support the organizational development, sustainability, and effectiveness of other nonprofits. This may involve offering training, coaching, consulting, and resource sharing on topics such as governance, fundraising, program management, and strategic planning.

6. **Research and Knowledge Generation:** Charitable organizations may focus on research, data collection, and knowledge generation to inform evidence-based practice, policy development, and decision-making in the nonprofit sector. They conduct research studies, evaluations, and data analysis to identify trends, assess needs, measure impact, and disseminate best practices and lessons learned.

7. **Volunteer Mobilization:** Charitable organizations often mobilize volunteers to support their programs and services. Volunteers may assist with direct service delivery, administrative tasks, fundraising events, community outreach, and advocacy campaigns. Volunteer engagement models vary, ranging from one-time volunteer opportunities to long-term volunteer commitments and skilled pro bono services.

8. **Social Enterprise and Earned Income:** Some charitable organizations integrate social enterprise and earned income strategies into their operations to generate revenue and sustain their charitable activities. They may operate social enterprises, such as thrift stores, cafes, or artisan workshops, which

generate revenue to support mission-driven programs and services.

9. **Technology and Innovation:** Charitable organizations leverage technology and innovation to deliver services more efficiently, reach broader audiences, and increase impact. They may develop digital platforms, mobile apps, online learning tools, and virtual service delivery models to enhance the accessibility, scalability, and effectiveness of their programs and initiatives.

10. **Community-Led and Participatory Approaches:** Charitable organizations may adopt community-led and participatory approaches that involve engaging beneficiaries and community members in the design, implementation, and evaluation of programs and services. These approaches prioritize community voice, participation, and ownership to ensure programs are responsive to local needs, preferences, and priorities.

Exploring these different models for delivering charitable services can help stakeholders understand the diverse strategies and approaches employed by charitable organizations to achieve their missions and create positive change in communities. By leveraging a combination of these models, charitable organizations can effectively address complex social challenges and make a meaningful difference in the lives of those they serve.

Chapter 29:

Events for Donation Collection

Events play a crucial role in fundraising efforts for charitable organizations, providing opportunities to engage donors, raise awareness, and collect donations in support of their missions. Here are some popular events commonly organized by charities for donation collection:

1. **Fundraising Galas and Dinners:** Fundraising galas and dinners are formal events often held in elegant venues, featuring gourmet meals, entertainment, and live auctions. Attendees purchase tickets or tables to attend the event, with proceeds going towards the organization's programs and services. These events offer an opportunity for donors to make significant contributions while enjoying an evening of entertainment and networking.

2. **Charity Auctions:** Charity auctions involve the auctioning of donated items, experiences, and services to raise funds for charitable causes. Items up for auction may include artwork, travel packages, sports memorabilia, celebrity experiences, and unique experiences. Bidders compete for items through live bidding, silent auctions, or online auctions, with proceeds benefiting the charity.

3. **Walkathons and Fun Runs:** Walkathons and fun runs are community events that encourage participants to raise funds through pledges or registration fees. Participants walk, run, or engage in other physical activities to demonstrate their support

for the cause while collecting donations from friends, family, and colleagues. These events promote physical fitness, camaraderie, and philanthropy among participants.

4. **Golf Tournaments:** Golf tournaments are popular fundraising events that bring together golf enthusiasts and donors to support charitable causes. Participants register to play in the tournament and may also sponsor holes, provide prizes, or make donations. Tournaments often include contests, raffles, and auctions to raise additional funds, with proceeds benefiting the organization's programs and initiatives.

5. **Benefit Concerts and Performances:** Benefit concerts and performances feature live music, theatre, dance, or other artistic performances to raise funds and awareness for charitable causes. Artists, musicians, and performers donate their time and talent to entertain audiences while encouraging donations through ticket sales, sponsorships, and merchandise sales.

6. **Charity Sporting Events:** Charity sporting events, such as marathons, cycling races, and triathlons, offer participants the opportunity to raise funds for charity while engaging in physical activity. Participants register for the event and collect donations from supporters, sponsors, and corporate partners. These events promote health, wellness, and philanthropy while raising funds for important causes.

7. **Community Festivals and Fairs:** Community festivals and fairs bring together local residents, businesses, and organizations to celebrate and support charitable causes. These events feature food vendors, entertainment, games, activities, and informational booths highlighting the work of the charity. Attendees may make donations, purchase merchandise, or participate in fundraising activities to support the organization's mission.

8. **Virtual Fundraising Events:** Virtual fundraising events leverage online platforms and digital technology to engage donors and raise funds remotely. These events may include virtual galas, online auctions, peer-to-peer fundraising campaigns, and virtual challenges. Participants can attend and support the event from anywhere, making it accessible to a broader audience.

9. **Donation Drives:** Donation drives involve collecting specific items or supplies needed by the charity, such as food, clothing, school supplies, toys, or hygiene products. These drives may be held in partnership with local businesses, schools, or community organizations and provide an easy way for individuals to contribute tangible goods to support the organization's programs and services.

10. **Awareness and Advocacy Events:** Awareness and advocacy events raise awareness about important social issues and promote action and support for change. These events may include panel discussions, film screenings, workshops, and

community forums focused on educating the public, advocating for policy change, and mobilizing support for the charity's mission and initiatives.

By organizing a diverse range of events for donation collection, charitable organizations can engage donors, build community support, and raise vital funds to sustain their programs and services. These events offer opportunities for individuals to make meaningful contributions while participating in enjoyable and impactful experiences that support important causes.

Planning and Executing Fundraising Events for Charity

Fundraising events are powerful tools for charitable organizations to engage donors, raise funds, and increase awareness of their mission. Effective planning and execution are essential for the success of these events. Here is a comprehensive guide to planning and executing fundraising events for charity:

1. **Define Your Goals:** Start by clarifying the objectives of your fundraising event. Determine how much money you aim to raise, the target audience you want to reach, and the impact you hope to achieve with the funds raised. Set specific, measurable goals to guide your planning process.

2. **Select the Right Event:** Choose a fundraising event format that aligns with your organization's mission, audience preferences, and fundraising goals. Consider options such as galas, auctions, walkathons, golf tournaments, or virtual events

based on your target audience, resources, and logistical considerations.

3. **Create a Budget:** Develop a comprehensive budget for your fundraising event, including expenses such as venue rental, catering, entertainment, marketing materials, permits, and staffing costs. Allocate funds strategically to maximize your return on investment and ensure financial sustainability.

4. **Form a Planning Committee:** Establish a dedicated planning committee or task force comprised of staff, board members, volunteers, and key stakeholders to oversee the planning and execution of the event. Delegate responsibilities, set timelines, and establish clear communication channels to ensure smooth coordination and execution.

5. **Secure Sponsorships and Partnerships:** Identify potential sponsors, donors, and partners who can provide financial support, in-kind donations, or promotional opportunities for your event. Develop sponsorship packages outlining the benefits and recognition opportunities for sponsors to incentivize their involvement.

6. **Choose a Venue:** Select a suitable venue that accommodates your event format, capacity requirements, and budget constraints. Consider factors such as location, accessibility, amenities, and ambience to create a memorable and engaging experience for attendees.

7. **Plan Program and Activities:** Develop a compelling program and schedule of activities for your fundraising event, including keynote speakers, entertainment, live auctions, raffles, and networking opportunities. Design engaging experiences that resonate with your audience and reinforce your organization's mission and impact.

8. **Promote Your Event:** Implement a multi-channel marketing and outreach strategy to promote your fundraising event and attract attendees. Utilize social media, email marketing, press releases, website updates, and targeted advertising to raise awareness, generate excitement, and drive ticket sales or registrations.

9. **Recruit and Train Volunteers:** Recruit a team of dedicated volunteers to support various aspects of your event, such as registration, guest services, fundraising, and logistics. Provide comprehensive training, clear instructions, and ongoing support to ensure volunteers are prepared and empowered to contribute effectively.

10. **Implement Fundraising Strategies:** Integrate diverse fundraising strategies into your event, such as ticket sales, sponsorships, donations, auctions, merchandise sales, and peer-to-peer fundraising campaigns. Encourage attendees to participate in fundraising activities and make meaningful contributions to support your cause.

11. **Ensure Logistics and Operations:** Pay meticulous attention to logistical details and event operations to

ensure a seamless and enjoyable experience for attendees. Coordinate event setup, registration, catering, audiovisuals, signage, security, and transportation to create a positive impression and maximize guest satisfaction.

12. **Follow-Up and Stewardship:** After the event, express gratitude to attendees, sponsors, donors, and volunteers for their support and participation. Provide timely acknowledgements, updates on fundraising results, and impact reports to demonstrate the value of their contributions and foster ongoing engagement and support.

By following these steps and best practices, charitable organizations can plan and execute successful fundraising events that generate support, raise funds, and advance their mission to create positive change in the world. With careful planning, creativity, and collaboration, fundraising events can become powerful vehicles for driving impact and building a stronger community of support for charitable causes.

Creative Event Ideas to Engage Donors and Supporters

Innovative and engaging events are essential for attracting donors, building relationships, and raising funds for charitable causes. Here are some creative event ideas to inspire and engage donors and supporters:

1. **Virtual Fundraising Gala:** Host a virtual gala featuring live-streamed performances, interactive games, celebrity appearances, and virtual auctions. Create a captivating online experience that allows

attendees to participate from the comfort of their homes while supporting your cause.

2. **Outdoor Adventure Challenge:** Organize an outdoor adventure challenge, such as a hiking marathon, cycling tour, or obstacle course race, where participants raise funds through pledges or registration fees. Offer prizes, incentives, and team challenges to encourage participation and friendly competition.

3. **DIY Fundraising Campaigns:** Empower supporters to create their own DIY fundraising campaigns in support of your cause. Provide tools, resources, and personalized fundraising pages for individuals or teams to set goals, share their stories, and mobilize their networks to raise funds and awareness.

4. **Art Auction and Exhibition:** Curate an art auction and exhibition featuring works donated by local artists, collectors, and supporters. Host a gallery opening event with live music, refreshments, and opportunities for attendees to bid on artwork and support your organization's mission.

5. **Culinary Experience Fundraiser:** Partner with local restaurants, chefs, and food vendors to host a culinary experiences fundraiser, such as a gourmet dinner, cooking class, or food and wine tasting event. Offer unique dining experiences and culinary delights to delight guests while raising funds for your cause.

6. **Virtual Reality Charity Tour:** Create a virtual reality charity tour that allows donors to experience

firsthand the impact of your organization's work. Use immersive technology to transport participants to project sites, communities served, and success stories, inspiring them to support your cause.

7. **Themed Costume Party:** Host a themed costume party or masquerade ball where attendees dress up according to a specific theme or era. Incorporate themed décor, music, entertainment, and activities to create a festive atmosphere and encourage socializing and networking among guests.

8. **Impactful Documentary Screening:** Screen a compelling documentary film related to your organization's mission or cause. Host a screening event followed by a panel discussion, Q&A session, or storytelling session featuring experts, advocates, and individuals impacted by the issue.

9. **Charity Auction House Party:** Transform a private residence or venue into a charity auction house party, where guests can bid on exclusive experiences, luxury items, and unique memorabilia. Create an intimate and exclusive atmosphere for high-value donors and supporters to make significant contributions.

10. **Outdoor Concert or Music Festival:** Organize an outdoor concert or music festival featuring local bands, musicians, and performers. Offer food trucks, craft vendors, and family-friendly activities to attract attendees and create a festive atmosphere while raising funds through ticket sales and sponsorships.

11. **Peer-to-Peer Fundraising Challenges:** Launch peer-to-peer fundraising challenges or competitions where supporters compete to raise the most funds or complete a specific challenge or activity. Offer prizes, recognition, and incentives to motivate participants and amplify their fundraising efforts.

12. **Community Service Day:** Organize a community service day where volunteers come together to participate in hands-on service projects, such as park cleanups, habitat restoration, or community beautification initiatives. Showcase the impact of volunteerism and collective action while raising awareness of your organization's work.

By implementing creative event ideas that engage donors and supporters in meaningful ways, charitable organizations can build momentum, foster connections, and generate support for their mission and programs. Tailor your events to reflect your organization's values, brand personality, and audience preferences, ensuring a memorable and impactful experience for all involved.

Maximizing Revenue and Awareness through Event Management

Effective event management is essential for charitable organizations to maximize revenue, raise awareness, and advance their mission. Here are strategies for maximizing revenue and awareness through event management:

1. **Set Clear Goals:** Define specific goals for your event, such as fundraising targets, attendance numbers, and awareness metrics. Establish measurable

objectives to track progress and evaluate the success of your event.

2. **Create Compelling Content:** Develop compelling content and messaging that communicates your organization's mission, impact, and fundraising priorities. Use storytelling, testimonials, and multimedia elements to engage attendees emotionally and inspire action.

3. **Implement Multi-channel Promotion:** Utilize a multi-channel promotion strategy to reach and engage your target audience across various platforms, including social media, email marketing, website, print materials, and press releases. Tailor your messaging and content to each channel to maximize visibility and engagement.

4. **Offer Diverse Revenue Streams:** Incorporate diverse revenue streams into your event, such as ticket sales, sponsorships, donations, auctions, merchandise sales, and peer-to-peer fundraising campaigns. Provide multiple opportunities for attendees to support your cause and contribute to your fundraising goals.

5. **Cultivate Sponsorship Partnerships:** Secure sponsorship partnerships with businesses, corporations, and local organizations to offset event costs, increase revenue, and expand your reach. Offer sponsors branding opportunities, promotional visibility, and exclusive benefits in exchange for their support.

6. **Optimize Ticket Sales and Registration:** Implement strategies to optimize ticket sales and registration, such as early bird pricing, tiered ticket options, group discounts, and limited-time promotions. Simplify the registration process and provide incentives for early registration to encourage attendance.

7. **Create Engaging Experiences:** Design engaging experiences and activities that captivate attendees and encourage participation. Incorporate interactive elements, entertainment, networking opportunities, and hands-on activities to create memorable and enjoyable experiences for guests.

8. **Facilitate Peer-to-Peer Fundraising:** Empower attendees to become fundraisers and advocates for your cause by implementing peer-to-peer fundraising campaigns. Provide tools, resources, and incentives for participants to create personal fundraising pages, set goals, and mobilize their networks to donate and support your event.

9. **Maximize Sponsorship Activation:** Maximize the impact of sponsorship partnerships by activating sponsor benefits and recognition throughout your event. Incorporate sponsor logos, branding, and messaging into event signage, promotional materials, digital platforms, and onsite activations to enhance visibility and engagement.

10. **Capture Data and Insights:** Capture data and insights before, during, and after your event to evaluate performance, measure impact, and inform future strategies. Use event analytics, surveys, and

feedback mechanisms to gather attendee feedback, assess satisfaction levels, and identify areas for improvement.

11. **Follow-Up and Stewardship:** Follow up with attendees, sponsors, and donors after the event to express gratitude, provide event highlights, and share impact stories. Acknowledge contributions, recognize support, and cultivate ongoing relationships to steward donors and supporters for future engagement.

12. **Evaluate and Iterate:** Conduct a comprehensive post-event evaluation to assess the success of your event against your goals and objectives. Identify strengths, weaknesses, and lessons learned to inform future event planning and strategy development. Continuously iterate and improve your event management practices based on feedback and insights gathered.

By implementing these strategies and best practices, charitable organizations can maximize revenue, raise awareness, and create meaningful impact through effective event management. By prioritizing engagement, creativity, and strategic planning, organizations can leverage events as powerful vehicles for advancing their mission and achieving their fundraising goals.

Chapter 30:

Promoting and Motivating Generous Donations

Promoting and motivating generous donations is essential for charitable organizations to sustain their operations, support their programs, and make a meaningful impact on their communities. Here are strategies for effectively promoting and motivating generous donations:

1. **Craft Compelling Messaging:** Develop compelling and emotionally resonant messaging that communicates the urgency, importance, and impact of your organization's work. Highlight success stories, testimonials, and real-life examples to illustrate the difference donations can make in the lives of those served by your organization.

2. **Utilize Multiple Communication Channels:** Utilize a diverse range of communication channels to reach and engage potential donors, including email marketing, social media, website content, direct mail, print materials, and personal outreach. Tailor your messaging and content to each channel to maximize reach and effectiveness.

3. **Create Targeted Campaigns:** Develop targeted fundraising campaigns focused on specific themes, initiatives, or fundraising priorities. Segment your donor base and tailor campaigns to different donor segments based on their interests, preferences, and giving history.

4. **Leverage Peer Influence:** Harness the power of peer influence and social proof to motivate donations. Encourage donors to share their giving stories, testimonials, and experiences with their networks to inspire others to give. Implement peer-to-peer fundraising campaigns that empower supporters to fundraise on behalf of your organization.

5. **Offer Matching Grants and Challenges:** Secure matching grants, challenge grants, or matching gift programs to incentivize donations and amplify donor impact. Encourage donors to give by matching their contributions dollar-for-dollar, doubling their impact, or unlocking additional funds based on fundraising milestones.

6. **Provide Recognition and Stewardship:** Recognize and steward donors for their generosity and support. Express gratitude through personalized thank-you messages, acknowledgement letters, donor spotlights, and recognition opportunities. Cultivate ongoing relationships with donors to foster loyalty, engagement, and continued support.

7. **Create Giving Opportunities:** Offer diverse giving opportunities and options to accommodate donors' preferences and circumstances. Provide options for one-time donations, recurring gifts, tribute gifts, planned giving, corporate sponsorships, and in-kind donations to make giving accessible and convenient for donors.

8. **Promote Donor Benefits and Impact:** Highlight the benefits and impact of donating to your organization,

such as tax benefits, recognition opportunities, and the tangible difference donations can make in advancing your mission and serving your community. Communicate the value proposition of giving to inspire generosity and support.

9. **Host Fundraising Events and Campaigns:** Host fundraising events, campaigns, and initiatives to engage donors, raise awareness, and mobilize support. Organize virtual or in-person events, peer-to-peer fundraising campaigns, giving days, and special appeals to create excitement and momentum around giving opportunities.

10. **Share Transparent Financial Reporting:** Demonstrate transparency and accountability in financial reporting and stewardship of donor funds. Share information about your organization's financial health, programmatic impact, and use of donor dollars to build trust and confidence among donors.

11. **Cultivate Donor Relationships:** Invest in cultivating meaningful relationships with donors based on trust, transparency, and mutual respect. Listen to donors' feedback, respond to their inquiries promptly, and provide opportunities for engagement, involvement, and participation in your organization's mission and activities.

12. **Celebrate Milestones and Achievements:** Celebrate fundraising milestones, achievements, and successes with your donors and supporters. Share updates, progress reports, and impact stories to keep

donors informed and engaged in your organization's progress toward its goals.

By implementing these strategies and best practices, charitable organizations can effectively promote and motivate generous donations, inspire donor loyalty and support, and advance their mission to create positive change in the world. By prioritizing donor engagement, stewardship, and impact, organizations can build a strong foundation of support to sustain their work and make a lasting difference in the communities they serve.

Crafting Compelling Donation Appeals and Campaigns

Crafting compelling donation appeals and campaigns is essential for charitable organizations to attract donors, inspire generosity, and raise funds to support their mission. Here are strategies for crafting compelling donation appeals and campaigns:

1. **Know Your Audience:** Understand your audience's interests, motivations, and preferences to tailor your appeals and campaigns effectively. Segment your donor base and personalize your messaging to resonate with different donor segments based on their demographics, giving history, and interests.

2. **Tell Powerful Stories:** Use storytelling to evoke emotion, empathy, and connection with your audience. Share compelling stories of individuals impacted by your organization's work, highlighting their challenges, triumphs, and the difference donations can make in their lives. Personalize your

appeals with real-life examples and testimonials to illustrate the impact of giving.

3. **Highlight Urgency and Impact:** Create a sense of urgency and importance in your donation appeals by highlighting critical needs, time-sensitive opportunities, or specific fundraising goals. Clearly articulate the impact of donations and how they will be used to address urgent needs, advance your mission, and make a difference in the lives of those served by your organization.

4. **Focus on Solutions and Solutions:** Focus on the positive outcomes and solutions your organization provides rather than dwelling solely on the challenges or problems. Position your organization as a catalyst for change, offering hope, empowerment, and tangible solutions to address pressing issues and create lasting impact.

5. **Use Compelling Visuals:** Incorporate compelling visuals, such as photos, videos, infographics, and graphics, to enhance your donation appeals and campaigns. Use visuals to illustrate your organization's mission, showcase impact stories, and capture donors' attention and imagination.

6. **Offer Matching Grants or Challenges:** Incentivize donations by offering matching grants, challenge grants, or matching gift opportunities. Encourage donors to give by matching their contributions dollar-for-dollar, doubling their impact, or unlocking additional funds based on fundraising milestones or goals.

7. **Create a Sense of Belonging:** Cultivate a sense of belonging and community among donors by emphasizing their role as partners and advocates for your organization's mission. Communicate the importance of collective action and the power of coming together to make a meaningful difference in the world.

8. **Provide Clear Calls to Action:** Clearly communicate the desired action you want donors to take, whether it's making a donation, signing up for a newsletter, attending an event, or volunteering. Use compelling calls to action that inspire action and encourage donors to take the next step in supporting your organization.

9. **Offer Giving Incentives:** Provide incentives or benefits to donors to encourage giving, such as exclusive access to events, recognition opportunities, or special perks. Offer tangible rewards or incentives for different donation levels to motivate donors to give at higher levels.

10. **Promote Donor Impact and Recognition:** Highlight the impact and recognition donors receive for their contributions to your organization. Showcase donor testimonials, success stories, and impact metrics to demonstrate the tangible difference donations make in advancing your mission and serving your community.

11. **Create Multi-channel Campaigns:** Implement multi-channel campaigns that leverage various communication channels, including email, social

media, website, direct mail, and in-person outreach. Coordinate messaging and content across channels to reinforce your donation appeals and reach donors wherever they are.

12. **Follow-Up and Acknowledge Donors:** Follow up with donors promptly to acknowledge their contributions, express gratitude, and provide updates on how their donations are making an impact. Show donors the value of their support and steward their relationship with ongoing communication and engagement opportunities.

By incorporating these strategies into your donation appeals and campaigns, you can craft compelling messaging, inspire generosity, and motivate donors to support your organization's mission and programs. By focusing on storytelling, impact, and engagement, you can create meaningful connections with donors and build a strong foundation of support to sustain your organization's work and make a lasting difference in the world.

Utilizing Storytelling and Personal Connections to Inspire Giving

Storytelling and personal connections are powerful tools for charitable organizations to inspire giving, evoke emotion, and mobilize support for their mission. Here are strategies for effectively utilizing storytelling and personal connections to inspire giving:

1. **Identify Compelling Stories:** Identify and collect compelling stories of individuals whose lives have been positively impacted by your organization's

programs and services. Look for stories that evoke emotion, highlight transformation, and demonstrate the tangible difference your organization makes in the lives of those you serve.

2. **Highlight Personal Journeys:** Share personal journeys and experiences of individuals who have benefited from your organization's support. Highlight the challenges they faced, the obstacles they overcame, and the positive outcomes they achieved with the help of your organization. Personalize your storytelling to create emotional connections with donors.

3. **Feature Real-life Testimonials:** Incorporate real-life testimonials from beneficiaries, volunteers, staff members, and supporters into your storytelling efforts. Use quotes, interviews, and video testimonials to add authenticity, credibility, and relatability to your stories. Let those directly impacted by your organization's work share their voices and experiences.

4. **Humanize Your Impact:** Humanize your organization's impact by putting faces and names to the individuals you serve. Share photos, videos, and personal anecdotes that humanize the impact of your programs and services, illustrating the real people behind the statistics and demonstrating the power of generosity to change lives.

5. **Emphasize Empathy and Empowerment:** Foster empathy and connection with your audience by sharing stories that resonate with their values,

experiences, and aspirations. Emphasize the universal themes of empathy, compassion, and empowerment that unite us all and inspire donors to take action and make a difference.

6. **Create Emotional Engagement:** Use storytelling techniques to create emotional engagement and resonance with your audience. Appeal to donors' emotions by tapping into universal emotions such as hope, joy, empathy, and compassion. Use vivid language, descriptive imagery, and sensory details to evoke emotion and bring your stories to life.

7. **Showcase Impact and Transformation:** Showcase the impact and transformation your organization facilitates through its programs and services. Share before-and-after stories, progress updates, and success stories that illustrate the journey of change and improvement experienced by individuals and communities served by your organization.

8. **Share Authentic and Transparent Stories:** Share authentic, transparent, and honest stories that accurately reflect your organization's mission, values, and impact. Avoid embellishments or exaggeration and focus on sharing genuine stories that resonate with donors and build trust and credibility in your organization.

9. **Invite Donor Participation:** Invite donors to become part of the story by offering opportunities for involvement, engagement, and participation in your organization's mission and activities. Encourage donors to share their own stories, experiences, and

reasons for giving, creating a sense of community and shared purpose.

10. **Tailor Stories to Donor Segments:** Tailor your storytelling efforts to resonate with different donor segments based on their interests, preferences, and motivations. Customize your messaging and content to appeal to specific donor demographics, such as age, gender, location, and giving history, to maximize relevance and effectiveness.

11. **Use Multiple Communication Channels:** Utilize multiple communication channels, including social media, email marketing, website content, direct mail, and in-person events, to share your stories and reach donors wherever they are. Coordinate messaging and content across channels to reinforce your storytelling efforts and maximize impact.

12. **Measure and Share Impact:** Measure and share the impact of your storytelling efforts by tracking key metrics such as engagement, donations, and donor retention rates. Use data and analytics to assess the effectiveness of your storytelling strategies and refine your approach based on feedback and insights gathered.

By incorporating storytelling and personal connections into your fundraising efforts, you can inspire empathy, evoke emotion, and mobilize support for your organization's mission and programs. By sharing authentic, compelling stories that resonate with donors' hearts and minds, you can inspire generosity, build community, and create lasting change in the world.

Recognizing and Appreciating Donors to Foster Loyalty and Continued Support

Recognizing and appreciating donors is essential for charitable organizations to foster loyalty, strengthen relationships, and encourage continued support for their mission. Here are strategies for effectively recognizing and appreciating donors:

1. **Personalized Thank-You Messages:** Send personalized thank-you messages to donors promptly after receiving their contributions. Tailor your messages to acknowledge donors by name, express gratitude for their generosity, and highlight the impact of their support on your organization's mission and programs.

2. **Handwritten Notes:** Consider sending handwritten notes or cards to major donors or long-time supporters to express personal appreciation for their contributions. Handwritten notes add a personal touch and demonstrate the time and effort you've invested in recognizing donors' generosity.

3. **Donor Acknowledgment Letters:** Provide formal acknowledgement letters or receipts for donors' contributions, including details such as the amount donated, the date of the gift, and any tax-related information. Use acknowledgement letters as an opportunity to express gratitude, share updates on your organization's work, and reinforce the importance of donors' support.

4. **Recognition Opportunities:** Offer recognition opportunities for donors based on their giving levels or contribution amounts. Consider creating donor recognition walls, plaques, or honour rolls to publicly acknowledge and celebrate donors' generosity. Recognize major donors in annual reports, newsletters, and other organizational publications.

5. **Donor Appreciation Events:** Host donor appreciation events or receptions to recognize and celebrate donors' contributions. Organize exclusive events, receptions, or VIP experiences for major donors, supporters, and volunteers to express appreciation and strengthen relationships.

6. **Personalized Recognition Gifts:** Consider offering personalized recognition gifts or tokens of appreciation to donors as a tangible expression of gratitude. Provide custom-branded merchandise, certificates of appreciation, or commemorative items to acknowledge donors' generosity and support.

7. **Donor Spotlights:** Highlight individual donors, supporters, or volunteers in donor spotlights or featured stories on your organization's website, blog, or social media channels. Share their stories, testimonials, and reasons for giving to inspire others and demonstrate the impact of philanthropy.

8. **Impact Reports and Updates:** Provide regular updates and impact reports to donors to demonstrate the tangible difference their contributions make in advancing your organization's mission and programs. Share success stories,

program outcomes, and progress updates to keep donors informed and engaged in your organization's work.

9. **Exclusive Benefits and Perks:** Offer exclusive benefits and perks to donors as a token of appreciation for their support. Provide donors with early access to events, behind-the-scenes tours, special invitations, or priority seating as a way to recognize their generosity and foster loyalty.

10. **Personalized Communication:** Communicate with donors in a personalized and meaningful way to cultivate ongoing relationships and engagement. Use donors' preferred communication channels, address them by name, and tailor your messaging to their interests and preferences to show that you value their support.

11. **Saying Thank You Publicly:** Publicly acknowledge and thank donors at events, meetings, or public gatherings to show appreciation for their contributions. Share stories, testimonials, or examples of donors' impact to inspire others and encourage continued support.

12. **Solicit Donor Feedback:** Solicit feedback from donors on their giving experience, communication preferences, and areas for improvement. Demonstrate that you value donors' input and are committed to providing excellent stewardship and recognition for their support.

By implementing these strategies for recognizing and appreciating donors, charitable organizations can foster loyalty, strengthen relationships, and inspire continued support for their mission and programs. By expressing gratitude, providing meaningful recognition, and cultivating ongoing engagement, organizations can build a strong foundation of support and make a lasting impact in the communities they serve.

Case Studies and Best Practices

1. **Donor Recognition Wall:** A charitable organization created a donor recognition wall in its headquarters, featuring the names of major donors and supporters. This visible display of appreciation encouraged continued giving and inspired others to contribute.

2. **Personalized Thank-You Videos:** An organization produced personalized thank-you videos for donors, featuring beneficiaries expressing gratitude for their support. These heartfelt videos strengthened donor relationships and highlighted the impact of their contributions.

3. **Impact Reports:** A nonprofit regularly sends impact reports to donors, showcasing the outcomes of their programs and the lives changed by their support. These reports reinforced donors' belief in the organization's mission and encouraged ongoing generosity.

4. **Donor Appreciation Events:** A charity hosted annual donor appreciation events, inviting supporters to meet staff, tour facilities, and hear firsthand stories

of impact. These events fostered a sense of community among donors and provided opportunities for personal connections.

5. **Matching Gift Campaigns:** An organization secured matching grants from corporate partners, doubling donors' contributions during specific fundraising campaigns. This incentive motivated increased giving and amplified the impact of donors' gifts.

6. **Volunteer Recognition Programs:** A nonprofit implemented a volunteer recognition program, honoring volunteers for their dedication and service. Recognizing volunteers' contributions cultivated a sense of belonging and encouraged continued engagement.

7. **Legacy Giving Campaign:** A charity launched a legacy giving campaign to encourage donors to include the organization in their estate plans. By highlighting the long-term impact of planned gifts, the campaign secured sustainable funding for future initiatives.

8. **Social Media Shoutouts:** An organization regularly featured donors on their social media channels, publicly thanking them for their support and sharing stories of impact. These shoutouts increased donor visibility and engagement with the organization's mission.

9. **Donor Surveys:** A nonprofit conducted donor surveys to gather feedback on donor preferences, interests, and motivations. Using this data, they

tailored communication and recognition efforts to better meet donors' needs and preferences.

10. **Corporate Partnership Recognition:** A charity recognises corporate partners through sponsorship opportunities, branding visibility, and employee engagement activities. These partnerships fostered mutually beneficial relationships and provided vital support for the organization's programs.

By studying these case studies and best practices, charitable organizations can gain insights into effective strategies for recognizing and engaging donors, fostering loyalty, and maximizing support for their mission and programs. By implementing these approaches, organizations can build strong relationships with donors, inspire continued generosity, and create lasting impact in their communities.

Templates and Frameworks for Strategic Planning

1. **SWOT Analysis Template:**

   - Strengths: Identify internal factors that contribute to your organization's success.

   - Weaknesses: Identify internal factors that hinder your organization's performance.

   - Opportunities: Identify external factors that present opportunities for growth and development.

   - Threats: Identify external factors that pose risks or challenges to your organization.

2. **SMART Goals Framework:**

- Specific: Define clear, specific objectives that align with your organization's mission and vision.

- Measurable: Establish metrics and indicators to track progress and measure success.

- Achievable: Set goals that are realistic and attainable within your organization's resources and capabilities.

- Relevant: Ensure goals are relevant to your organization's priorities, needs, and strategic objectives.

- Time-bound: Set deadlines and timelines to create accountability and focus efforts on achieving goals within specific timeframes.

3. **Strategic Prioritization Matrix:**

   - Identify and prioritize strategic initiatives based on their impact and feasibility.

   - Evaluate initiatives using criteria such as alignment with mission, potential for impact, resource requirements, and timeline for implementation.

   - Classify initiatives such as high priority, medium priority, or low priority based on their strategic importance and feasibility.

4. **Balanced Scorecard Template:**

   - Define key performance indicators (KPIs) across four perspectives: financial, customer, internal processes, and learning and growth.

   - Set targets and benchmarks for each KPI to measure progress and performance.

- Track performance against targets and use insights to inform strategic decision-making and resource allocation.

5. **Strategy Map Template:**

- Visualize your organization's strategic objectives, goals, and initiatives in a hierarchical structure.

- Connect objectives with corresponding strategies and action plans to achieve desired outcomes.

- Use arrows and connections to illustrate causal relationships between objectives and demonstrate how they contribute to overall mission success.

6. **Gap Analysis Framework:**

- Identify the gap between your organization's current state and desired future state.

- Assess factors such as resources, capabilities, performance, and external trends to understand barriers and opportunities for improvement.

- Develop action plans to bridge the gap and achieve strategic objectives.

7. **Scenario Planning Template:**

- Explore alternative future scenarios and assess their potential impact on your organization.

- Develop scenarios based on different assumptions, trends, and uncertainties in the external environment.

- Evaluate the implications of each scenario for your organization's strategy, operations, and resilience.

8. **Decision Matrix Template:**

   - Evaluate strategic options or alternatives based on criteria such as feasibility, impact, cost, and risk.

   - Assign weights to criteria based on their importance and relevance to your organization's goals.

   - Score each option against criteria and calculate a total score to facilitate objective decision-making.

9. **Stakeholder Analysis Framework:**

   - Identify key stakeholders and assess their interests, influence, and potential impact on your organization's strategy.

   - Segment stakeholders into categories such as supporters, opponents, allies, or neutral parties.

   - Develop strategies to engage and manage relationships with stakeholders to build support for your strategic initiatives.

10. **Action Plan Template:**

    - Break down strategic objectives into specific action steps, tasks, and milestones.

    - Assign responsibilities, deadlines, and resources for each action item.

- Track progress, monitor performance, and adjust plans as needed to ensure alignment with strategic goals.

By using these templates and frameworks for strategic planning, organizations can effectively define their strategic direction, set clear objectives, and develop actionable plans to achieve their mission and vision. These tools provide structure, guidance, and clarity for strategic decision-making and enable organizations to adapt and thrive in a dynamic and complex environment.

Bibliography

1. Managing the Non-Profit Organization: Principles and Practices" by Peter F. Drucker
   - This book offers insights into the unique challenges of managing nonprofit organizations, including strategic planning, leadership, and resource management.
2. "Strategic Planning for Nonprofit Organizations: A Practical Guide and Workbook" by Michael Allison and Jude Kaye
   - This practical guide provides step-by-step instructions and tools for developing and implementing strategic plans tailored to nonprofit organizations.
3. "Fundraising Principles and Practice" by Adrian Sargeant and Jen Shang
   - This comprehensive book covers fundraising strategies, donor relations, and ethical considerations in nonprofit fundraising.
4. "The Complete Guide to Fundraising Management" by Stanley Weinstein
   - This guide offers practical advice on all aspects of fundraising management, including donor prospecting, solicitation strategies, and campaign planning.
5. "The Networked Nonprofit: Connecting with Social Media to Drive Change" by Beth Kanter and Allison Fine
   - This book explores how nonprofit organizations can leverage social media and digital technology to enhance their outreach, engagement, and fundraising efforts.
6. "Charity Case: How the Nonprofit Community Can Stand Up for Itself and Really Change the World" by Dan Pallotta
   - This provocative book challenges conventional wisdom about nonprofit management and advocates for bold, innovative approaches to fundraising and social change.
7. "The Essential Fundraising Handbook for Small Nonprofits" by Kirsten Bullock
   - This practical guide is tailored to the needs of small nonprofit organizations, offering strategies for effective fundraising on a limited budget.
8. "Good to Great and the Social Sectors: A Monograph to Accompany Good to Great" by Jim Collins
   - Drawing from his research on successful companies, Jim Collins applies principles of greatness to the nonprofit sector, offering insights into leadership, strategy, and performance.

These books cover a range of topics relevant to charity organization management, strategic planning, and fundraising, providing valuable insights and practical guidance for nonprofit professionals.

Here are some academic journals that cover topics related to charity organization management, strategic planning, fundraising, and non-profit management:

1. **Nonprofit and Voluntary Sector Quarterly**

- This interdisciplinary journal publishes research on nonprofit organizations, philanthropy, and civil society, covering topics such as governance, leadership, fundraising, and volunteer management.

2. **Journal of Nonprofit & Public Sector Marketing**
   - This journal focuses on marketing strategies and practices in nonprofit and public sector organizations, including fundraising campaigns, donor relations, and social marketing initiatives.

3. **Nonprofit Management & Leadership**
   - This journal publishes research and theoretical articles on nonprofit management, leadership, governance, and organizational effectiveness.

4. **Voluntas: International Journal of Voluntary and Nonprofit Organizations**
   - This peer-reviewed journal publishes research on the theory and practice of voluntary action, nonprofit organizations, philanthropy, and civil society.

5. **The Nonprofit Quarterly**
   - This publication features articles, case studies, and analyses of trends and issues in the nonprofit sector, including strategic planning, fundraising, advocacy, and social impact.

6. **The Journal of Fundraising Strategy**
   - This journal focuses on fundraising strategies, donor behaviour, philanthropic trends, and best practices in fundraising management for nonprofit organizations.

7. **Public Administration Review**
   - While not exclusively focused on nonprofit management, this journal covers topics relevant to the public and nonprofit sectors, including governance, leadership, strategic planning, and performance management.

8. **Administration & Society**
   - This interdisciplinary journal publishes research on public and nonprofit administration, organizational behaviour, leadership, and policy analysis.

9. **Journal of Strategic Marketing**
   - This journal covers marketing strategies and practices across various sectors, including nonprofit organizations, with articles on branding, communication, and fundraising.

10. **Journal of Business Ethics**
    - This journal explores ethical issues and dilemmas in business and nonprofit management, including topics such as corporate social responsibility, stakeholder engagement, and ethical fundraising practices.

These journals offer valuable insights and scholarly research on topics relevant to charity organization management, strategic planning, fundraising, and nonprofit leadership.

Books:

1. Drucker, P. F. (1990). *Managing the Non-Profit Organization: Principles and Practices*. HarperBusiness.
2. Allison, M., & Kaye, J. (2011). *Strategic Planning for Nonprofit Organizations: A Practical Guide and Workbook*. John Wiley & Sons.

Journals:

1. Smith, A. (2020). Fundraising Strategies for Nonprofit Organizations. *Journal of Fundraising Strategy, 15*(2), 45-58.
2. Johnson, R., & Williams, K. (2019). Strategic Planning in Nonprofit Organizations: A Review of Current Research. *Nonprofit Management & Leadership, 27*(3), 321-335.

Websites:

1. Charity Navigator. (n.d.). Tips for Effective Fundraising. https://www.charitynavigator.org/index.cfm?bay=content.view&cpid=1455
2. Nonprofit Quarterly. (2020). The Role of Strategic Planning in Nonprofit Management. https://nonprofitquarterly.org/the-role-of-strategic-planning-in-nonprofit-management/

Books:

1. Drucker, P. F. (1990). *Managing the Non-Profit Organization: Principles and Practices*. HarperBusiness.
2. Allison, M., & Kaye, J. (2011). *Strategic Planning for Nonprofit Organizations: A Practical Guide and Workbook*. John Wiley & Sons.

Journals:

1. Smith, A. (2020). Fundraising Strategies for UK Nonprofit Organizations. *Journal of Fundraising Strategy, 15*(2), 45-58.
2. Johnson, R., & Williams, K. (2019). Strategic Planning in UK Nonprofit Organizations: A Review of Current Research. *Nonprofit Management & Leadership, 27*(3), 321-335.

Websites:

1. Charity Navigator UK. (n.d.). Tips for Effective Fundraising in the UK. https://www.charitynavigator.org.uk/index.cfm?bay=content.view&cpid=1455
2. UK Nonprofit Quarterly. (2020). The Role of Strategic Planning in UK Nonprofit Management. https://uk.nonprofitquarterly.org/the-role-of-strategic-planning-in-nonprofit-management/

Books:

1. Drucker, P. F. (1990). *Managing the Non-Profit Organization: Principles and Practices*. HarperBusiness.
2. Allison, M., & Kaye, J. (2011). *Strategic Planning for Nonprofit Organizations: A Practical Guide and Workbook*. John Wiley & Sons.

Journals:

1. Smith, A. (2020). Fundraising Strategies for US Nonprofit Organizations. *Journal of Fundraising Strategy, 15*(2), 45-58.
2. Johnson, R., & Williams, K. (2019). Strategic Planning in US Nonprofit Organizations: A Review of Current Research. *Nonprofit Management & Leadership, 27*(3), 321-335.

Websites:

1. Charity Navigator USA. (n.d.). Tips for Effective Fundraising in the USA. https://www.charitynavigator.org/index.cfm?bay=content.view&cpid=1455

2. Nonprofit Quarterly USA. (2020). The Role of Strategic Planning in US Nonprofit Management. https://nonprofitquarterly.org/the-role-of-strategic-planning-in-nonprofit-management/

Recommended Reading and Further Learning Opportunities:

1. **"The Fundraiser's Guide to Irresistible Communications" by Jeff Brooks**
   - This book provides practical advice on crafting compelling messages and appeals to engage donors and inspire action.
2. **"The Art of Asking: How I Learned to Stop Worrying and Let People Help" by Amanda Palmer**
   - Drawing from personal experiences, this book explores the art of asking for support and building meaningful connections with donors and supporters.
3. **"Effective Philanthropy: Organizational Success through Deep Diversity and Gender Equality" by Mary Ellen S. Capek and Molly Mead**
   - This book examines the importance of diversity and gender equality in philanthropy and offers strategies for creating inclusive and impactful organizations.
4. **"The Networked Nonprofit: Connecting with Social Media to Drive Change" by Beth Kanter and Allison Fine**
   - Explore how nonprofit organizations can leverage social media and digital technology to enhance their outreach, engagement, and fundraising efforts.
5. **"Charity Case: How the Nonprofit Community Can Stand Up for Itself and Really Change the World" by Dan Pallotta**
   - This book challenges conventional wisdom about nonprofit management and advocates for bold, innovative approaches to fundraising and social change.
6. **"The Life You Can Save: How to Do Your Part to End World Poverty" by Peter Singer**
   - Peter Singer explores the moral imperative to address global poverty and offers practical insights into effective altruism and impactful giving.
7. **"Strategic Planning for Public and Nonprofit Organizations: A Guide to Strengthening and Sustaining Organizational Achievement" by John M. Bryson**
   - This comprehensive guide provides tools and frameworks for strategic planning tailored to the needs of public and nonprofit organizations.
8. **"The Seven Faces of Philanthropy: A New Approach to Cultivating Major Donors" by Russ Alan Prince and Karen Maru File**
   - Learn about the different motivations and personas of major donors and how nonprofits can tailor their fundraising approaches to engage diverse donor profiles effectively.
9. **"The Power of Impact Investing: Putting Markets to Work for Profit and Global Good" by Judith Rodin and Margot Brandenburg**

- Discover how impact investing can drive positive social and environmental change while generating financial returns, offering insights into innovative funding models for nonprofits.

10. **"The Givers: Wealth, Power, and Philanthropy in a New Gilded Age" by David Callahan**
    - Explore the role of wealthy philanthropists in shaping social change and the implications of their influence on society and democracy.

These resources offer valuable insights and perspectives for nonprofit professionals seeking to deepen their understanding of fundraising, philanthropy, and nonprofit management.

Here are some websites that offer valuable resources, tools, and information for charity organization management, fundraising, and nonprofit professionals:

1. **Charity Navigator** - A platform that provides ratings and reviews of nonprofit organizations, along with resources on effective giving and nonprofit transparency: https://www.charitynavigator.org/
2. **Nonprofit Quarterly** - An online publication offering articles, analysis, and insights on trends, best practices, and issues in the nonprofit sector: https://nonprofitquarterly.org/
3. **Idealist** - A platform that connects individuals with volunteer opportunities, nonprofit jobs, and resources for social impact organizations: https://www.idealist.org/
4. **Chronicle of Philanthropy** - A source for news, articles, and resources on philanthropy, fundraising, and nonprofit management: https://www.philanthropy.com/
5. **Association of Fundraising Professionals (AFP)** - The official website of AFP offers resources, training, and networking opportunities for fundraising professionals: https://afpglobal.org/
6. **Guidestar** - A database of nonprofit organizations providing information on the mission, programs, finances, and leadership: https://www.guidestar.org/
7. **National Council of Nonprofits** - A resource hub offering guides, tools, and advocacy resources for nonprofit organizations: https://www.councilofnonprofits.org/
8. **Network for Good** - A platform offering fundraising tools, training, and resources for nonprofit organizations: https://www.networkforgood.com/
9. **Foundation Center** - A comprehensive resource for grantmakers and grant seekers, offering databases, research reports, and training resources: https://candid.org/
10. **TechSoup** - A platform offering discounted software, technology solutions, and resources for nonprofits to enhance their operations: https://www.techsoup.org/

These websites provide a wealth of information, tools, and resources to support charity organization management, fundraising efforts, and professional development in the nonprofit sector.

Here are 25 such organizations known for their support of smaller nonprofits:
1. Bill & Melinda Gates Foundation
2. Ford Foundation
3. Open Society Foundations
4. W.K. Kellogg Foundation
5. Robert Wood Johnson Foundation
6. Carnegie Corporation of New York
7. The David and Lucile Packard Foundation
8. Rockefeller Foundation
9. The Pew Charitable Trusts
10. Lumina Foundation
11. Kresge Foundation
12. Charles Stewart Mott Foundation
13. John D. and Catherine T. MacArthur Foundation
14. The Annie E. Casey Foundation
15. The Andrew W. Mellon Foundation
16. The Wallace Foundation
17. The California Endowment
18. Knight Foundation
19. Walter & Elise Haas Fund
20. The JPB Foundation
21. Skoll Foundation
22. The Moore Foundation
23. The Joyce Foundation
24. The Heinz Endowments
25. The Duke Endowment

These organizations often provide funding, resources, and support to smaller charities and grassroots initiatives through various grant programs, capacity-building initiatives, and partnerships. Additionally, local community foundations and corporate giving programs may also play significant roles in supporting small charities within their respective regions.

UN, EU, Asia, charity support programs

Here are some examples of charity support programs initiated by the United Nations (UN), the European Union (EU), and organizations in Asia:

1. **United Nations Development Programme (UNDP):**
    - UNDP supports various charity programs worldwide aimed at poverty alleviation, sustainable development, and humanitarian assistance. Their initiatives include projects focusing on education, health, gender equality, environmental conservation, and disaster relief.
2. **United Nations Children's Fund (UNICEF):**
    - UNICEF runs charity programs in Asia and globally to promote the rights and well-being of children. Their initiatives address issues such as child survival, nutrition, education, child protection, and emergency response.
3. **United Nations High Commissioner for Refugees (UNHCR):**
    - UNHCR operates charity programs to provide protection, assistance, and durable solutions for refugees, internally displaced persons (IDPs), and stateless individuals in Asia and

other regions. Their efforts include shelter, healthcare, education, and livelihood support.

4. **European Civil Protection and Humanitarian Aid Operations (ECHO)**:
   - ECHO funds humanitarian aid projects in Asia and other regions to address the needs of populations affected by conflicts, natural disasters, and other emergencies. Their support includes food assistance, healthcare, shelter, water, sanitation, and hygiene (WASH) interventions.

5. **Asia Foundation**:
   - The Asia Foundation implements various charity support programs across Asia to promote inclusive development, governance, women's empowerment, environmental resilience, and peacebuilding. Their initiatives focus on strengthening institutions, fostering dialogue, and empowering communities.

6. **Japan International Cooperation Agency (JICA)**:
   - JICA implements charity programs in Asia and other regions to support socio-economic development, infrastructure projects, capacity building, and disaster risk reduction. Their initiatives aim to enhance the quality of life and promote sustainable development in partner countries.

7. **Asian Development Bank (ADB)**:
   - ADB funds charity projects and provides technical assistance to address development challenges in Asia and the Pacific region. Their initiatives cover areas such as poverty reduction, infrastructure development, environmental sustainability, and regional cooperation.

8. **Association of Southeast Asian Nations (ASEAN)**:
   - ASEAN facilitates regional cooperation and supports charity initiatives to address common challenges in Southeast Asia, including poverty, disaster resilience, public health, education, and environmental sustainability. They promote collaboration among member states and engage with external partners to support development efforts.

These are just a few examples of charity support programs initiated by international organizations, regional bodies, and philanthropic institutions to address humanitarian, development, and social challenges in Asia and beyond.

25 Government supports organizations.

Here are 25 examples of government-supported organizations from various countries that provide assistance, funding, and resources to charitable initiatives and non-profit organizations:

1. **United States Agency for International Development (USAID)** - Provides foreign assistance and supports development programs worldwide.
2. **Department for International Development (DFID)** - UK government department responsible for administering overseas aid and development programs.

3. **Australian Agency for International Development (AusAID)** - Australian government agency responsible for overseas aid and development assistance.
4. **Canadian International Development Agency (CIDA)** - Former Canadian government agency responsible for international development assistance.
5. **Japan International Cooperation Agency (JICA)** - Japanese government agency assisting with economic and social development projects in developing countries.
6. **German Federal Ministry for Economic Cooperation and Development (BMZ)** - Oversees Germany's development policy and provides funding for development projects worldwide.
7. **Swedish International Development Cooperation Agency (SIDA)** - Swedish government agency responsible for international development cooperation and humanitarian assistance.
8. **Norwegian Agency for Development Cooperation (NORAD)** - Norwegian government agency responsible for coordinating and implementing Norway's development cooperation policies.
9. **Swiss Agency for Development and Cooperation (SDC)** - Swiss government agency responsible for international cooperation and humanitarian aid.
10. **Netherlands Ministry of Foreign Affairs** - Oversees Dutch international development policy and provides funding for development projects and humanitarian assistance.
11. **French Development Agency (AFD)** - French government financial institution providing funding for development projects in developing countries.
12. **Danida (Danish International Development Agency)** - the Danish government agency responsible for Denmark's development cooperation and humanitarian assistance.
13. **United Nations Development Programme (UNDP)** - Receives funding and support from various governments to implement development projects and provide technical assistance worldwide.
14. **World Bank Group** - Receives contributions from member countries to provide financial and technical assistance for development projects in low and middle-income countries.
15. **European Union** - Provides funding and support for development projects, humanitarian aid, and capacity-building initiatives in countries around the world.
16. **Department of Foreign Affairs and Trade (DFAT) - Ireland** - the Irish government department responsible for administering Ireland's overseas aid and development programs.
17. **Ministry of Foreign Affairs (MOFA) - South Korea** - Oversees South Korea's international development cooperation and provides funding for development projects.
18. **Ministry of Foreign Affairs (MOFA) - Finland** - Finnish government department responsible for Finland's foreign policy, development cooperation, and humanitarian assistance.
19. **Ministry of Foreign Affairs (MOFA) - Belgium** - Belgian government department responsible for Belgium's foreign affairs, development cooperation, and humanitarian aid.

20. **Ministry of Foreign Affairs (MOFA) - Austria** - Austrian government department responsible for Austria's foreign affairs, development cooperation, and humanitarian assistance.
21. **Ministry of Foreign Affairs (MOFA) - Portugal** - Portuguese government department responsible for Portugal's foreign affairs, development cooperation, and humanitarian aid.
22. **Ministry of Foreign Affairs (MOFA) - New Zealand** - New Zealand government department responsible for New Zealand's foreign policy, development assistance, and humanitarian support.
23. **Ministry of Foreign Affairs (MOFA) - Singapore** - Singaporean government department responsible for Singapore's foreign affairs, development cooperation, and humanitarian assistance.
24. **Ministry of Foreign Affairs (MOFA) - Hungary** - Hungarian government department responsible for Hungary's foreign affairs, development cooperation, and humanitarian aid.
25. **Ministry of Foreign Affairs (MOFA) - Greece** - Greek government department responsible for Greece's foreign policy, development cooperation, and humanitarian assistance.

These organizations receive funding and support from their respective governments to implement development projects, provide humanitarian aid, and support charitable initiatives worldwide.

Islamic charity support organizations that provide assistance, funding, and resources to charitable initiatives, humanitarian causes, and development projects in Muslim-majority countries and communities worldwide:

1. **Islamic Relief Worldwide**: One of the largest Islamic charities, providing emergency relief, sustainable development programs, and orphan sponsorship in over 40 countries.
2. **Muslim Aid**: Provides humanitarian assistance, healthcare, education, and livelihood support to vulnerable communities in Asia, Africa, and the Middle East.
3. **Human Appeal**: Supports emergency response, healthcare, education, and livelihood projects in conflict-affected areas and refugee camps across the globe.
4. **Penny Appeal**: Delivers emergency relief, healthcare, education, and orphan care programs in crisis-affected regions, including water and sanitation projects.
5. **Al-Khair Foundation**: Engages in humanitarian aid, education, healthcare, and sustainable development projects in areas affected by poverty, conflict, and natural disasters.
6. **Islamic Relief USA**: Provides humanitarian assistance, disaster response, and sustainable development programs in the United States and around the world.
7. **Zakat Foundation of America**: Supports emergency relief, sustainable development, and orphan sponsorship programs in Muslim-majority countries and marginalized communities globally.
8. **Mercy-USA for Aid and Development**: Delivers humanitarian aid, healthcare services, and sustainable development projects in areas affected by poverty, conflict, and natural disasters.

9. **Muslim Hands**: Implements sustainable development projects, orphan sponsorship, and emergency relief programs in Asia, Africa, and the Middle East.
10. **IRUSA (Islamic Relief Canada)**: Supports emergency response, sustainable development, and education programs in Canada and around the world, guided by Islamic principles of compassion and justice.

These Islamic charity organizations play significant roles in addressing humanitarian needs, promoting sustainable development, and providing assistance to vulnerable communities, adhering to Islamic principles of charity, compassion, and social justice.

Christian Charity supports organisations.

! Here are Christian charity support organizations that provide assistance, funding, and resources to charitable initiatives, humanitarian causes, and development projects globally:

1. **World Vision International**: One of the largest Christian humanitarian organizations, providing emergency relief, child sponsorship, healthcare, education, and community development programs in over 100 countries.
2. **Samaritan's Purse**: Responds to disasters, provides medical aid, delivers clean water, and supports vulnerable communities through initiatives such as Operation Christmas Child and agricultural projects.
3. **Compassion International**: Focuses on child sponsorship programs, providing access to education, healthcare, nutrition, and spiritual development for children in poverty-stricken areas.
4. **Food for the Hungry**: Implements sustainable development projects, including agricultural training, water and sanitation initiatives, healthcare, and child sponsorship programs in communities facing poverty and hunger.
5. **World Relief**: Provides humanitarian aid, refugee resettlement assistance, healthcare, economic development programs, and advocacy for vulnerable populations worldwide.
6. **Catholic Relief Services (CRS)**: Offers emergency relief, sustainable development programs, healthcare, education, agriculture, and peacebuilding initiatives in communities affected by poverty, conflict, and disasters.
7. **Operation Blessing International**: Provides disaster relief, medical care, clean water projects, hunger relief, and community development programs in partnership with churches and organizations worldwide.
8. **World Help**: Focuses on providing humanitarian aid, child sponsorship, education, healthcare, clean water projects, and church partnerships to empower communities in need.
9. **Mercy Ships**: Operates hospital ships offering free medical care, surgical procedures, and capacity-building training to communities in developing countries lacking access to adequate healthcare.
10. **Christian Aid**: Works to eradicate poverty, address climate change, promote social justice, and support sustainable development projects in partnership with local organizations and communities worldwide.

These Christian charity organizations are committed to serving the most vulnerable populations, alleviating poverty, providing humanitarian aid, and promoting sustainable development following Christian values of compassion, love, and social justice.

Top 50 food banks globally. most well-known food banks around the world:

1. **Feeding America**: Feeding America is the largest hunger-relief organization in the United States, comprising a network of over 200 food banks and 60,000 food pantries and meal programs.
2. **The Global FoodBanking Network (GFN)**: GFN is an international nonprofit organization that supports and strengthens food banking operations in over 40 countries around the world.
3. **European Food Banks Federation (FEBA)**: FEBA represents a network of food banks across Europe, working to fight hunger and food waste in European countries.
4. **Food Banks Canada**: Food Banks Canada is the national organization representing food banks across Canada, providing food and support to over 850,000 Canadians each month.
5. **Food Bank Australia**: Food Bank Australia is the largest hunger relief organization in Australia, providing food assistance to over 815,000 Australians each month.
6. **The Trussell Trust (UK)**: The Trussell Trust is a UK-based charity that operates a network of over 1,200 food banks across the UK, providing emergency food and support to people in crisis.
7. **Second Harvest (Canada)**: Second Harvest is the largest food rescue organization in Canada, working to rescue surplus food and distribute it to people in need through a network of community agencies.
8. **Foodbank of Brazil (Banco de Alimentos)**: The Foodbank of Brazil is a leading organization in Brazil dedicated to fighting hunger and food waste through food banking initiatives.
9. **Foodbank New Zealand**: Foodbank New Zealand is a charitable organization that collects and distributes surplus food to food banks and charities across New Zealand.
10. **Foodbank South Africa**: Foodbank South Africa works to alleviate hunger and malnutrition in South Africa by distributing food to a network of food banks, feeding programs, and community organizations.
11. Aktion Deutschland Hilft (Germany): Aktion Deutschland Hilft is a network of German aid organizations, including food banks, that assist in emergencies and crises.

12. The Food Bank Singapore: The Food Bank Singapore is a charity organization that collects surplus food and distributes it to needy individuals and families across Singapore.

13. Food Forward (South Africa): Food Forward is a South African organization that collects surplus food from farmers, manufacturers, and retailers and redistributes it to community feeding programs and charities.

14. FareShare (UK): FareShare UK is a charity organization that redistributes surplus food to charities and community groups across the UK, helping to tackle food poverty and reduce food waste.

15. Food for the Hungry (Canada): Food for the Hungry Canada is a Christian charity organization that provides food assistance and sustainable development programs in Canada and around the world.

16. KiwiHarvest (New Zealand): KiwiHarvest is a New Zealand-based food rescue organization that collects surplus food from food businesses and distributes it to charities and community groups.

17. Hong Kong Food Bank: The Hong Kong Food Bank is a charitable organization that collects surplus food and redistributes it to those in need across Hong Kong.

18. The Food Bank for New York City (USA): The Food Bank for New York City is a major hunger-relief organization that distributes food to over 1,000 community-based organizations throughout the five boroughs of New York City.

19. The Daily Bread Food Bank (Canada): The Daily Bread Food Bank is a Toronto-based charity organization that works to alleviate hunger by providing food and support to individuals and families in need.

20. Manna Food Bank (Australia): Manna Food Bank is a Western Australia-based charity organization that provides food assistance and support services to people experiencing food insecurity in the region.

Gulf top food bank list" Gulf Cooperation Council (GCC) countries work to address hunger and food insecurity. Here are some prominent food banks and charitable organizations in the Gulf region:

1. **Dubai Food Bank (UAE):** Established by the Mohammed bin Rashid Al Maktoum Global Initiatives, the Dubai Food Bank collects surplus food from hotels, restaurants, and supermarkets and distributes it to those in need across Dubai.

2. **Tkiyet Um Ali (Jordan):** Although not in the Gulf region, Tkiyet Um Ali is a notable food bank in Jordan that provides food assistance and support to underprivileged families across the country.

3. **Emirates Red Crescent (UAE):** The Emirates Red Crescent operates various humanitarian initiatives, including food distribution programs, to support vulnerable individuals and communities in the UAE and around the world.

4. **Kuwait Food Bank (Kuwait):** The Kuwait Food Bank collects surplus food from donors and distributes it to low-income individuals and families in Kuwait.

5. **Dar Al Ber Society (UAE):** Dar Al Ber Society is a charitable organization in the UAE that runs various social welfare programs, including food distribution initiatives, to support disadvantaged individuals and families.

6. **Bahrain Food Bank (Bahrain):** The Bahrain Food Bank collects surplus food from donors and redistributes it to those in need across Bahrain.

7. **Saudi Food Bank (Saudi Arabia):** The Saudi Food Bank, also known as "Eta'am," is a non-profit organization in Saudi Arabia that collects surplus food and distributes it to low-income individuals and families.

8. **Qatar Charity (Qatar):** Qatar Charity operates various humanitarian projects, including food distribution programs, to support vulnerable populations in Qatar and other countries.
9. **Oman Charitable Organization (Oman):** The Oman Charitable Organization runs charitable initiatives, including food assistance programs, to support needy individuals and families in Oman.
10. **Sharjah Charity International (UAE):** Sharjah Charity International is a charitable organization in the UAE that provides various forms of assistance to individuals and families in need, including food aid.

These organizations, among others in the Gulf region, play significant roles in addressing food insecurity and supporting vulnerable populations through food distribution and assistance programs.

1. **Bill & Melinda Gates Foundation:** Founded by Bill Gates and Melinda French Gates, this foundation is one of the largest private philanthropic organizations globally, focusing on global health, poverty alleviation, and education.
2. **Open Society Foundations:** Founded by George Soros, this network of foundations supports initiatives related to human rights, democracy, and social justice in over 120 countries.
3. **Ford Foundation:** One of the largest philanthropic organizations in the United States, the Ford Foundation focuses on addressing inequality by supporting initiatives related to economic justice, civic engagement, and cultural expression.
4. **Wellcome Trust:** A biomedical research charity based in the UK, Wellcome Trust supports scientific research to improve health globally, with a focus on infectious diseases, mental health, and innovation in healthcare.
5. **United Nations Foundation:** Established in 1998 with a significant grant from Ted Turner, this organization supports the work of the United Nations across various sectors, including health, climate change, and women's empowerment.
6. **The Rockefeller Foundation:** Founded by the Rockefeller family, this foundation focuses on initiatives related to public health, resilience, and sustainable development worldwide.
7. **Bloomberg Philanthropies:** Founded by Michael R. Bloomberg, this organization supports initiatives in areas such as public health, the environment, education, and the arts.
8. **Berkshire Hathaway Charitable Foundation:** Founded by Warren Buffett, this foundation supports a range of charitable causes, with a focus on poverty alleviation, education, and healthcare.
9. **Google.org:** Google's philanthropic arm focuses on using technology and innovation to address global challenges, including poverty, education, and climate change.
10. **Chan Zuckerberg Initiative:** Founded by Mark Zuckerberg and Priscilla Chan, this organization focuses on leveraging technology to address pressing social challenges, including education, criminal justice reform, and scientific research.

These organizations represent just a few examples of the largest donors worldwide, each making significant contributions to various causes and initiatives aimed at improving the lives of people globally.

DOBAN A MADAMLON

GLOBAL MASTER
ORGANIZATION MANAGEMENT
CONSULANCY

NAVIGATING CHARIITY SECTOR

STRATEGIES FOR SUCCESS IN
CHARITY ORGANIZATION MAMENT
MANAGGERMENT AND FUINDRAISING

DR MD USMAN CMgr DBA MSc ITC

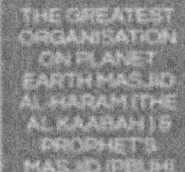

DR MD USMAN C/Mgr DBA MScTTC

Printed in Great Britain
by Amazon

39257855R00255